Encountering The Goddess

SUNY Series in Hindu Studies

Wendy Doniger, Editor

Encountering The Goddess

A Translation of the *Devī-Māhātmya* and A Study of Its Interpretation

Thomas B. Coburn

STATE UNIVERSITY OF NEW YORK PRESS

Production by Ruth East
Marketing by Bernadette LaManna

Published by
State University of New York Press, Albany

Printed in the United States of America

For information, address State University of New York
Press, State University Plaza, Albany, N.Y. 12246

Library of Congress Cataloging-in-Publication Data

Coburn, Thomas B.
Encountering the goddess : a translation of the Devī-māhātmya and a study of its interpretation / Thomas B. Coburn.
p. cm. — (SUNY series in Hindu studies)
Includes bibliographical references.
ISBN 0-7914-0445-5 (alk. paper). — ISBN 0-7914-0446-3 (pbk. : alk. paper)
1. Puranas. Mārkaṇḍeyapurāṇa. Devīmāhātmya—Criticism, interpretation, etc. 2. Puranas. Mārkaṇḍeyapurāṇa. Devīmāhātmya--Commentaries—History and criticism. I. Puranas. Mārkaṇḍeyapurāṇa. Devīmāhātmya. English. 1991. II. Title. III. Series.
BL1140.4.M376C64 1991 71098
294.5′925—dc20 90-30574
CIP

10 9 8 7 6 5 4 3 2 1

For
Ruth and John
Brooke and Jesse

Contents

Illustrations ix
Preface xi

1. Introduction 1

PART I: The Text in Its Context

2. The Historical Setting 13
1. Introduction
2. Sanskrit and Sanskritization
3. The Names of the Goddess
4. The Myths in the *Devī-Māhātmya*
5. The Divine Protector or Protectress

3. The Text in Translation 29
1. A Note on the Translation
2. The Translation

PART II: Encounters With the Goddess

4. The Legacy of a Text 87

5. Encounter with the Text I—The Ritual and Philosophy of the *Aṅga*s 99
1. Introduction
2. The Armor, the Stopper, the Bolt: Kavaca, Argalā, and Kīlaka
3. The Secrets Pertaining to Primordial Matters, Subsequent Modifications, and Forms: The Prādhānika, Vaikṛtika, and Mūrti Rahasyas

6. Encounter with the Text II—The Commentaries 119
1. Introduction
2. Bhāskararāya and Nāgoji Bhaṭṭa
3. Bhāskararāya's *Guptavatī*: "Containing What is Hidden"
4. Comparative Considerations

7. Encounters in the Contemporary World 149
1. Introduction
2. Scholar and Translator
3. Pūjāri and Professor
4. "Standing at the Feet of the Mother"
5. Conclusion

Appendix: Translation of the *Aṅga*s 175
Notes 195
Glossary 231
Bibliography 235
Index 247

Illustrations

Figures

4.1 Aihole (Bijapur-Mysore), sandstone, late sixth century. Goddess breaking the buffalo's neck with her knee. 94

4.2 Bādāmi (Bijapur-Mysore), sandstone, late sixth century. Four-armed Goddess raising the buffalo by his hind-quarters. 95

4.3 Mahābalipuram, granite, second quarter of the seventh century. Buffalo-headed human Mahiṣa cringing before the Goddess. 96

4.4 Tiruvalañjali, granite, first half of the tenth century. Goddess standing on the head of the slain buffalo demon. Courtesy, Tanjore Art Gallery. 97

4.5 Ālāmpur, red sandstone, eighth century. Goddess slaying Mahiṣa in human form as he emerges from his buffalo shape. Courtesy, Ālāmpur Museum. 98

5.1 Diagram of relationships in the Prādhānika Rahasya 113

5.2 Diagram of relationships in the Vaikṛtika Rahasya 113

5.3 The *Devī-Māhātmya/Saptaśatī* Caṇḍī *yantra* 115

6.1 The Śrīcakra *yantra.* Courtesy, University of Chicago Press. 127

Preface

All serious writing, I suspect, is in some measure autobiographical. Whatever subject matter we choose is evidence of ideas that have somehow caught our fancy, traces of things which we have thought about for a while. I am aware of such a personal dimension to this book, not only because of the many people who have contributed to its completion, but also because it reflects part of my own intellectual odyssey over a number of years.

Like many of my contemporaries, I was captivated as an undergraduate by the study of books, particularly historically significant books, and, among them, the books of religion, especially the Bible. The detailed study of Jewish and Christian scripture, with its "source hypotheses" and the like, was intrinsically interesting and challenging. Finding myself some years later in the process of becoming a comparativist or historian of religion, deeply interested in the great Goddess of India, I was still drawn to the study of written documents, but with an uneasiness about the terms of comparison: The status of written records seemed to vary cross-culturally, but we simply took for granted the legitimacy, and the significance, of comparing them. Over the past decade or so, a fair number of scholars in widely varying fields have begun to pay attention to such matters, and this book is, in part, my contribution to that discussion. Since I introduce some of the issues in the discussion early on in chapter 1, I will not anticipate them here. The following very general orientation may, however, be helpful.

What we are about is trying to understand the range of attitudes that we human beings have had toward written documents, particularly those that have been religiously significant. Not all cultures and times share the assumptions that we in the modern West have on this matter. If we were to display the range of opinions along a spectrum, I suspect that the modern West would fall somewhere in the middle. And I have candidates for defining the two ends of the spectrum.

At one end sits the old wheelwright described by the Taoist master, Chuang Tzu. He had criticized his ruler's obsession with "the words of the Sages," and explained his criticism by talking about why he was still working in his old age:

> When I am making a wheel, if my stroke is too slow, then it bites deep but is not steady; if my stroke is too fast, then it is steady, but does not go deep. The right pace, neither slow nor fast, cannot get into the hand unless it comes from the heart. It is a thing that cannot be put into words; there is an art in it that I cannot explain to my son. That is why it is impossible for me to let him take over my work, and here I am at the age of seventy, still making wheels. In my opinion it must have been the same with the men of old. All that was worth handing on, died with them; the rest, they put into their books. . . . What you [are reading therefore is nothing but] the lees and scum of bygone men.[1]

Surely it is hard to imagine a more severe devaluing of the written word than this!

At the other end of the spectrum sits a young woman. In order to understand her, we must be aware of the great debate that divided Europe during the eighteenth century over the new and widespread enthusiasm for reading. On one side were those who feared not just for morality, but for public health: among the adverse effects were cited "'susceptibility to colds, headaches, weakening of the eyes, heat rashes, gout, arthritis, hemorrhoids, asthma, apoplexy, pulmonary disease, indigestion, blocking of the bowels, nervous disorder, migraines, epilepsy, hypochondria, and melancholy.'" On the other side were those who maintained that, although reading was ill-advised after eating or while standing up, one could through proper disposition of the body "make reading a force for good." Neither group, however, disputed the highly physical nature of the reading process. Our young woman represents what is surely the ultimate affirmation of such a view, for she "'ate a New Testament, day by day, and leaf by leaf, between two sides of bread and butter, as a remedy for fits.'"[2]

Most of our human attitudes toward the written word fall, I suggest, somewhere between these two extremes. This book is intended, in a comparative context, to explore some Indian views on these matters, and also to inquire into Hindu encounters with the Goddess. As we shall see, the two issues are intimately intertwined.

I am greatly indebted to many people who have contributed to the writing of this book. Foremost among them are the Hindus with whom I have read commentaries and had extended discussions about the *Devī-Māhātmya*, its liturgy and function: the late Ambika Datta Upādhyāya, Ram Shankar Bhattacharya, Hrishikesh Bhattacharya, and A. N. Jani. The substance of our conversations, at various times and places, was matched only by the personal warmth that accompanied them. Without them, there would be no book.

During the fall of 1981, J. N. Tiwari provided wise counsel and keen analysis at an important juncture, as I pursued and refined my inquiry in Varanasi. The Mahārāja of Benaras, H. H. Vibhuti Narain Singh Kashiraj, was generous in sharing material from his family library at Fort Ramnagar.

I am grateful to the American Institute of Indian Studies for a Senior Research Fellowship during 1981-1982, and to the National Endowment for the Humanities for support during the summer of 1982 at a seminar on "Scripture as Form and Concept." St. Lawrence University has provided a Faculty Research Grant, which took me to India in the summer of 1987, and several smaller grants in support of completing this manuscript.

The American Institute of Indian Studies has also provided the photographs that constitute the figures in chapter 4. Michael Meister, Kanta Bhatia, and Michael Rosse were gracious in expediting access to materials in the Institute's archive at the University of Pennsylvania, as was V. R. Nambiar in sending the photographs from Varanasi. I am indebted to the Tanjore Art Gallery and the Ālāmpur Museum for allowing inclusion of photographs of sculptures in their collections, figures 4.4 and 4.5, respectively, and to Douglas Brooks and the University of Chicago Press for figure 6.1.

Douglas Brooks has kindly read and commented on parts of this study, and generously shared his own learning and forthcoming work. My understanding of Bhāskararāya, in particular, would be much diminished but for him. Misunderstandings are mine alone. Mackenzie Brown has also read and offered helpful comments on the manuscript. I most appreciate the willingness of Cynthia A. Humes to correspond on the substance of her doctoral dissertation prior to its completion, and I trust I have not misrepresented her highly promising work.

Gail Colvin and Laurie Olmstead of the St. Lawrence University word processing department have, with wonderful good cheer, transcribed my field notes, and cleverly coaxed the final draft of the manuscript from reluctant software. Jim Benvenuto produced the copy of figures 5.3 and 6.1. Michael Battaglia has diligently constructed most of the bibliography.

During the years that I have been working on this project, I have come to learn in unanticipated ways what it means to be a father, and what to be a son. The experience has been extraordinary, thanks chiefly to the individuals who make me both of those. It is with deep appreciation, and love, that this book is dedicated to my parents and my sons. At the same time, I am mindful that great siblings help enormously in effecting the continuity between generations. I sense their presence—Judy, Mike, and Sarah—hovering between the two lines on the dedication page.

It has been my great good fortune for the past few years to keep company with Leigh Berry. Her contribution to this project has been to share her wit, good humor, and enthusiasm for whatever it is that needs doing. That spirit is infectious. It seems as if I've known her forever.

Canton, New York
July 1989

1

Introduction

Some fifteen hundred years ago, under circumstances largely unknown to us, somewhere in northwest India, several thousand words were arranged into a more or less unified composition. The language of these words was Sanskrit, and they were arranged in versified form. Over the ensuing centuries, these words attracted to themselves a number of designations, the most popular being *Devī-Māhātmya* and *Durgā-Saptaśatī*. The former designation may be translated "The Specific Greatness (or Virtue) of (the) Goddess," while the second means "Seven Hundred (Verses) to Durgā." Through the years these words have been elaborated upon in a variety of ways, in both word and deed, in commentary and liturgy. They have been inscribed on individual hearts, that is, they have been memorized. They have been written down in more graphic form, in manuscripts. Eventually they appeared in printed editions. Judging from the volume of the manuscript evidence, these particular words have been enormously popular through the centuries, and they remain among the best known devotional words in contemporary India. If we were to conceptualize this kind of phenomenon by saying that virtually all cultural and religious traditions generate and preserve artifacts of various sorts, then clearly the *Devī-Māhātmya* has been one of the major verbal artifacts that has been left in the Indian subcontinent.

What shall we make of this fact? How shall we do justice to these particular words, composed in a specific time and place, leaving an enormous legacy within India proper, beckoning contemporary

Westerners who would understand a culture other than their own, and—we should particularly note in a global environment that has recently been paying increased attention to matters of gender—presenting an intrinsically arresting view of ultimate reality as feminine?

A great deal clearly depends on who is meant by the "we" that is asking these questions.

In presenting the matter in this way, I should indicate immediately that this book is not primarily concerned with the complex and fascinating matter of "point of view" that has so claimed the attention of artists and humanists, and humanistic scholarship, in recent years. It is not a venture into literary criticism. It is neither intended as an inquiry into philosophical theology, nor is it meant to contribute directly to that area of scholarly discourse known as hermeneutics. There has been a great deal of interest lately in how one ought to interpret texts, particularly religious texts. This discussion is perhaps most readily associated with the names of Martin Heidegger, Paul Ricoeur, and Hans-Georg Gadamer, joined now by many others, and the debate will, no doubt, continue for some time. I have listened to these discussions with interest, and it may be that those who are engaged in them will find something worthy of attention in the current volume. But by training and inclination I am neither philosopher nor literary critic. The interests that have led me to the current study lie elsewhere.

There are, in fact, three such interests.

Foremost among them has been a desire to contribute in some way to what is surely one of the massive revolutions of our day, that is, the way in which we think and behave with regard to matters of gender. While there remain those who would think of recent developments in the study and experience of women as a fad, I am of the persuasion that something of great historical moment is afoot here. I have followed the various intellectual and social dimensions of this revolution with great interest and concern, though I recognize that I am not necessarily the best person to press the case here, or elsewhere, for the importance of feminist concerns. What I can admit to, however, is the sense that on this matter, as elsewhere, careful scholarship has important contributions to make, both intellectually and humanistically. And so I have done some research, part of which has already appeared as a book, directed largely at scholars in Indian studies, examining the crystallization of the Hindu Goddess tradition.[1] The sense has persisted, however, that there are issues running through this research that would be of broader interest. This sense has been reinforced by my students, especially the women, with whom I have shared excerpts of my own translation of the *Devī-Māhātmya*. Their reports of what it did for them—particularly its tremendous enrichment of their dream-life—have encouraged me in the current undertaking. That undertaking is to make available an English translation of the *Devī-Māhātmya* that for the first time pays careful attention to historical factors in the composition, translation, and interpretation of the text. It is also the first translation in nearly a century by someone who is a native speaker of English.[2] In this undertaking, I shall not attempt to identify implications for the gender revolution beyond offering an occasional suggestion. To do more would require a competence I cannot claim. I am content here to lay a foundation with this translation, and invite others to draw out the further ramifications for our thinking about matters of gender.

There is a second revolution that is also now on the horizon, and it constitutes my second interest. This revolution deals with the way in which we think about the place of books in religious life. It therefore has a very direct bearing on what is involved in the translation of a written document. It is hazardous to attempt description of a movement that is barely under way, but the basic issue might be put as follows.

At first glance, it appears obvious that the religious traditions of the world have scriptures. Virtually all of the major traditions, and many of the minor, have left literary deposits, produced written documents, and the mere fact of their "writtenness" invites comparison between one tradition and another. The logic behind F. Max Müller's massive editorial undertaking at the end of the last century—the publication in English translation of the fifty volumes of the Sacred Books of the East—is a compelling one. A similar logic runs through much contemporary thinking, both popular and scholarly. In recent years, a style of religious life has emerged, on a very broad scale, in which the defining feature is commitment to the content of a particular book as ultimate truth, as "God's Word" in a quite literal sense. The most vivid instances, perhaps, are found in the Christian tradition, but they have their parallels elsewhere: the phenomenon is a global one. In academic circles, too, fascination with the written word persists. Not only do we focus upon written materials in our teaching and research, but we also carry this fascination over into our own conviction about the very nature of truth, by identifying "publication," appearance in print, as the criterion of worthwhile knowledge.

The roots of this ready association of "religions" with "scriptures," and of this virtual obsession with the written word, are complex. They include the Renaissance, with its emphasis on classical texts, the Reformation, with its elevation of the Bible as the locus of God's ongoing revelation, and Gutenberg's development of a printing press with moveable type, with its consequences for the spread of literacy. To trace these roots is not my purpose here.[3] It is enough to note that this association of "religions" with "scriptures" is so obvious as scarcely to merit comment.

Recently, however, there has begun to emerge a self-consciousness about the ease with which we assume this connection between religions and books, a recognition that things are otherwise in nonliterate cultures, and that they have been otherwise in literate cultures. We are coming to see that our assumptions about books, their nature, and their relation to religion are scarcely universal. James Barr, one of the leaders of this new awareness in the study of the Christian tradition, has put the matter vividly with his observation that, in biblical times, a "Bible" was not a volume. Rather, it was "a cupboard or chest with pigeon-holes, or a room or cave with a lot of individual scrolls."[4] Not only are such antecedents of our "books" being noted, but we are also becoming increasingly aware that there are alternative evaluations of the place of books and written documents in human life, particularly in religious life. The evidence from India is especially challenging in this regard. Some 2,500 years ago, we find expressed a sentiment that has been dominant throughout the later history of the subcontinent: "A pupil should not recite [the sacred oral composition that is] the Veda after he has eaten meat, seen blood or a dead body, had intercourse or engaged in writing."[5] In other words, the act of writing is on a par with the most polluting and inauspicious of acts. To engage in it disqualifies one from the heart of the religious life. In the face of such a sentiment, what could possibly be the significance of translating a written text, originating in India, from one language to another? Are there not a host of prior questions that clamor for attention? Would there not be a profound irony, even absurdity, in presenting for contemporary Western appreciation a text that embodies a powerful vision of the Goddess, without also paying attention to what Hindus have done with this artifact? Since there appears to be great variety both *within* any one religious tradition in the assessment of a given religious document and *across* cultures in the way written documents are regarded, is it not incumbent upon us to take note of this variety?

These are difficult questions. To them there is at present no simple answer. So novel is our self-consciousness about scripture as a global phenomenon, so diverse are the evaluations of the data, and so woven into our own cultural assumptions is the value of literacy that the revolution cannot be said to have more than barely begun. Although movement is apparent on many fronts, no fully satisfactory solution to these searching dilemmas is currently apparent.[6]

There are certain implications for the task immediately at hand, however, that would seem appropriate in light of this newly dawning awareness. While it will always be tempting for those who are literate to read translated texts for their *content*, this would appear to be fully justifiable, and sufficient, only when the culture of the reader and the culture where the text originated ascribe similar significance to writing, and to the products of written expression. This may seem like a bizarre statement, but it is not necessarily the case that what is most significant about a verbal composition is its content. It may well be that what is most noteworthy is its *form*. Poets, I suspect, have always known this. Certainly this awareness has been more in evidence when a verbal composition has been regarded as religious than when it has been viewed as a secular phenomenon. What is striking is the extent to which this emphasis has been carried in India. Louis Renou, giant among the last generation of Indologists, has suggested that this tendency, this emphasis on the formal qualities of verbal composition, has been pushed further in India than elsewhere.[7] He has also noted that this characteristically Indian preoccupation with form rather than meaning has meant that "at all times, recitation constituted the principal, if not the exclusive, object of Vedic teaching, the same as today . . . whilst the interpretation of the texts is treated as a poor relation."[8] Renou is admittedly speaking here of the Indian attitude specifically toward the Veda, the primal verbal artifact in the Hindu tradition. Elsewhere, however, I have noted certain functional parallels between the *Ṛg Veda* and the *Devī-Māhātmya*,[9] the text that claims our attention in the present study. Not the least of the grounds for seeing such parallels is the way in which the tradition has "made sense" of these compositions. The *Devī-Māhātmya* has gathered around itself no fewer than sixty-seven commentaries, the most common concern of which is with how the verbal material, with its modest number of variants, should be properly divided so as to arrive at the required 700 verses for recitation. It is proper and precise recitation, not cognitive mastery nor substantive exegesis, that has been the primary concern of the Hindu tradition as it has embraced the verbal phenomenon that is the *Devī-Māhātmya.*[10] The specific nature of some of the commentaries is a matter that will claim our attention later on. For the moment, however, it is sufficient simply to notice the divergence between an emphasis upon the content of the text—to which we may be tempted precisely because of its striking portrayal of ultimate reality as feminine—and an emphasis on its form—which is more representative of how Hindus have approached the text.

Having noticed this divergence, we are then in a position to draw a tentative conclusion regarding the implications of our dawning awareness of "scripture" as a global phenomenon for our aspiration to translate the *Devī-Māhātmya.* For all of its renown in India, the *Devī-Māhātmya* is neither a "classical text" in the sense known to Western humanists, nor is it a "scripture" in the sense known to Protestant Christians. Any translation that is done within the context of our emerging knowledge about the variety and complexity of the phenomenon of "writtenness" must pay attention to the way Hindus have encountered the Goddess, to the sense they have made of this text. For this reason, after translating the *Devī-Māhātmya* below in chapter 3, we turn in subsequent chapters to an examination of the interpretive apparatus that has gathered around the text through the centuries. My goal is thus first, to make the text available for contemporary readers, both Western and other, and second, to do so in a way that calls attention to what Hindus have done with this verbal phenomenon.[11] My hope is thus to provide here a model for the way in which any "scripture" might be studied.

I have, finally, a third interest that has determined the shape of this study. I mentioned earlier that the translation that I provide below is the first translation of the *Devī-Māhātmya* to pay close attention to *historical* factors. What does this mean, and why is it worthy of special consideration in a specifically Indian context?

Basically, I am concerned to distinguish an historical approach to the *Devī-Māhātmya* from two other ways of dealing with this and other texts in the so-called popular strand of Hinduism. One is associated with a dominant trend in recent Western scholarship on India. The other is apparent in earlier Indian translations of the *Devī-Māhātmya* into English. Both call for brief exploration.

For some years now, the intellectual movement known as structuralism has been applied to the analysis of Indian material with extraordinarily rich results. The structuralist movement as a whole ranges across many disciplines and is of great complexity, but its basic vision is simple. A structure, in the words of one of its most brilliant expositors, Jean Piaget, is "a system of transformations" that is "closed," that is, self-contained and self-regulating.[12] What structuralism seeks to do is to identify the particular laws that govern the transformations within a given system. It is mythological material that in significant measure constitutes the fabric of popular Hinduism, so the structural study of India has often been inspired by the vision of Claude Lévi-Strauss, the structural anthropologist who has lavished such great attention on the study of myth.[13] Simply to cite the names of those who have been drawn to this kind of inquiry is to identify many of the dominant figures in the study of Hinduism over the past two decades:

Madeleine Biardeau, Veena Das, Alf Hiltebeitel, Stella Kramrisch, Wendy Doniger O'Flaherty, Hans Penner, and David Shulman, among others.[14] While the specific applications of structuralist thought to Indian culture vary considerably, there is no doubt they have enabled us to discern order in the face of nearly overwhelming complexity. At a quite practical level, anyone who has grappled with a particularly obscure and intransigent textual passage must admit with the structuralists that comparing it with similar passages in other texts can provide unsuspected insights into the original. There has been a relatively happy marriage, in other words, between the transtemporal world of the Hindu epics and Purāṇas,[15] and the ahistorical bent of structuralist thought. By virtue of the latter, we now understand a great deal more clearly the dynamics of the former. This understanding will surely grow further in the years ahead.

And yet there are limits, it would appear, to the kind of understanding that is produced by structuralist methods.[16] This is not the place for a full discussion of such limits, nor is such discussion essential to my purpose. I would, however, cite the remarks of the dean of contemporary Talmudic studies, for if we seek a religious literature that rivals the Purāṇas in complexity, the Talmud is surely a prime candidate. In assessing the merits of structuralism, Jacob Neusner writes:

> Structuralism asks the right questions. But it does not stand to hear all the answers its questions precipitate. . . . Structure without context, that is, the social and economic, material context defined by concrete history, is insufficient either for description or for explanation. . . . We may amply describe a structure within the framework of religions and show how a system is constituted and how it functions. We may notice the fundamental concerns of the stories we have examined and show how the way in which the story is told highlights what the story wishes to tell us. But without careful attention to the historical context in which the story, as part of a system of values, actually functions, we still cannot explain what is important about it. That is, we do not know how to describe and make sense of the system, the world-view and way of life, of which the story is a part. What is still more important, through (mere) structuralism we cannot account for changes within the system itself. Literature is a part of society, and if we do not know what particular stimulus made it necessary or even inevitable that a story such as the one before us should be told, we cannot make sense of it.[17]

Given India's proverbial aversion of attention from historical detail, the kind of knowledge to which Neusner aspires will be very hard to come by. Doubtless one of the reasons for the success of structuralism in dealing with Indian data, as noted above, is the convergence between the nontemporal quality of Indian culture and that of structuralist method. Providing an alternative leverage on the data, one that pays greater attention to matters of chronology, will not be easy. The necessary tools, such as critical editions of Purāṇic materials, are only gradually becoming available, their significance continues to be debated, and it will be a long while yet before they reveal the broader context that Neusner exhorts us to explore. We need not be daunted, however, simply because our aspirations cannot as yet be fully met. One must, after all, begin somewhere. Moreover, as I hope to show, any movement toward realizing those aspirations provides an historical counterpoint to the structuralist spectacular that is both instructive and salutary.[18]

There is also a particular rationale for departing from a structural mode of analysis in the specific case of the *Devī-Māhātmya.* Although this text is woven quite naturally into the fabric of the *Mārkaṇḍeya Purāṇa*, it cannot be considered a "typical" Purāṇic text. I have considered this matter at some length elsewhere,[19] but the critical facts at this juncture are these. Unlike most Purāṇic texts, the *Devī-Māhātmya* has a high degree of textual integrity: the additional verses and variant readings that are so characteristic of the Purāṇas are far fewer in our text. The *Devī-Māhātmya* has also had a tremendously vital independent life, apart from its appearance in the *Mārkaṇḍeya Purāṇa.* While there are several dozen manuscripts of the entire *Purāṇa*, those of the *Devī-Māhātmya* as an autonomous text are virtually "innumerable."[20] Finally, very few commentaries have been written on the Purāṇas. The exceptions are the *Bhāgavata, Viṣṇu*, and *Liṅga Purāṇa*s, the Kāśī Khaṇḍa of the *Skanda Purāṇa*, and chapters 81-93 of the *Mārkaṇḍeya Purāṇa.*[21] It is these chapters of the *Mārkaṇḍeya* that constitute the *Devī-Māhātmya* and, as we noted earlier, this text has attracted to itself a minimum of sixty-seven commentaries. Only one other Purāṇic text has more than a fraction of this number, and that is the magnificent testament to the divine cowherd Krishna in the tenth book of the *Bhāgavata Purāṇa.*[22] In other words, while the Purāṇic tendency has been toward fluidity, the *Devī-Māhātmya* has shown striking stability. In the midst of Purāṇic flux, it has been fixed. Although we have seen that there are major differences between classical India and the modern West in the evaluation of written documents, it would appear that the *Devī-Māhātmya* has been more like scripture in the Protestant sense than are the Purāṇas in general precisely because it is compact, boundaried and therefore capable of being "canonized."[23] In order to do justice to the text, it is necessary to take account of its fixed, reified quality. We cannot simply assimilate it to other Purāṇic texts and proceed to identify their common structural properties. The text has functioned as a relatively autonomous phenomenon, and respect for the integrity of the text requires that we treat it as such.[24]

It is in this context that we should, finally, glance at the two English translations of the *Devī-Māhātmya* that have been made within the past generation, those of Agrawala and Jagadīśvarānanda, for while they have their merits, both are seriously flawed for any effort to arrive at an historical understanding of the *Devī-Māhātmya*. The problem in both cases is that the translators have brought to their work interpretative schema that are demonstrably later than the *Devī-Māhātmya* itself. This is not in itself surprising. Indeed, the way in which verbal artifacts or "scriptures" function in most traditions is by allowing, even enticing, later generations to bring *their* concerns to the text. It is precisely in this kind of dialogue that the great verbal artifacts live on. However, if we would understand analytically how a given text has functioned over time, then we must be prepared to drive a wedge, as it were, between the sense of a text at the time of its composition and the senses that later commentators and translators have drawn out of it. There will, presumably, be a measure of continuity between any text and its later interpreters, but, given the inevitable variations in circumstance, it is virtually impossible for this continuity to be utter.

To obtain this kind of historical leverage on a written document is also a tall order. Having obtained it, its significance remains much debated. This is, in fact, one of the reasons for the current ferment in Biblical studies: The precise bearing of the exquisitely detailed knowledge of original texts that Biblical scholars have been accumulating for over a century on later (including contemporary) generations is not obvious.[25]

However, it now appears possible to obtain this kind of leverage on the *Devī-Māhātmya* in at least a preliminary fashion. One of the purposes of my earlier study of the *Devī-Māhātmya* was to examine the Vedic and epic antecedents of the language that is used in this sixth-century text. What we are now in a position to do is to use this information to translate the text in a way that will approximate its sense at the time of its composition. We can translate the text in a way that avoids reading in more than is justified by demonstrably earlier usage of language and mythology. Then using this translation as a baseline, we may go on to see how later commentators and translators and ritual specialists have engaged with the text. We can come to see how the text has lived on, in various ways, in the lives of some Hindus for these many centuries.[26] We can come to a more historical appreciation of the *Devī-Māhātmya*'s status in Indian life than has heretofore been obtained by either scholars or translators.

The agenda, then, for subsequent chapters is as follows. In the next chapter, I shall situate the *Devī-Māhātmya* in the Hindu tradition, sketching in broad strokes the background out of which the text emerges. In chapter 3 I shall translate the *Devī-Māhātmya*, using language and terminology that are appropriate to the time of its composition. Chapter 4 will orient us to the second half of our inquiry by exploring what it means to talk about the historical legacy of any given text, with special attention to the dynamics of Indian culture. Chapter 5 will then examine some of the interpretative devices, the *aṅga*s or "limbs," that have gathered around our particular text, primarily for ritual purposes. In chapter 6 we shall consider some of the issues that arise in commentaries on the text, focusing especially on two commentaries composed in the eighteenth century. Finally, chapter 7 will present a sampling of how some contemporary Hindus engage with the text, with attention to festival life, focusing on three individuals in particular, and concluding with some general reflections on the ongoing life of verbal compositions. Such an agenda integrates the three personal interests that have been introduced in this chapter around a single goal of presenting the *Devī-Māhātmya* as a living document, providing some sense of how it has lived in India over the past fifteeen hundred years, and presenting a translation that will enable it to continue its life under the striking conditions that are presented now in the contemporary world.

PART I

The Text in Its Context

2

The Historical Setting

Introduction

It has become something of a commonplace to speak of Western civilization as the offspring of the marriage between Athens and Jerusalem. While this is hardly a precise formulation, it does have a kind of rough-hewn simplicity, for it identifies the two obvious strands that have been woven into the cultural fabric that is customarily identified as "the West." These are, of course, the Hellenistic heritage associated with classical Greece and Rome, on the one hand, and the Semitic heritage of Judaism and early Christianity, on the other. While those who would know more of the details of Western civilization soon find that it is necessary to refine such a portrait, there is no doubt that, in broad strokes, it captures the key features of one of the world's great civilizations.

A similar kind of portrait—done, as it were, by the same artist—exists for Indian civilization. Like its Western counterpart, it hardly does justice to the rich texture of the subject, but as a preliminary approximation, it provides a passable likeness, recognizable to those who know the subject, and a useful introduction for those who do not. This portrait conceives of Indian civilization as the offspring of the marriage between the Indo-Europeans or Aryans, who entered India in the latter half of the second millenium B.C.E., and the pre-Aryan inhabitants of the Indian subcontinent.

For our purpose in this chapter, namely, providing the historical backdrop to the emergence of the *Devī-Māhātmya* in the sixth century C.E., it is not necessary to enter into the lively debate about how the two partners in this marriage came to meet one another. Suffice it to say that the details of this encounter remain a good deal more obscure than is the case with the marriage that spawned Western civilization. What is important to note is the radically different appraisal that the Aryans and the pre-Aryans appear to offer of the place of goddesses, and of female gender, in religious life. Let us explore this matter a little further, then turn to the specific antecedents of the *Devī-Māhātmya.*

Ever since the discovery in the 1920s of the remains of a pre-Aryan civilization along the banks of the Indus River, the interpretation of those remains has been problematical. Not the least of the difficulties is the fact that an apparent script, incised along with animal, human, and hybrid figures on small terracotta seals, has so far resisted a translation "that two people can agree on."[1] There are on these seals and elsewhere indications that the powers of fertility were regarded as extraordinary, and that a corresponding worship of feminine power was known, but debate on these matters continues. The basic facts are these. First, at the level of what might be described as folk art, there are a great many small terracotta female figures, wide-hipped, full-breasted, scantily clad, often with ornate headdresses. Second, a number of more refined sculptural pieces, in varying styles and of both sexes, include a striking bronze "dancing girl." Third, the carefully crafted seals show a number of suggestive scenes: a female in a tree, being approached by another figure and animal; a nude female figure, with her legs apart and a plant issuing from her womb; a nude or partially clothed female in various interactions with male, animal, and theriomorphic figures; a figure seated on a raised platform, with legs folded, complex headgear, and surrounded by wild animals. Fourth, a number of ring-shaped and cylindrical stones invite interpretation as aniconic representations of female and male sexual power, the *yoni* and *liṅga* of later times.[2] There are a number of thorny questions about these data—whether it is appropriate to call the distinctive female figures "goddesses"; the relationship between Indus Valley and Middle Eastern civilizations; the nature of continuity between Indus Valley and later religious life in India, particularly the significance of the cross-legged figure, who has traditionally been called "proto-Śiva" on the basis of his apparent resemblance to the deity of later times, but who has more recently been seen as a male surrogate for various female powers,[3] and so forth—but these need not detain us here. What is clear is that the feminine figured prominently in the visual representation by which the Indus Valley people gave expression to their concerns. In particular, there seems to be acknowledgement of the mystery of fertility, especially as it appears in women, and a sense that this power provides a linkage between the human, natural, and animal realms. Given the proximity of Indus civilization to the drama of the agricultural cycle, based as it was on farming of the flood plain, such an intuition seems quite natural.

What is striking, by contrast, is both the cosmic, celestial orientation of the Aryans, and the relative dearth of feminine conceptions of the divine in their world view. The heart of the religious life of the migratory, martial Aryans was sacrifice, offered in various forms to a variety of deities. The hymns composed for use in the sacrifice, collectively known as the *Ṛg Veda*, constitute the earliest stratum of Sanskrit literature. These hymns received rich elaboration, in both liturgy and commentary, in the millenium after the Aryan entry into India, but the fundamental orientation on the matter of the gender of the divine persists. There are, indeed, Vedic goddesses, with particular names and qualities—Uṣas, Vāc, Sarasvatī, Pṛthivī, Aditi, Rātrī—but these "are goddesses with a small 'g' rather than the singular embodiment that we might write with a capital."[4] Kinsley summarizes the situation as follows:

> Although many goddesses are mentioned in the *Ṛg-veda*, none is as central to the Ṛg-vedic vision of reality as [the gods] Agni, Soma, or Indra, and only Uṣas among the goddesses could be considered on a par with the male deities of the second rank. . . . Although there are many female deities they do not, either individually or collectively, represent the "center" of Ṛg-vedic religion. In most cases they are mentioned infrequently and must have played minor roles compared to the great male gods of the *Ṛg-veda*.[5]

Some of these Vedic goddesses are, indeed, known subsequently throughout the Hindu tradition. However, "many of the most important goddesses of the later tradition are not found at all in Vedic literature or are simply mentioned by name in passing," and it is certainly clear that "there is no one great goddess in Vedic literature."[6]

It is this striking richness of the pre-Aryan material regarding the place of the feminine in religious life, and the corresponding poverty of the Aryan, that has, in part, nurtured the image of Indian civilization as the joint creation of non-Aryan and Aryan. It is not the case that the former was obliterated by the latter, nor that the latter was absorbed by the former. Rather a complex process of interaction set in, the specific details of which, as I have indicated, remain quite unclear. What is clear, however, is that, after roughly 500 years, during which the Aryan vision was the most visible and perhaps dominant religious movement in the subcontinent, a series of alternatives began to emerge.

The earliest and most radical of these movements were those that were self-conscious in their rejection of the Vedic heritage of the Aryans. From them have emerged two distinct strands in the religious heritage of India, the Buddhist and the Jain, both of which encouraged renunciation of the world in order to attain self-knowledge, and to escape from a potentially endless cycle of rebirths. Somewhat later, during the last centuries B.C.E., there occurred a wide range of religious creativity that remained deliberately linked to the Vedic-Sanskritic tradition, a process that Thomas Hopkins has nicely described as "the Brahmanical synthesis."[7] The major features of this creativity were the articulation of a pattern of order, or *dharma*, that was manifested socially in the phenomenon of caste, and the emergence of devotion to a personal god (*bhakti*) as the fulfilment of human life. It is texts like the *Bhagavad Gītā* that present this synthetic, world-affirming vision, and they do so in a way that parenthetically validates world-renunciation for the minority that may be drawn to it. Finally, in the first centuries of the Christian Era, the long silence that ensued on the suggestive testimony of the Indus Valley is broken by a variety of literary and iconographic evidence, and "from the third or fourth century . . . the religion of the Goddess becomes as much a part of the Hindu written record as the religion of God."[8] The *Devī-Māhātmya* is not the earliest literary fragment attesting to the existence of devotion to a goddess figure, but it is surely the earliest in which the object of worship is conceptualized as Goddess, with a capital *G*.[9]

As noted in the previous chapter, our primary concern in this book, apart from providing a good new translation of the *Devī-Māhātmya*, is to examine how the subsequent tradition has engaged with the text. If we are to have a sense of how the text was heard or read at the time of its crystallization, however, it would clearly be helpful to have some sense of the previously distinct elements that are here being crystallized. The glossary that is found at the end of this volume provides brief accounts of earlier usage of the major terms applied to the Goddess in the *Devī-Māhātmya*, and those who are interested in detailed analysis of this material may consult my earlier study.[10] In the balance of this chapter, we will consider in more general terms four aspects of the integrative vision presented in our text. The first pertains to the fact that the language of our text is Sanskrit, and the other three pertain to its specific antecedents in naming the deity, in myth, and in the notion of a divine protector or protectress from adversity.

Sanskrit and Sanskritization

The easiest way to grasp the significance of the *Devī-Māhātmya*'s being composed in Sanskrit is to return to the notion of "the Brahmanical synthesis" referred to above. At the risk of great oversimplification, the heart of that synthesis may be described as a simultaneous twofold movement: on the one hand, there is the effort to broaden the appeal of the Aryan world view by enfolding into it various elements of popular origin; on the other hand, there is the effort to provide those elements with a new dignity in the form of verbal compositions in Sanskrit, the language that was one of the major "carriers" of Aryan culture. One of the reasons for the complexity and encyclopedic quality of the Sanskrit Purāṇas is that they are the meeting ground for these two mutually reinforcing inclinations.[11]

It is not enough, however, to understand Sanskrit simply as the language of aristocracy, prestige, and learning in classical India, or as the rough equivalent of Latin in the European Middle Ages. It is, of course, all of these. But it is more. J. A. B. van Buitenen has nicely drawn out the rich symbolic significance of "Sanskritization" in two ways. First, he notes that "whereas for us [in the West], knowledge is something to be *discovered*, for the Indian knowledge is to be *recovered*." In this recovery process, there exist several "lifelines" that afford access to the original revelation. "Sanskrit is felt to be one of the lifelines, and Sanskritization in its literal sense, the rendering into Sanskrit, is one of the prime methods of restating a tradition in relation to a sacral past."[12] Second, van Buitenen notes that Indian use of the term "Sanskrit/Saṃskritic"

> has reference to a rather complex notion of normative self-culture, of which it is more or less consciously felt that the Sanskrit language was its original vehicle. It carries with it associations of a sacral character. . . . [In some contexts] a meaning of "refining or perfecting one's nature and conduct by ritual means" becomes central, . . . [so that] "Sanskritic" is that which is the most ancient, therefore the most pure, and therefore hierarchically the most elevated; it thus provides a norm for exclusive personal or group conduct—exclusive for its purity and elevation—that most effectively proves itself in securing correct descent, backward by relating oneself to an ancient lineage or an ancient myth and forward by safeguarding the purity of future offspring.[13]

As we turn now to more specific instances of the *Devī-Māhātmya*'s Vedic and epic inheritance, we should not lose sight of the fact that, in its original context, virtually every word of the text served to demonstrate the primordial nature of its vision of the Goddess—because it was in Sanskrit. Every syllable assimilated her to the sacrality of the Sanskritic world, and distanced her from the uncouth profaneness of non-Aryan hoi polloi.[14]

The Names of the Goddess

One of the ways in which our text conveys its integrative vision of the Goddess is through the application to her of familiar names and characterizations.[15] In light of the text's being the first comprehensive statement of her identity, these would resonate appropriately in the minds and hearts of those who were familiar with the Sanskritic heritage, adding nuance and richness to what they might already know.

The simplest way in which this is accomplished is through identifying the Goddess with various nouns of feminine gender. Such is the logic of the hymnic verses in the fifth chapter of the text where the refrain—"The Goddess who abides in all creatures in the form of. . . "—is completed with a series of feminine nouns, and with the offering of praise. This enables our text to draw upon a range of characterizations, such as intelligence, faith, knowledge, graceful reticence, wisdom, prosperity, tranquillity, and contentment. None of these brings any dramatic associations from its earlier usage, contributing rather to the general portrait of the Goddess.

At other times, however, these feminine nouns carry important weight. *Śrī*, for instance, a common noun meaning "wealth, good luck, or fortune," and its frequent synonym, *lakṣmī*, are also proper names for particular goddesses from late Vedic times onward. As a distinct deity, Śrī appears to be "a pre-Aryan goddess of fertility and other phenomena relative to it . . . , whose symbol is the lotus, the plant growing in mud and slime, and whose cult, mythology and iconography show a variety of traits characteristic of deities concerned with fertility and prosperity in general."[16] In its earliest usage, *lakṣmī* in the sense of "fortune" is ambivalent, capable of being good or bad, but by the time of our text, the beneficent qualities predominate, with any negative residue conceived and personified as her opposite, Alakṣmī: in the *Devī-Māhātmya*, the Goddess is both. The words *śrī* and *lakṣmī* also carry an association with kingship, and as goddesses they are both related, often as consorts, to lord Viṣṇu, who is commonly conceived in regal terms.

Our text also uses various adjectives to re-present elements of the Sanskritic heritage in association with the Goddess. Once again such usage is often quite innocent, as when she is described as blessed, supreme, auspicious, abiding, boon-granting, and beautiful. But in some instances a striking series of associations, a dramatic refocusing on the familiar, is apparent. This is most in evidence where an adjective that is well-known in its masculine form—for instance, *aindra*, "belonging or related to [the great Vedic god] Indra"—is now used in the feminine. Such instances would have previously been limited to modifying feminine nouns (butter libations, hymnic verses, etc.), but now a much more dramatic assertion is made. What is now "related to Indra" is another familiar feminine noun, *śakti*, "power or ability." This power, however, is now understood to be a universal phenomenon, the fundament of the universe that is *identical* with the Goddess. Whatever aptitude and potency we may have been accustomed to ascribing to Indra is now asserted to be a manifestation of the Goddess, a portion of her potency that is the "power essence" (*śakti*) of the male deity. And it is not just Indra whose aptitude is seen to be derivative, for she is also "related to" Viṣṇu, Śiva, Brahmā, and the several incarnations of Viṣṇu in this same internal, a priori fashion.[17] The *Devī-Māhātmya* does not argue this point logically, but demonstrates it in chapters 8, 9, and 10 of the narrative. What might once have been thought to be "mere" adjectives, descriptive of various aspects of human experience, are now seen to be applicable in new ways to the Goddess, the very foundation of all experience.

Finally, there are a few major names, or clusters of names, that call for an explicit introductory remark.

The Goddess is *Ambikā* and *Ambā*, "Mother" or "Mother dear." To call her by these names, which are both common and proper nouns, is to underscore her fertile and maternal qualities, but it is also to link her with the figure of Rudra-Śiva, as he came to prominence in late Vedic texts. She is known there as "the dispenser of happiness," he as "the fragrant bestower of husbands," but they are also associated with the autumn, as a time of fever and death.

The Goddess is also *Svadhā* and *Svāhā*. These two designations are ritual exclamations drawn from the heart of the Vedic sacrificial tradition. *Svadhā* was originally a physical offering, but it subsequently comes to be the verbal utterance "svadhā," offered to satisfy one's deceased ancestors. *Svāhā* is a simple ritual benediction—"hail! praise be!"—offered hundreds of times in Vedic literature to a range of divine figures. Though the *Devī-Māhātmya* never directly identifies the Goddess with the Vedic goddess of speech, Vāc, there is an implicit association of the two, for in the same verses in which she is addressed as *Svadhā* and *Svāhā*, she is called *nityā*, "the inwardly eternal one," (1.54) and her utterance is said to satisfy all the gods at all sacrifices (4.7).

In addition, the Goddess is *Prakṛti, Māyā,* and *Śakti.* These terms mean, respectively, "matter or nature," "trick or illusion," and "power or ability." Each has a modest but significant history in the earlier literature, particularly in the two texts that first proclaim the importance of devotion to a personal deity, the *Śvetāśvatara Upaniṣad* and the *Bhagavad Gītā.* There are distinctions between these three terms, but in general it might be said that, by the time of our text, they had collectively come to designate a secondary or lesser form of reality, an instrument that is ontologically connected to the male deity, on which he relies in the creation of the universe. The words also refer to the results of God's creative activity, which he unfolds, or projects, or exfoliates out of his own primary reality. The inheritance that these designations bring to the *Devī-Māhātmya*, then, is that of being master concepts for immanence, and for a reality that is less-than-fully divine: This reality is a manifestation of divine power, but it also obscures its fullness and tricks us. Prior to our text *Prakṛti-Māyā-Śakti* is thus something that both partially reveals and partially hides a male God.

Bhadrakālī, Kātyāyanī, and *Durgā* are also names that the *Devī-Māhātmya* applies to the Goddess. What they have in common is that there are fragmentary allusions to figures with these names in the later strata of Vedic literature, but we get no more than hints of their identity. *Bhadrakālī* consistently appears in the context of the blessing of a house, as the deity invoked at the foot of the bed. The family name "Kātyāyana" is associated with a lineage of venerable sages, and *Kātyāyanī* is known as the mother of famous teachers. *Durgā* has a complex earlier history as an adjective, and as a masculine and neuter noun, with a basic connotation of "hard-to-go-by;" its derivative meanings include "inaccessible, unassailable, adversity, difficult passage, mountain fortress," where the reference may be to difficulty, and/or to a means of overcoming difficulty. By the time of our text, the feminine form has referred in Vedic circles both to a goddess with these qualities and to hymnic verses that provide protection. There are also two hymns in the *Mahābhārata* that are directed to a goddess named *Durgā,* who abides in the mountains, is "fond of liquor, flesh, and beasts," and who provides refuge from adversity. Although these hymns have been excised from the critical edition of the epic, they would appear to be older than the *Devī-Māhātmya* and so to feed into the synthesis that our text is accomplishing.[18]

The Goddess in our text is also *Pārvatī*, and one of her forms is *Kālī*. Although both designations later become applied to major goddesses in their own right,[19] evidence that is clearly older than our text is very slim. Although it is common knowledge throughout the epic that Śiva has a consort, she is rarely called "Pārvatī." But the great dramatist Kālidāsa, a century or so before our text, knows Śiva's consort unequivocally by this name. There are inauspicious associations to the word *kālī*, an adjective meaning "black," in the Vedic context, but only one passing personification. The *Mahābhārata* connects a black goddess with the night of destruction, and the name Kālī is used in its hymns to Durgā.

Finally, we should note that our text occasionally refers to several forms of the Goddess collectively as "the mothers" (*mātṛs*) or "the band of mothers" (*mātṛgaṇa*).[20] This occurs in the third episode, where the Goddess has multiplied her forms for battle by calling forth the "power essence" (*śakti*) from each of the male deities. It is to the seven deities thus summoned, plus a messenger who emanates from the Goddess herself, that this designation is applied. The primary association that such a label has at the time of the *Devī-Māhātmya*'s composition derives from the occasional appearance in the *Mahābhārata* of a horde of females known as "the Mothers." Of indeterminate number, with lists of names running into the hundreds, and intertwined with Śiva and the nascent mythology of Skanda, they are "mothers" in a euphemistic sense. They "generally appear as a formidable group of fighting, ferocious, and bloodthirsty beings,"[21] but in them the maternal instinct also runs deep. Consequently, there is deep ambivalence about "the Mothers," for they are sensed to lurk within the shadows of childhood's vulnerability, with the potential both to protect and to kill. J. N. Tiwari summarizes the epic and early Purāṇic material aptly when he writes that "the Mātṛs were originally a group of analogous goddesses of cruel, demoniacal aspect, outside the brahmanical tradition . . . ; when confronting the brahmanical society, it was by their group character rather than by specific names that they were recognizable."[22] In the process of being absorbed into that society—a process clearly to be observed in the *Devī-Māhātmya*—the Mothers became delimited in number, given specific names, "acquired much of their kindly nature," and became conceptualized in relation to male deities through the emerging theology of *śakti*.[23]

The Myths in the Devī-Māhātmya

The basic structure of the *Devī-Māhātmya* is that of a "frame story" and three mythological narratives of the Goddess's salvific activity that are recounted within the two halves of the frame.[24] With regard to the frame story, we may recall that, in addition to its vital life as an independent verbal phenomenon, the *Devī-Māhātmya* also exists as chapters 81-93 of the *Mārkaṇḍeya Purāṇa*.[25] What the frame story does is to provide a thread of continuity between the substance of our text and the earlier and later portions of that Purāṇa. One of the characteristics of a Purāṇa, in the classical definition of the term, is that it should provide an account of "Manu-intervals," cosmic cycles, each of which is presided over by a semidivine figure known as a "Manu." Though not all Purāṇas include such material, the *Mārkaṇḍeya* does: the narrator, named Mārkaṇḍeya, begins his account of the first Manu, Svayambhu, "the Self-born," in chapter 53 and continues to describe the first seven Manu-intervals through the next twenty-six chapters, ending with the Vaivasvata or current age. In the brief chapter 80, Mārkaṇḍeya then promises to tell of the seven Manus of the future, and chapter 81, the first chapter of the *Devī-Māhātmya*, begins to make good on this promise with its discussion of Sāvarṇi's birth. The very last verse of the *Devī-Māhātmya* reminds hearers and readers of its starting point, and chapter 94 of the *Mārkaṇḍeya Purāṇa* turns to the ninth and subsequent Manus. This kind of elaborate expansion upon a simple cue is typical of Purāṇic style, reflecting in part, no doubt, the bardic quality that underlies and is woven into the texts as they now exist. It has also been described as the *upabṛṃhaṇam* or "confirming elaboration" of the primordial Vedic revelation that the Purāṇas are believed to provide.[26]

When the sage who appears in the frame story seeks to instruct his two distraught pupils about the identity of the Goddess, he does so by telling three stories of her exploits. Each of these has been known, in varying degrees, in earlier literature, but none had ever been used to glorify the Goddess to such an extent, nor is there evidence for the prior association of these stories with one another.

The *Devī-Māhātmya*'s first myth, that of Madhu and Kaiṭabha, is perhaps the most dramatic of the three, not just because of its brevity and understatement, but because of its bold appropriation and reinterpretation of a familiar tale. Throughout the *Mahābhārata* it is common knowledge that once upon a time lord Viṣṇu slew two demons named Madhu and Kaiṭabha. The basic epic version of the story is that, once when the universe was in its state of dissolution, all that existed was the universal ocean. On it Viṣṇu lay gently sleeping, stretched out on a couch formed by his serpent, Śeṣa. Two demons, Madhu and Kaiṭabha, arose from the wax in Viṣṇu's ear and began to harass the creator-god Brahmā, who was seated on a lotus that grew from Viṣṇu's navel. Brahmā awoke Viṣṇu, and a battle of both brawn and wits ensued between Viṣṇu and the demons. In a punning finale, Madhu and Kaiṭabha ask to be slain in a place where the earth (*urvī*) is not covered with water: Viṣṇu raises his two thighs (*ūrvī*) and decapitates them on the surface. From the marrow of their bones was formed the universe.

Much could be said about this myth, but the following will be sufficient. It is clearly concerned with creation and cosmogony, about the movement from the condition of disintegration to that of the manifestation of the universe. There is vivid appreciation of both the beneficent and the martial qualities of Viṣṇu, for he responds when implored, and he forcibly intervenes to ward off the impending chaos. And, finally, there is a sense of trickery and illusion, of the principals trying to outsmart one another, and Viṣṇu's triumph is as much a vindication of his knowledge, his freedom from illusion, as it is of his grace and power. Whatever one makes of the details—or of any one version—of this myth, its clear purpose is to celebrate the glories of lord Viṣṇu. So successful is it that one of Viṣṇu's commonest names, applied pervasively throughout the *Mahābhārata*, is that of Madhusūdana, "the slayer of Madhu."[27]

In the case of the *Devī-Māhātmya*'s second myth, the story of Mahiṣa, the situation is quite different. Here the evidence pertaining to the myth's earlier history is far more ambiguous, suggesting a mythology in transition. Indeed, one might say that, against this backdrop, the *Devī-Māhātmya*'s account of the Goddess's triumph over Mahiṣa constitutes the *locus classicus*, the definitive textual statement which "fixes" the association of Goddess and demon for the subsequent tradition.

The *Mahābhārata* knows but a single discursive account of the Mahiṣa story, in its first version of the birth of the god Skanda, where the slaying of Mahiṣa is the crowning episode in giving identity to this "new" divine figure.[28] The entire account is very complicated, for, as van Buitenen has remarked, though the notion of divine incarnations is a familiar one in the epic, "the birth of a completely *new* God is unique."[29] There are correspondingly various candidates for the parentage of Skanda, and we have not yet arrived at the consensus that will be apparent by the time of Kālidāsa, in the fourth century C.E., that he is the offspring of Śiva and Pārvatī. Elsewhere in the *Mahābhārata*, there are passing references to Skanda as slayer of Mahiṣa, but in the somewhat later interpolated material in the epic and its supplement, the *Harivaṃśa*, both Śiva (once) and a goddess, perhaps Durgā, (three times) are ascribed this role. The *Vāmana Purāṇa*, which is roughly contemporary with the *Devī-Māhātmya*, knows two versions of a myth in which a demon named Mahiṣa is slain by a goddess, but despite some interesting resemblances to the *Devī-Māhātmya*'s account, she is here clearly a local goddess, for the praise she receives in hymns is relatively modest, and she has merely a transitory relationship to the gods. Finally, we may note that the iconographic evidence confirms the suspicion that is aroused by the literary: that there has been a variety of ways of conceiving a goddess/Goddess in combat with a buffalo (*mahiṣa*) demon. Some of these, which portray the demon theriomorphically, date from the early centuries of the Christian era, while others, which show him anthropomorphically, or in hybrid form, or with the Goddess on his severed head, are somewhat later.[30] In any case, by the seventh century the association of the Goddess, under the name Caṇḍī or Caṇḍikā, with a demonic antagonist named Mahiṣa is so firm that their struggle can form the very backbone of a major literary composition, Bāṇa's *Caṇḍīśataka*.

Finally, we may note that the *Devī-Māhātmya*'s third myth, that of Śumbha and Niśumbha, recounted at some length in our text, is almost unknown in earlier Sanskrit literature. There is no relevant evidence at all from Vedic and epic sources, but there is a hint of such a myth in early sources dealing with the story of Krishna, the cowherd god (Krishna Gopāla): the *Harivaṃśa*, the *Viṣṇu Purāṇa*, and a play ascribed to Bhāsa, the *Bālacarita*. Following the lead of Charlotte Vaudeville, I have concluded elsewhere that what we appear to have in the Śumbha-Niśumbha myth is a tale from the mythology of the non-Aryan peoples of north India.[31] These peoples both were and are devotees of the great Goddess, and it was among them that the heroic exploits of Krishna Gopāla first came to be known. Those exploits, of course, subsequently underwent major elaboration in cult, literature, and theology, in both north and south India. Meanwhile, the Goddess's involvement with Śumbha and Niśumbha also found its way out of folk tradition into Sanskrit, and received elaboration in such texts as the *Devī-Māhātmya*.

The Divine Protector or Protectress

There is a final matter that requires comment before turning to translation of the text. A striking feature of the *Devī-Māhātmya* is the way in which it goes on from describing the Goddess's past redemptive activity in the three myths to promise more such activity in the future, particularly when devotees call upon her in adversity. We must glance briefly at the precedents for this kind of promise.

In some measure, of course, elements of supplication and requests for beneficence are as old as the hymns of the *Ṛg Veda*. What we are interested in, however, is the more specific kind of protection that is provided when the world order is about to crumble, on either a grand or a minor scale. And here it is clear that the major antecedent to the *Devī-Māhātmya* is in the *Bhagavad Gītā*, in particular in Viṣṇu's proclamation of what comes to be known as the doctrine of the *avatāra* ("descent, incarnation"):

> Although being unborn (and) having an eternal soul (*ātman*), (and) even though I am Lord of creatures,
> Having resorted to my own material nature (*prakṛti*), I come into being by means of my own magic power (*māyā*).
> For whenever the proper state of affairs (*dharma*) declines, O son of Bhārata,
> Whenever disorder is on the rise, then do I send myself forth.
> For protection of the good, and for destruction of evil-doers,
> To make a firm foundation for *dharma*, I come into being in age after age.[32]

David Kinsley has argued appropriately that the Goddess in the *Devī-Māhātmya* must not be understood as simply the feminine form of masculine deities.[33] One could not agree with this more, for the vision of our text clearly has a powerful integrity of its own. Nonetheless, we also must not overlook the extent to which there appears to have been an interplay of the traditions of the Goddess and of Viṣṇu-Krishna as divine protector or protectress.

This interplay and common theme of regally protecting the world are evident in a variety of ways.

There is, first of all, the fact that when our text describes the crystallization of the Goddess out of the *tejas* of the enraged gods at the beginning of the second chapter, there is a clear model for such an event in the way *The Laws of Manu* had several centuries earlier described the place of the king in human affairs:

> . . . When these creatures, being without a king, through fear dispersed in all directions, the Lord created a king for the protection of this whole (creation),
> Taking (for that purpose) eternal particles [of the various deities,

> namely,] of Indra, of the Wind, of Yama, of the Sun, of Fire, of Varuṇa, of the Moon, and of the Lord of Wealth (Kubera). Because a king has been formed of particles of those lords of the gods, he therefore surpasses all created beings in lustre [*tejas*];
> And, like the sun, he burns eyes and hearts; nor can anyone on earth even gaze on him.

The resemblance between Goddess and king, moreover, extends beyond a shared image of origin to their common ability to assume a variety of forms, and to their common character as both valorous and irrascible.

> Having fully considered the purpose, (his) power, and the place and time, he [the king] assumes by turns many (different) shapes for the complete attainment of justice.
> He, in whose favour resides Padmā, the goddess of fortune, in whose valour dwells victory, in whose anger abides death, is formed of the lustre of all (gods).[34]

What has thus previously been affirmed of the king on a mundane scale is now in the *Devī-Māhātmya* affirmed to be true of the Goddess on a cosmic scale.[35]

There are, in addition, more particular connections between Krishna and the Goddess. We have remarked in the previous section on the intimate historical connection between the cowherd Krishna (Krishna Gopāla) and the worship of the Goddess in north India during the early centuries of the Christian era.[36] It is also well known that the theology of Viṣṇu-Krishna as articulated in the *Bhagavad Gītā* and later draws freely upon regal conceptualizations in its portrait of the Lord. What is less often noticed is the easy rapprochement that was apparently felt by the editors of the *Mahābhārata* between this portrait of God and the emerging figure of the Goddess. Specifically, we should note that some of the earliest evidence for the emergence of the worship of the Goddess consists of two hymns to Durgā that have been inserted into the *Mahābhārata*, and one of these has been inserted immediately prior to the *Bhagavad Gītā*.[37] In the critical edition of the *Mahābhārata*, the *Bhagavad Gītā* begins in chapter 23 of book 6 (the Bhīṣma Parvan). At the very end of chapter 22, a number of manuscripts insert what has become known as the *Durgā Stotra*. The context, of course, is exactly the same as that of the *Bhagavad Gītā*, with Arjuna and Krishna surveying the battle lines for the impending combat. The inserted text begins as follows:

> Having seen the army of the sons of Dhṛtarāṣṭra drawn up for battle,
> Krishna spoke (these) words for the sake of Arjuna's well-being:
> "Having become pure, O great-armed one, being about to engage in battle,
> Recite the *Durgā Stotra* for the sake of conquering (your) enemies."

Arjuna then recites the thirteen verses of the *Durgā Stotra*, after which the Goddess appears to him, assures him of victory, and then vanishes. The inserted text concludes with a *phala-śruti* or statement of the results for one who, like Arjuna, recites the *Durgā Stotra:* "He never knows any fear . . . , and has no enemies. . . . In controversy he obtains victory . . . , he inevitably crosses over difficulty . . . ; he is always victorious in battle."

The conclusion seems inevitable: The conception of deity as periodically incarnate for the sake of redeeming the world has been employed in the service of both Krishna and the Goddess. That this is more than a mere structural similarity is suggested by the affinity that the *Mahābhārata*'s editors apparently felt between this early hymn to Durgā and the text and message of the *Bhagavad Gītā.* That this affinity is not merely casual is suggested by the fact that virtually all the other early hymns to the Goddess as found in the *Mahābhārata* and *Harivaṃśa* contain this same emphasis on salvific activity in the teeth of adversity. This same characterization is, of course, found throughout the *Devī-Māhātmya* and is particularly emphasized in chapter 12, immediately after the Goddess's Krishna-like future incarnations have been enumerated.[38] Finally, we may note that as early as the ninth century the verses of the *Bhagavad Gītā* were observed to amount to 700 in number.[39] It is this fact, taken together with the considerations we have just reviewed, that prompts me to suspect it is the 700 verses of the *Bhagavad Gītā* that have served as a model for the later tradition's understanding of the *Devī-Māhātmya* as comprising "700 (Verses) to Durgā," that is, *Durgā-Saptaśatī.*[40]

The synthesis that is accomplished in the *Devī-Māhātmya* is therefore extraordinarily and uniquely broad. It reaches deep into the Sanskritic heritage, identifying the Goddess with central motifs, names, and concepts in the Vedic tradition. It appropriates one familiar myth on behalf of the Goddess, and enfolds several less well-known tales into its vision. It locates the Goddess in relation to a full range of contemporary theistic and sectarian movements, familiar ones such as those of Śiva and Viṣṇu, and more recent ones such as those of Skanda and Krishna Gopāla. It is to the translation of this text that we now turn.

3

The Text in Translation

A Note on the Translation

Selecting a text for translation and then translating it appear, on the face of it, to be straightforward tasks: one takes the verbal creation that has caught one's fancy and, with a judicious balance of literalness and interpretation, effects its recreation in a different language. And yet translators have noted for centuries that translation always entails some measure of distortion (*traduttori, traditori*), and, as the Western tradition of humanistic scholarship has known since at least the Renaissance, immediately on the desire to translate a given text follows the thorny matter of determining the relative merits of different manuscripts, the significance of variant readings, the possibility of constituting a critical edition, and so forth. The problems are, if anything, compounded when this Western tradition turns its attention to other parts of the world, and I must therefore say a brief word about how I have dealt with such matters in translating the *Devī-Māhātmya*.

We have seen in the two previous chapters that the *Devī-Māhātmya* forms a part of the fluid and dynamic corpus that is the Purāṇas, but that it has also had a relative textual stability that makes it unlike most Purāṇic texts. The nature and significance of critical editions of Purāṇic texts is a matter that has been much debated in recent years,[1] and the laborious task of constituting such editions is beginning to bear fruit. Since the Oriental Institute in Baroda is just now undertaking the critical edition of the *Mārkaṇḍeya Purāṇa*, it might appear desirable to postpone translation of the *Devī-Māhātmya* until that edition becomes available. I have decided against such a course of action, however, and that for three reasons. First, it will be a good half dozen years before the Oriental Institute's work is done, and the intrinsic interest of the text seems to me to warrant more immediate availability. Second, over the course of the past ten years I have examined several dozen versions of the *Devī-Māhātmya* and there is remarkable comparability between them. It is, of course, possible that the critical edition will radically alter our understanding of the text,[2] but at this point I suspect such alterations will be modest. Third, I have indicated earlier that, alongside of translating a major Goddess text, my aspiration in this book is to provide an indication of how some Hindus have engaged with the text since the time of its composition. Materials for such a sketch of how the *Devī-Māhātmya* has functioned in Indian life are currently available, and it seems likely that they will be little altered by constitution of the critical edition. Since one of my goals is to indicate how fruitful it is to ask questions about a text's *consequences* rather than its *sources*, to make such a study contingent on availability of an "original" text would be to betray my own effort to shift the emphasis of textual scholarship.

The version of the text that I have translated below has therefore been selected primarily with an eye toward its relative familiarity. Rather than constituting or using a critical edition, I have tried to identify a vulgate. Since a number of editions might meet this criterion, I have added the further stipulation that, in order to facilitate our subsequent discussion of how the text has been received, it should be readily correlated with the well-known commentaries. One edition then immediately stands out above the others: that edited by Harikṛṣṇaśarma, published with seven commentaries by Veṅkateśvara Press in the early years of this century, and recently republished by Buṭālā and Co.[3] It is this edition that is the basis for the following translation. I have emended it only in the case of obvious misprints, and I have taken its inclusion or exclusion of verses as normative.

The reader should also be aware that, for all of its narrative drama and theological power, the literary merits of the *Devī-Māhātmya* in the original Sanskrit are not overwhelming.[4] Although some of the hymnic passages are indeed elegant, and complex, most of the text is composed in the *anuṣṭubh* (*śloka*) metre of eight syllables per quarter that is standard for epic and Purāṇic composition. Susceptible to sophisticated development, this metre is also highly serviceable for narrative purposes, and it is in this latter capacity that it is employed in our text. I have thought it dishonest to remove this simple, straightforward, sometimes tedious style entirely from the translation, though I have tried to temper it—as the Purāṇas themselves do—with the occasional well-turned phrase, and, of course, with the hymns.

A related matter pertains to the obvious repetitiveness of phrase, and of grammatical construction, that runs through our text. This appears to be a function of what scholars have come to call "formulaic construction," where a formula is a stock phrase spontaneously used by an oral poet in the process of recreating a familiar story to meet the simultaneous demands of narrative development and metre.[5] The nature of oral composition, and of the relationship between orality and literacy, has received a great deal of attention in recent years.[6] It is a matter to which we ourselves shall return in chapter 5, in connection with the ritual recitation of the *Devī-Māhātmya.* For the moment, however, it is sufficient to notice two things. First, this repetitiveness is an intrinsic part of our text and therefore, like the literary simplicity of the narrative, should not be unduly masked by our translation. Second, in affirming the bardic qualities of portions of our text, we must still leave open the question of whether it was "originally" an oral or a literary composition. There is some doubt as to whether Western theories of oral poetry are applicable to Indian material without serious revision, and the Purāṇas themselves seem to represent a transitional stage, from the earlier appreciation of the predominantly oral nature of verbal reality to the emergence of a "cult of the book," which subsequently parallels (rather than replaces) the Indian emphasis on the oral mode of expression.[7]

Finally, there is one small, but obvious and important way in which the format of the translation below reflects a concern of the later interpretative tradition. We have already seen that an alternative title for the *Devī-Māhātmya* is the *Durgā-Saptaśatī,* "700 (Verses) to Durgā." In fact, the latter title is usually preferred when the text circulates as an independent document, apart from the *Mārkaṇḍeya Purāṇa.* We shall return to this matter in chapter 6 when we consider some of the commentaries, for one of their major concerns is with how a text can be said to have 700 verses when the prima facie evidence is that it has somewhat fewer than 600: the Harikṛṣṇaśarma edition translated below, for instance, has 579 verses. There are various ways of overcoming this difficulty, the most common of which is to count half-verses as wholes, and to consider interlocutory phrases like *ṛṣir uvāca* ("the seer said") as verses in their own right. In order to exemplify this treatment of the text, I have taken a contemporary Gujarati edition[8] that closely follows the judgment of the most important Sanskrit commentator, Bhāskararāya, and indicated in [brackets] how the verses are divided and enumerated so as to arrive at the requisite 700.

The Translation

Mārkaṇḍeya[9] said: [1]

1.1 Sāvarṇi, who is Sūrya's son, is said to be the eighth Manu.
Hear about his birth from me, speaking at length, [2]

1.2 How by the power of Mahāmāyā, Sāvarṇi, the illustrious
Son of the sun, came to be the overlord of a Manu-interval. [3]

1.3 Once upon a time, in the Svārociṣa (Manu) interval, born in the family of Caitra,
There was a king over the whole earth, named Suratha. [4]

1.4 While he was protecting all creatures well, like his own sons,
The Kolāvidhvaṃsin kings became his enemies. [5]

1.5 There was a battle between him, possessed of mighty forces, and them.
He was conquered in battle by the Kolāvidhvaṃsins, though they were inferior (to him). [6]

1.6 Returning to his own city, he became ruler of (only) his own country.
Then the illustrious one was (again) overcome by mighty enemies. [7]

1.7 By the mighty, wicked ministers of the weak (king), evil in their intent,
The treasury and army were seized, right there in his own city. [8]

1.8 Then the king, deprived of his authority, under the pretext of going hunting,
Mounted his horse and went off to the dense forest alone. [9]

1.9 There he saw the hermitage of Medhas, best of the twice-born,[10]
Crowded with wild beasts that had been domesticated, resplendent with disciples of the sage. [10]

1.10 Honored by the sage, he dwelt there for some time,
Wandering here and there in the hermitage of the best of sages. [11]

1.11 He then reflected, his mind afflicted with egoism: [12]
"The city that was formerly well protected by my ancestors has been lost by me.

1.12 Is it now protected according to *dharma* (virtue) by my wicked subjects or not? [13]
I do not know. My best elephant, brave, always in rut,

1.13 Has fallen into the hands of my enemies. What kind of treatment will he receive? [14]

Those who constantly followed me with favors, riches, and food

1.14 Now are surely making compliance with other kings. [15]
By those spendthrifts constantly spending funds

1.15 The treasury that was accumulated by me with great difficulty will be destroyed." [16]
The king continually pondered this and other matters.

1.16 Then he saw a *vaiśya* (member of the merchant caste) alone in the vicinity of the Brahman's hermitage. [17]
He asked him: "Who are you? Why have you come here?

1.17 Why do you appear grieving (and) of sad mind?" [18]
Having listened to the words of the king, spoken in friendship,

1.18 The *vaiśya* bowed down in obeisance (and) replied to the king. [19]

The *vaiśya* said: [20]

"I am a *vaiśya* named Samādhi, born in a wealthy family,

1.19 Banished by my wicked sons and wife because of their greed for my wealth. [21]
Without my own people, sons and wives, having had my wealth taken from me,

1.20 I have come to the woods in grief, and abandoned by my beloved kinsmen. [22]
Abiding here I do not know whether this state of affairs is essentially good or bad

1.21 For my sons, my kinfolk and wives. [23]
Do things currently go well or ill for them at home? [24]

1.22 How are my sons? Are they behaving themselves or not?" [25]

The king said: [26]

"Why is your mind lovingly attached to those [27]
Greedy sons and wives who deprived you of your wealth?" [28]

The *vaiśya* said: [29]

1.23 "The very words that you have spoken have occurred to me!
What can I do? My mind is not inclined toward hardness. [30]

1.24 To the same very ones who banished me, having abandoned love for their father

And affection for husband and kinsman, to them is my mind drawn in affection. [31]

1.25 O wise one, though knowing this (to be a fact), I do not understand.
I do not understand how the mind is inclined to love relatives who are bereft of good qualities. [32]

1.26 On their account my sigh comes forth, and my dejection. [33]
What can I do since my heart has not hardened toward those unloving ones?" [34]

Mārkaṇḍeya said: [35]

1.27 Then together they approached the sage, O wise one, [36]
That *vaiśya* named Samādhi and the best of kings. [37]

1.28 Having displayed etiquette that was proper and worthy of him,
The *vaiśya* and the king sat down and told him their tales. [38]

The king said: [39]

1.29 "Venerable sir, I wish to ask you one thing. Please speak [40]
Since my mind has gone to grief, without being restrained by my thoughts. [41]

1.30 I am selfishly attached to my departed kingdom, even to all parts of the kingdom,
Knowing matters to be otherwise, as if I were ignorant. How can this be, O best of sages? [42]

1.31 And this fellow was spurned by his sons and wives, likewise abandoned by his servants,
Forsaken by his own people. Nevertheless he remains affectionately inclined toward them. [43]

1.32 Thus, both he and I are utterly miserable:
The mind is drawn by egoism toward an object, even though its faults are seen. [44]

1.33 How does it happen, O illustrious one, that there is delusion even for men of knowledge,
That this delusion has (come upon) him and me, (who are) blind to discrimination?" [45]

The seer said: [46]

1.34 "O illustrious one, there is knowledge for every creature in the sphere of sense-objects,
And sense-objects proceed in various ways. [47]

1.35 Some creatures are blind by day, likewise others are blind by night,
And some creatures see equally well by day and by night. [48]

1.36 It is true that men have knowledge, but are they alone?
For all cattle, birds, and animals have knowledge, too. [49]

1.37 The knowledge that beasts and birds have, men also have.
And that which men have, they have, too; they are both equal to each other. [50]

1.38 Look at these birds: even though they have the knowledge that they are themselves afflicted by hunger,
They are intent on dropping grain into the beaks of their young. [51]

1.39 O best of men, human beings have a craving for offspring,
Out of greed expecting them to reciprocate; do you not see this? [52]

1.40 Just in this fashion do they fall into the pit of delusion, the maelstrom of egoism,
Giving (apparent) solidity to life in this world through the power of Mahāmāyā. [53]

1.41 There should be no surprise in this, (for) the Yoganidrā (yogic sleep) of the lord of the worlds,
Hari (i.e., Viṣṇu), is (this same) Mahāmāyā, and through her is this world being deluded. [54]

1.42 This blessed Goddess Mahāmāyā, having forcibly seized the minds
Even of men of knowledge, leads them to delusion. [55]

1.43 Through her is created the entire three-tiered universe,[11] that which both does and does not move.
Just she is the gracious giver of boons to men, for the sake of (their) release. [56]

1.44 She is the supreme, eternal knowledge that becomes the cause of release [57]
From bondage to mundane life; she is indeed the queen (governing) all who have power." [58]

The king said: [59]

1.45 "O reverend one, who is this Goddess whom you call Mahāmāyā?
How was she born? What is her work, O twice-born one? [60]

1.46 This Goddess, her nature, her own form (*svarūpā*), her origin, [61]
All this I wish to know from you, O best of Brahma-knowers." [62]

The seer said: [63]

1.47 "She is eternal, having as her form the world. By her is all this pervaded. [64]
Also, her birth is in many forms. Hear about this from me. [65]

1.48 When she becomes manifest for the sake of accomplishing the work of the gods,
Then, even though she is called 'eternal,' she is said to be 'born in the world.' [66]

1.49 When the universe dissolved into the primordial waters at the end of the age, the blessed lord Viṣṇu,
Having stretched out (his serpent) Śeṣa (as a couch), entered into (*abhajat*) Yoganidrā (i.e., entered the sleep of *yoga*). [67][12]

1.50 Then two terrible Asuras named Madhu and Kaiṭabha
Arose from the dirt in Viṣṇu's ear (and) set out to slay Brahmā. [68]

1.51 Brahmā Prajāpati dwelt in a lotus in Viṣṇu's navel,
And having seen the two fierce Asuras and the sleeping Viṣṇu, [69]

1.52 With single-pointed concentration, for the sake of awakening Viṣṇu,
He praised Yoganidrā, who had made her abode in the eyes of Viṣṇu. [70]

1.53 The lord of splendor (praised) the blessed sleep of Viṣṇu,
The incomparable queen of all, supportress of the world, who causes its maintenance and destruction." [71]

Brahmā said: [72]

1.54 "You are Svāhā, you are Svadhā, you are the exclamation *vaṣaṭ*, having speech as your very soul.
You are the nectar of the gods, O imperishable, eternal one; you abide with the threefold syllabic moment (*mātrā*)[13] as your very being. [73]

1.55 (You are) the half-*mātrā*, steadfast, eternal, which cannot be uttered distinctly.

You are she; you are Sāvitrī (the Gāyatrī *mantra*); you are the Goddess, the supreme mother. [74]

1.56 By you is everything supported, by you is the world created;

By you is it protected, O Goddess, and you always consume (it) at the end (of time). [75]

1.57 At (its) emanation you have the form of creation; in (its) protection (you have) the form of steadiness;

Likewise at the end of this world (you have) the form of destruction, O you who consist of the world! [76]

1.58 You are the great knowledge (*mahāvidyā*), the great illusion (*mahāmāyā*), the great insight (*mahāmedhā*), the great memory,

And the great delusion, the great Goddess (*mahādevī*), the great demoness (*mahāsurī*). [77]

1.59 You are the primordial material (*prakṛti*) of everything, manifesting the triad of constituent strands,[14]

The night of destruction, the great night, and the terrible night of delusion. [78]

1.60 You are *śrī*, you are the queen, you modesty, you intelligence, characterized by knowing;

Modesty, well-being, contentment, too, tranquillity and forebearance are you. [79]

1.61 Terrible with your sword and spear, likewise with cudgel and discus,

With conch and bow, having arrows, sling, and iron mace as your weapons, [80]

1.62 Gentle, more gentle than other gentle ones, exceedingly beautiful,

You are superior to the high and low, the supreme queen. [81]

1.63 Whatever and wherever anything exists, whether it be real or unreal, O you who have everything as your very soul,

Of all that, you are the power (*śakti*); how then can you be adequately praised? [82]

1.64 By you the creator of the world, the protector of the world, who (also) consumes the world (i.e., lord Viṣṇu)

Is (here) brought under the influence of sleep (*nidrā*); who here is capable of praising you? [83]

1.65 Since Viṣṇu, Śiva, and I have been made to assume bodily form
By you, who could have the capacity of (adequately) praising you? [84]

1.66 May you, praised in this fashion, O Goddess, with your superior powers
Confuse these two unassailable Asuras, Madhu and Kaiṭabha, [85]

1.67 And may the imperishable lord of the world be quickly awakened, [86]
And may his alertness be used to slay these two great Asuras." [87]

The seer said: [88]

1.68 The Goddess of darkness (*tāmasī*), praised there in this fashion by the creator
For the sake of awakening Viṣṇu so he would slay Madhu and Kaiṭabha, [89]

1.69 Having gone forth from his eyes, nose, arms, heart, and breast,
Presented herself in front of Brahmā, of unmanifest birth. [90]

1.70 And Viṣṇu, lord of the universe, released by her, arose
From his couch on the single ocean; then he saw the two (demons), [91]

1.71 Madhu and Kaiṭabha, of wicked soul, tremendously virile and valorous,
Their eyes red with anger, endeavoring to slay Brahmā. [92]

1.72 Having gotten up, the wise (and) blessed Viṣṇu fought with the two of them
For five thousand years, striking (them) with his arms. [93]

1.73 Intoxicated by their excessive might, deluded by Mahāmāyā, those two [94]
Said to Viṣṇu: "Choose a boon from us." [95]

The blessed (Viṣṇu) said: [96]

1.74 "May the two of you, who are pleased with me, be slain by me. [97]
What good is any other boon here? Just this do I choose." [98]

The seer said: [99]

1.75 (Thinking) "We have been deceived," and having seen the entire universe to consist solely of water,
The two of them addressed the lotus-eyed Viṣṇu: [100]

1.76 ["We are delighted by this battle with you; we are proud to die at your hands."][15]
"Slay us on a place where the earth is not flooded with water."[101]

The seer said: [102]

1.77 Having said, "So be it," the blessed one who carries conch, discus, and club,
Put the two of them on his lap, and cut off their heads with his discus. [103]

1.78 This is how she, when praised by Brahmā, came into being.
Hear again of the majesty of this Goddess. I will tell you. [104]

****

The seer said: [1]

2.1 In days of yore there was a battle between the gods and Asuras that lasted a full hundred years,
When Mahiṣa was chief of the Asuras and Indra (chief) of the gods. [2]

2.2 Then the army of the gods was conquered by the valorous Asuras,
And having conquered all the gods, Mahiṣa became Indra ("the chief"). [3]

2.3 Then the conquered gods, having put the lotus-born Prajāpati in front,
Went to the place where Śiva and Viṣṇu were. [4]

2.4 The thirty (gods) told them of the extent of the gods' defeat,
How it all happened, and likewise the conduct of Mahiṣāsura: [5]

2.5 "He himself now wields sovereignty over Sūrya, Indra, Agni, Vāyu, Candra, Yama,
And over Varuṇa and the others. [6]

2.6 All the hosts of gods, expelled from heaven by the wicked Mahiṣa, Wander on earth like (mere) mortals. [7]

2.7 We have told you what the enemy of the gods has done, And we have taken refuge (in you). Please put your mind on doing away with him!" [8]

2.8 Having heard these words of the gods, the slayer of Madhu (Viṣṇu) Became angry, and Śiva too, with furrowed brows and twisted faces. [9]

2.9 Then from Viṣṇu's face, which was filled with rage, Came forth a great fiery splendor (*tejas*), (and also from the faces) of Brahmā and Śiva. [10]

2.10 And from the bodies of the other gods, Indra and the others, Came forth a great fiery splendor, and it became unified in one place. [11]

2.11 An exceedingly fiery mass like a flaming mountain Did the gods see there, filling the firmament with flames. [12]

2.12 That peerless splendor, born from the bodies of all the gods, Unified and pervading the triple world with its lustre, became a woman. [13]

2.13 From Śiva's splendor her mouth was produced, Her tresses from that of Yama, her arms from the splendor of Viṣṇu. [14]

2.14 From that of Soma (the moon) came her two breasts, from that of Indra her waist, From that of Varuṇa her legs and thighs, from that of the earth her hips. [15]

2.15 From the splendor of Brahmā her two feet (were produced), from the splendor of the sun her toes, From that of the Vasus her fingers, from that of Kubera her nose. [16]

2.16 Her teeth were produced from the splendor of Prajāpati, And her three eyes came from the splendor of Agni. [17]

2.17 Her eyes were the splendor of the two twilights, and her ears that of the wind, And whatever was born from the splendor of the other gods, that, too, was the auspicious (Goddess). [18]

2.18 Having seen her who was born from the rays of the splendor of all the gods,
The gods who were tormented by Mahiṣa rejoiced. [19]

2.19 Having withdrawn a trident from (his own) trident, Śiva gave it to her,
And Krishna gave her a discus, having pulled it out of his own discus. [20]

2.20 And Varuṇa gave her a conch, Agni a spear,
And Vāyu gave a bow and two quivers filled with arrows. [21]

2.21 Indra, lord of the immortals, (gave) a thunderbolt, having pulled it out of his own thunderbolt;
The thousand-eyed one gave her a bell from his elephant, Airāvata. [22]

2.22 From the staff of death, Yama gave a staff, Varuṇa a noose,
And Prajāpati gave a string of beads, Brahmā an ascetic's water-jar. [23]

2.23 The sun put his own rays into all the pores of her skin
And Kāla gave her a sword and spotless shield. [24]

2.24 The sea of milk (gave) a flawless necklace and two unaging garments,
A heavenly crest-jewel, two earrings and bracelets, [25]

2.25 A heavenly half-moon (ornament), armlets on all her arms,
Two spotless anklets, likewise a neck-ornament without parallel, [26]

2.26 And bejewelled rings on all her fingers. [27]
Viśvakarma gave her an utterly flawless axe,

2.27 Likewise weapons of various forms, and unbreakable armor. [28]
A garland of unwithering lotuses on her head, and another on her breast

2.28 And an exceedingly brilliant lotus did the ocean give her. [29]
The Himālaya (gave) a lion as her mount, and various jewels.

2.29 Kubera gave a drinking-cup filled with wine, [30]
And Śeṣa, lord of all the snakes, who supports this earth,

2.30 Gave her a serpent-necklace, ornamented with great jewels. [31]
Honored by the other gods with ornaments and weapons,

2.31 She bellowed aloud with laughter again and again. [32]
The entire atmosphere was filled with her terrible noise,

2.32 And with that measureless, overwhelming (noise) a great echo arose. [33]
All the worlds quaked, and the oceans shook.

2.33 The earth trembled, and mountains tottered. [34]
And the gods, delighted, cried, "Victory!" to her whose mount is a lion.

2.34 And sages praised her, their bodies bowed in devotion. [35]
Having seen the triple world trembling, the enemies of the gods,

2.35 With all their armies prepared for battle, their weapons upraised, rose up together. [36]
Mahiṣāsura, having fumed in anger, "Ah, what is this?!,"

2.36 Rushed toward the sound, surrounded by all the Asuras. [37]
Then he saw the Goddess, filling the triple world with her radiance,

2.37 Causing the earth to bow down at the tread of her feet, scratching the sky with her diadem, [38]
Making all the nether regions tremble at the sound of her bowstring,

2.38 Standing (there) filling all the directions with her thousand arms. [39]
Then there began a battle between the Goddess and the enemies of the gods,

2.39 With the atmosphere illuminated by the weapons and missiles that were hurled in abundance. [40]
The great Asura Cikṣura, Mahiṣāsura's general,

2.40 Fought, and Cāmara, outfitted with an army of four divisions, along with others, [41]
The great Asura named Udagra, with sixty thousand chariots,

2.41 Mahāhanu with ten million fighting, [42]
The great Asura Asiloman with fifty million,

2.42 Bāṣkala fought in battle with sixty million (chariots), [43]
Parivārita with many multitudes of thousands of elephants and horses.

2.43 Surrounded in battle by ten million chariots, the one named Viḍāla [44]
Fought, with five billion (chariots).

2.44 He fought in battle there, surrounded with chariots, [45]
And myriads of others surrounded by chariots, elephants, and horses,

2.45 (All the) great Asuras fought there in battle with the Goddess. [46]
With countless chariots and elephants

2.46 And horses surrounded, Mahiṣāsura was there in battle. [47]
With iron maces and javelins, with spears and cudgels,

2.47 With swords, battle-axes, and pikes they fought with the Goddess in battle. [48]
Some threw spears, while others (threw) nooses.

2.48 They attacked the Goddess in order to slay her with blows from their clubs. [49]
These weapons and arms the Goddess Caṇḍikā

2.49 Broke as if in play, showering down her own weapons and arms. [50]
The Goddess, being praised by gods and seers, appeared unruffled.

2.50 The queen released weapons and arms at the bodies of the Asuras. [51]
The lion-mount of the Goddess, with shaken mane, angry,

2.51 Roamed among the armies of the Asuras, like fire in the forest. [52]
The breaths that Ambikā released while fighting in battle,

2.52 These immediately became her hosts, by the hundred and thousand. [53]
They fought with axes, javelins, swords, and pikes,

2.53 Sustained by the power of the Goddess, destroying the Asura hordes. [54]
Some of her throng caused battle drums to resound, and others conches,

2.54 And others tabors in the great festival of battle. [55]
Then the Goddess with her trident, club, and showers of spears,

2.55 With sword and the like slew the great Asuras by the hundreds, [56]
And she felled others who were deluded by the sound of her bell.

2.56 And having bound some Asuras on the ground with her noose, she dragged them along. [57]
Others were cut in two by sharp blows from her sword.

2.57 Still others, crushed by the fall of her club, lay on the ground, [58]
And some, much smitten by her mace, vomited blood.

2.58 Some fell to the ground, their chests rent by her spear. [59]
Others were destroyed on the field of battle, cut by the flood of arrows.

2.59 (Merely) a semblance of an army, those tormentors of the gods breathed their last. [60]
The arms of some were broken, and others had broken necks.

2.60 The heads of some fell (to the ground), others were pierced in the middle, [61]
And other great Asuras, with their legs cut off, fell to earth.

2.61 Others were cut in half by the Goddess, having (in each part) a single arm, eye, and leg. [62]
Some, when their heads were cut off, fell (and) rose again.

2.62 Headless trunks, (still) grasping the best of weapons, fought with the Goddess,
And others danced in battle, keeping time to the sound of the drums, [63]

2.63 Headless trunks, with broken heads, with sword, spear, and double-edged sword still in hand.
Other great Asuras cried out, "Stop! Stop!" to the Goddess. [64]

2.64 The earth became impassable with the fallen chariots, elephants, horses, and Asuras
Which had come together there where the great battle occurred. [65]

2.65 Great rivers with torrents of blood from the elephants, Asuras, and horses
Flowed there in the midst of the Asura army. [66]

2.66 Thus did Ambikā lead to destruction the great army of the Asuras,
Just as a great fire does a pile of grass and wood. [67]

2.67 And (her) lion, tossing its mane and uttering a terrible roar,
Rooted around searching for breaths still coming from the bodies of the enemies of the gods. [68]

2.68 In this way did the battle take place between the Asuras and the hosts of the Goddess,
So that the gods were pleased with them, releasing showers of flowers from heaven. [69]

****

The seer said: [1]

3.1 Having seen his army being slain, the great Asura
General Cikṣura went forth in anger to fight Ambikā. [2]

3.2 The Asura rained a shower of arrows on the Goddess in battle,
Just as a cloud showers the summit of Mount Meru with rain. [3]

3.3 The Goddess, having broken his multitudes of arrows just in play,
Killed the horses and the driver of the horses with (her) arrows. [4]

3.4 And straightaway she broke his bow and upraised banner,
And she pierced the limbs of the broken-bowed one with arrows. [5]

3.5 With his bow broken, without chariot, with his horses slain, and his charioteer dead,
The Asura ran at the Goddess, armed with sword and shield. [6]

3.6 Having hit the lion on the head with a sharp-edged sword,
He of great speed struck the Goddess on the left arm. [7]

3.7 On touching her arm, the sword exploded, O prince.
Then he seized his lance, his eyes red with anger. [8]

3.8 The great Asura then hurled the flaming (weapon) at Bhadrakālī
As if it were the disc of the sun with shimmerings from the sky. [9]

3.9 On seeing the flying lance, the Goddess released (her own) lance.
By it the Asura's weapon was shattered into a hundred pieces, and the great Asura, too. [10]

3.10 When the valorous leader of Mahiṣa's army was slain,
The afflicter of the gods (named) Cāmara came forward, mounted on an elephant. [11]

3.11 He released a spear at the Goddess. Ambikā quickly caused it to
Fall to the ground splendorless, dashed by her roar. [12]

3.12 Having seen his spear fall shattered, filled with anger,
Cāmara hurled a lance. Even it she broke with arrows. [13]

3.13 Then (her) lion, rising up, fastened on the space between the frontal lobes of the elephant.
In hand-to-paw combat he fought fiercely with (Cāmara), the enemy of the gods. [14]

3.14 The fighting pair fell from the elephant to the earth.
Locked in battle the two fought with dreadful blows. [15]

3.15 Then having leapt up into the sky and descended (again) quickly,
The lion severed Cāmara's head with a blow from his paw. [16]

3.16 Udagra was slain in battle by the Goddess with rocks, trees, and so forth.
And Karāla was felled with her teeth, fists, and palm. [17]

3.17 The angry Goddess pulverized Uddhata with blows from her club,
Bāṣkala with her javelin, and Tāmra (and) Andhaka with arrows. [18]

3.18 The supreme three-eyed Goddess with her trident slew
Ugrāsya and Ugravīrya and likewise Mahāhanu. [19]

3.19 She caused Biḍāla's head to fall from his body with her sword;
She led both Durdhara and Durmukha to the abode of death with arrows. [20]

3.20 When his own army was thus being destroyed, Mahiṣāsura
In his own buffalo form caused (the Goddess's) troops to tremble. [21]

3.21 Some (he slew) with the blow of his snout, others with the stampings of his hooves;
Others (were) lashed with his tail, still others torn by his horns. [22]

3.22 Others by his (sheer) speed, his bellow, his wheeling about,
Still others by the wind of his breaths did he knock to the surface of the earth. [23]

3.23 Having cast down the hosts of Pramathas, the Asura
Ran forth to slay the great Goddess's lion. Then Ambikā became infuriated. [24]

3.24 In anger he of great valor, pounding the earth with his hooves,
Hurled up mountains with his horns and bellowed. [25]

3.25 The earth, trampled by his rapid whirlings, was crushed,
And the ocean, flailed by his tail, flooded everywhere. [26]

3.26 Clouds were torn into pieces, rent by his swaying horns.
Mountains by the hundreds, thrown about by his breath, fell from the sky. [27]

3.27 Having seen the great onrushing Asura, inflated with anger,
Caṇḍikā got angry in order to slay him. [28]

3.28 Hurling a snare at him, she bound the great Asura.
Thus bound in the great battle, he abandoned his buffalo form. [29]

3.29 Immediately thereupon he became a lion. As soon as Ambikā cut off his head,
He appeared as a man, with sword in hand. [30]

3.30 Instantly the Goddess cut the man to shreds with her arrows,
Along with his sword and shield. Then he became a great elephant. [31]

3.31 With his trunk he dragged the great lion and roared;
The Goddess cut off the trunk of the dragging one with her sword. [32]

3.32 At this point, the great Asura resumed his buffalo form again.
Thus, he caused the three worlds, along with what does and does not move, to tremble. [33]

3.33 Then the angry Caṇḍikā, mother of the world, quaffed a superior beverage,
And again and again she laughed, with reddened eyes. [34]

3.34 The Asura, puffed up and drunk with might and power, bellowed
And with his horns hurled mountains at Caṇḍikā. [35]

3.35 Pulverizing what he threw with a volley of arrows,
With passion in her face that was flushed with intoxication, she uttered fevered words. [36]

The Goddess said: [37]

3.36 "Roar, roar for a moment, O fool, while I drink (this) nectar!
When you are slain here by me, it is the gods who soon will roar!" [38]

The seer said: [39]

3.37 Having spoken thus and springing up, she mounted the great Asura.
Having struck him with her foot, she beat him with her spear. [40]

3.38 Then he, struck with her foot, came forth out of his own mouth,
Completely hemmed in by the valor of the Goddess. [41][16]

3.39 That great Asura, who had come forth halfway fighting, was felled by the Goddess,
Who had cut off his head with a great sword. [42]

3.40 Then the whole demon army, crying "Alas, alas!" perished,
And all the throngs of gods attained the highest bliss. [43]

3.41 The gods together with the great heavenly seers praised the Goddess.

The leaders of the Gandharvas sang, and throngs of Apsarases danced. [44]

****

The seer said: [1]

4.1 When the exceedingly brave (and) wicked (Mahiṣa) and the army of the enemies of the gods were slain by the Goddess, throngs of gods, led by Indra,

Praised her with their voices, their necks and shoulders bowed in reverence, their bodies made beautiful by shuddering in ecstacy. [2]

4.2 "To the Goddess by whom this world was spread out through her own power, whose body is comprised of the powers of all the hosts of gods,

To Ambikā, worthy of worship by all gods and great seers, are we bowed down in devotion; may she bring about auspicious things for us. [3]

4.3 May she whose peerless splendor and might the blessed Viṣṇu, Brahmā, and Śiva cannot describe,

May she, Caṇḍikā, fix her mind on the protection of the entire world, and on the destruction of the fear of evil. [4]

4.4 May she who is Śrī herself in the abodes of those who do good, Alakṣmī (in the abodes) of those whose soul is wicked, intelligence in the hearts of the wise,

Faith (in the hearts) of the good, modesty (in the heart of) one of good birth, to you who are she are we bowed down: protect the universe, O Goddess! [5]

4.5 How can we describe this unthinkable form of yours? Or your abundant, surpassing valor which destroys Asuras?

Or such deeds as (you do) in battles among all the throngs of Asuras and gods, O Goddess? [6]

4.6 (You are) the cause of all the worlds; although possessed of the three qualities (*guṇa*s), by faults you are not known; (you are) unfathomable even by Hari, Hara, and the other gods.

(You are) the resort of all, (you are) this entire world that is composed of parts, for you are the supreme, original, untransformed Prakṛti. [7]

4.7 By means of whose utterance, every deity attains satisfaction at all sacrifices, O Goddess,

You are Svāhā, and, (as) the cause of satisfaction of the multitude of Manes, you are proclaimed by men to be Svadhā. [8]

4.8 You who are the cause of release and of inconceivable austerities, your name is repeated by sages, who hold the essence of truth because they have restrained their senses,

Intent upon *mokṣa* with all faults shed: you are this blessed, supreme knowledge, O Goddess. [9]

4.9 Having sound as your very soul, the resting-place of the utterly pure *Ṛg* and *Yajur* (hymns) and of the *Saman*s, delightfully recited with the *Udgītha*,[17]

The Goddess (are you), the blessed triple (Veda), acting for the existence and production of all worlds, the supreme destroyer of pain. [10]

4.10 O Goddess, you are insight, knowing the essence of all scripture, you are Durgā, a vessel upon the ocean of life (that is so) hard to cross, devoid of attachments.

(You are) Śrī, whose sole abode is in the heart of Kaiṭabha's foe (Viṣṇu); you are Gaurī, whose abode is made with the one who is crowned with the moon (Śiva). [11]

4.11 Slightly smiling, spotless, like the orb of the full moon, as pleasing as the lustre of the finest gold (is your face).

Wondrous it is that when the Asura Mahiṣa saw (this) face, he suddenly struck it, his anger aroused. [12]

4.12 But, O Goddess, the fact that Mahiṣa, having seen (your face) angry, terrible with knitted brows, in hue like the rising moon, did not immediately

Give up his life is exceedingly wondrous—for who can live, having seen Death enraged? [13]

4.13 O Goddess, may you, the supreme one, be gracious to life; enraged, you (can) destroy (whole) families in a trice.

This is now known, since the extensive power of the Asura Mahiṣa has been brought to an end. [14]

4.14 Honored are they among nations, riches are theirs, honors are theirs, and their portion of *dharma* does not fail,

Fortunate are they, with devoted children, servants, and wives, on whom you, the gracious one, always bestow good fortune. [15]

4.15 O Goddess, a virtuous man always attentively performs all righteous actions on a daily basis,

And then he goes to heaven by your grace: are you not thus the bestower of rewards on the three worlds, O Goddess? [16]

4.16 O Durgā, (when) called to mind, you take away fear from every creature; (when) called to mind by the healthy, you bestow an exceedingly pure mind.

O you who destroy poverty, misery, and fear, who other than you is always tender-minded, in order to work benefits for all? [17]

4.17 Since these (foes) are slain, the world attains happiness; although they have committed (enough) sin to remain in hell for a long time,

It is with the thought—'Having met death in battle, may they go to heaven'—that you assuredly slay (our) enemies, O Goddess. [18]

4.18 Having, in fact, seen them, why do you not (immediately) reduce all the Asuras to ashes, since you hurl your weapon at enemies?

'Let even enemies, purified by (my) weapons, attain (heavenly) worlds'—such is your most gracious intent even toward those who are hostile. [19]

4.19 Although the eyes of the Asuras were not destroyed by the terrible flashings of the light-mass of your sword, or by the abundant lustre of your spearpoint,

While they looked at your face, which was like a portion of the radiant moon, that very thing happened (i.e., their eyes were destroyed). [20]

4.20 Your disposition, O Goddess, calms the activity of evildoers, and this incomprehensible form (of yours) is unequalled by others,

And (your) valor slays those who have robbed the gods of their prowess: thus was compassion shown by you even towards enemies. [21]

4.21 With what may this prowess of yours be compared? Where is there (such a) form, exceedingly charming (yet) striking fear into enemies?

Compassion in mind and severity in battle are seen in you, O Goddess, who bestow boons even upon the triple world. [22]

4.22 This whole world was rescued by you, through the destruction of (its) enemies; having slain (them) at the peak of battle,

The hosts of enemies were led to heaven by you, and our fear, arising from the frenzied foes of the gods, was dispelled: hail to you! [23]

4.23 With (your) spear protect us, O Goddess! And with (your) sword protect (us), O Ambikā!

Protect us with the sound of (your) bell, and with the twang of your bowstring! [24]

4.24 In the east protect (us) and in the west, O Candikā; protect (us) in the south

By the wielding of your spear, likewise in the north, O queen. [25]

4.25 With your gentle forms that roam about in the triple world,

And with the exceedingly terrible ones, protect us, and also the earth. [26]

4.26 And with the weapons, O Ambikā, sword, and spear, and club, and the rest,

Which lie in your sprout(-like) hands, protect (us) on every side." [27]

The seer said: [28]

4.27 Thus was the supportress of the world praised by the gods with heavenly flowers growing in Indra's pleasure garden,

And praised with perfumes and ointments. [29]

4.28 With devotion was she censed by all the thirty (gods) with heavenly incenses.

With gracious face she spoke to all the prostrate gods. [30]

The Goddess said: [31]

4.29 "O all (you) thirty (gods), whatever is desired from us, let that be chosen."

["I (will) gladly give (it since I am) well worshipped with these hymns of praise."] [32]

The gods said: [33]

"All has been done by you. Nothing is left,

4.30 Since this enemy of ours, Mahiṣāsura, was slain. [34]

But if a boon is to be given to us by you, O great queen,

4.31 (Let it be that) whenever you are remembered by us, may you destroy (our) greatest misfortunes. [35]

And whatever mortal praises you with these hymns, O one whose face is without blemish,

4.32 May you, O Ambikā, who are resorted to by us, the grantress of everything, [36]

Be concerned with his growth through wealth, wife, success, (etc.,) by means of riches, prosperity, and power." [37]

The seer said: [38]

4.33 Thus graciously solicited by the gods both for their own well-being and for that of the world,
Having said, "I consent," Bhadrakālī disappeared, O king. [39]

4.34 Thus has it been related, O king, how she, the Goddess, was formerly produced
From the bodies of the gods, desiring the well-being of the three worlds. [40]

4.35 On another occasion she came to be born (from) the body of Gaurī
For the sake of destroying the wicked Daityas and Śumbha and Niśumbha, [41]

4.36 And for the sake of protecting the worlds (as the) benefactress of the gods.
Hear this story (now) related by me. I will tell it to you properly. [42]

****

The seer said: [1]

5.1 Once upon a time, the two demons, Śumbha and Niśumbha, who had an inflated sense of themselves and their power,
Took away Indra's three worlds and shares in the sacrifice. [2]

5.2 Similarly they took away the powers of the sun, the moon,
Kubera, Yama, and Varuṇa. [3]

5.3 The two of them took over Vāyu's authority and Agni's proper action.
Then the gods, fallen from their kingdoms, were scattered about and defeated. [4]

5.4 All the gods, bereft of authority and conquered by those two
Great Asuras, remembered the invincible Goddess. [5]

5.5 "A boon was given us by her, saying, 'Whenever I am remembered by you in crises,
I will instantly put an end to all adversities.'" [6]

5.6 Having made up their minds, the gods went to the Himālaya, lord of mountains.
They then praised there the Goddess who is Viṣṇu's *māyā.* [7]

The gods said: [8]

5.7 "Hail to the Goddess, hail eternally to the auspicious great Goddess!
Hail to Prakṛti, the auspicious! We who are restrained bow down to her. [9]

5.8 To the terrible one, hail! To the eternal Gaurī, the supportress, hail!
And to the moonlight, to the blissful one having the form of the moon, hail eternally! [10]

5.9 To the auspicious one (are we) bowed down; to growth, to success, to Kūrmī, alleluia, alleluia!
To Nairṛti, to the Lakṣmī of kings, to you, Śarvāṇī, hail, hail! [11]

5.10 To Durgā, the inaccessible further shore, the essential one who accomplishes all,
To fame, likewise the black one, the smokey one, hail eternally! [12]

5.11 To the one who is exceedingly gentle and exceedingly terrible (are we) bowed down: hail, hail!
Hail to the support of the world, to the Goddess (who is) action: hail, hail! [13]

5.12 The Goddess who is known as the *māyā* of Viṣṇu in all creatures,
Hail to her, [14] hail to her, [15] hail to her: hail, hail! [16]

5.13 The Goddess who is designated 'consciousness' in all creatures,
Hail to her, [17] hail to her, [18] hail to her: hail, hail! [19]

5.14 The Goddess who abides in all creatures in the form of intelligence,
Hail to her, [20] hail to her, [21] hail to her: hail, hail! [22]

5.15 The Goddess who abides in all creatures in the form of sleep,
Hail to her, [23] hail to her, [24] hail to her: hail, hail! [25]

5.16 The Goddess who abides in all creatures in the form of hunger,
Hail to her, [26] hail to her, [27] hail to her: hail, hail! [28]

5.17 The Goddess . . . shadow,
Hail to her, [29] hail to her, [30] hail to her: hail, hail! [31]

5.18 The Goddess . . . power,
Hail to her, [32] hail to her, [33] hail to her: hail, hail! [34]

5.19 The Goddess . . . thirst,
Hail to her, [35] hail to her, [36] hail to her: hail, hail! [37]

5.20 The Goddess . . . patience,
Hail to her, [38] hail to her, [39] hail to her: hail, hail! [40]

5.21 The Goddess . . . birth,
Hail to her, [41] hail to her, [42] hail to her: hail, hail! [43]

5.22 The Goddess . . . modesty,
Hail to her, [44] hail to her, [45] hail to her: hail, hail! [46]

5.23 The Goddess . . . tranquillity,
Hail to her, [47] hail to her, [48] hail to her: hail, hail! [49]

5.24 The Goddess . . . faith,
Hail to her, [50] hail to her, [51] hail to her: hail, hail! [52]

5.25 The Goddess . . . loveliness,
Hail to her, [53] hail to her, [54] hail to her: hail, hail! [55]

5.26 The Goddess . . . Lakṣmī,
Hail to her, [56] hail to her, [57] hail to her: hail, hail! [58]

5.27 The Goddess . . . activity,
Hail to her, [59] hail to her, [60] hail to her: hail, hail! [61]

5.28 The Goddess . . . memory,
Hail to her, [62] hail to her, [63] hail to her: hail, hail! [64]

5.29 The Goddess . . . compassion,
Hail to her, [65] hail to her, [66] hail to her: hail, hail! [67]

5.30 The Goddess . . . contentment,
Hail to her, [68] hail to her, [69] hail to her: hail, hail! [70]

5.31 The Goddess . . . mother,
Hail to her, [71] hail to her, [72] hail to her: hail, hail! [73]

5.32 The Goddess . . . error,
Hail to her, [74] hail to her, [75] hail to her: hail, hail! [76]

5.33 She who is the inner controller of the senses in all creatures,
And constantly in the elements, to the Goddess who is the fact of universal presence, hail, hail! [77]

5.34 She who abides, having pervaded this whole world in the form of mind,
Hail to her, [78] hail to her, [79] hail to her: hail, hail! [80]

5.35 Praised of yore by the gods because refuge was desired, similarly praised by the lord of gods day after day,

May she, the queen, the cause of what is bright, accomplish for us bright things, auspicious things: may she destroy misfortunes. [81]

5.36 She, the ruler, is now reverenced by us, the gods, who are tormented by haughty demons.

And at this very moment, she who has been called to mind by us, whose bodies are prostrated in devotion, destroys all misfortunes." [82]

The seer said: [83]

5.37 Thus (entreated) by the gods who are filled with praise and the like,
Pārvatī then went to bathe in the waters of the Ganges, O king. [84]

5.38 She of beautiful brows said to the gods: "Who is being praised here by you?"

An auspicious (*śivā*) (form) came forth from the sheath of her body (and) said: [85]

5.39 "This hymn is made to me by those who have been vanquished by Śumbha,

The gods who have assembled (here), conquered by Niśumbha in battle." [86]

5.40 Since Ambikā came forth from the body sheath (*kośa*) of Pārvatī,
She is sung of in all the worlds as "Kauśikī." [87]

5.41 When she had come forth, Pārvatī became black (*kṛṣṇā*).
Known as "Kālikā," she makes her abode in the Himālayas. [88][18]

5.42 Then the two servants of Śumbha and Niśumbha, Caṇḍa and Muṇḍa, saw

Ambikā wearing this supreme mind-boggling form. [89]

5.43 They told Śumbha about her: "O king, a certain woman dwells (there),

Exceptionally beautiful, causing the Himālayas to glow. [90]

5.44 Such a form has never been seen anywhere by anyone.
You should find out who this goddess is and seize her, O king! [91]

5.45 She is a jewel among women; with the most beautiful limbs, illuminating all the directions with her lustre,

She abides there; O lord of demons, you really must see her! [92]

5.46 O lord, the jewels and gems, the elephants, horses, and so on
That exist in the three worlds, they all now shine here in your own abode. [93]

5.47 You have taken the jewel of elephants, Airāvata, away from Indra,
And also this Pārijāta tree and the horse Uccaiḥśravas. [94]

5.48 This wondrous gem of a chariot, yoked to swans, which was taken away from Brahmā,
Stands here in your courtyard. [95]

5.49 This treasure called 'Great Lotus' was taken away from Kubera,
And the ocean gave you a garland of unwithering lotuses. [96]

5.50 Varuṇa's royal umbrella, which showers down gold, now stands in your house,
And this best of chariots, which formerly belonged to Prajāpati. [97]

5.51 This spear named 'Giver of Death' was taken by you from the lord of death, O king.
The noose of the lord of waters, Varuṇa, is in the possession of your brother. [98]

5.52 To Niśumbha belong all the jewels that have been produced from the ocean,
And Agni gave you two garments purified by the fire himself. [99]

5.53 In this fashion, O lord of demons, have all valued possessions been taken away by you.
This beauty is a jewel among women: why don't you seize her?!" [100]

The seer said: [101]

5.54 Then, having heard these words of Caṇḍa and Muṇḍa, Śumbha
Sent the great demon Sugrīva as a messenger to the Goddess, [102]

5.55 Saying, "Having approached her, speak words on my behalf
So that, being won over, she will be readily enchanted." [103]

5.56 He then went to the resplendent mountainous place where the Goddess dwelt,
And spoke sweet words to her with honeyed voice. [104]

The messenger said: [105]

5.57 "Śumbha is the lord of demons, the supreme lord in the three worlds.
I am a messenger sent by him here into your presence. [106]

5.58 He whose command is always obeyed where celestials dwell,
He has conquered all the enemies of the demons. Hear what he says. [107]

5.59 'All the three worlds are mine; all the gods have come under my sway.
I enjoy all the sacrificial portions that belong to each god. [108]

5.60 All the finest jewels in the triple world have come into my power, with no exceptions.
Similarly the jewel of elephants, the very mount of the lord of gods, has been taken away. [109]

5.61 The jewel of horses, born from the churning of the ocean,
Named Uccaiḥśravas, has been reverentially delivered over to me by the gods. [110]

5.62 And whatever other valuables exist among gods, Gandharvas and serpents,
All these things are mine, O fair one. [111]

5.63 We regard you as the jewel among women in the world, O Goddess.
You should come to us, for we are the enjoyer of jewels. [112]

5.64 Choose either me or my valorous younger brother, Niśumbha,
For you are indeed a jewel, O one of tremulous eyes. [113]

5.65 By taking me you will acquire supreme, unparalleled dominion.
Having reflected on this with your keen intellect, come be my wife.'" [114]

The seer said: [115]

5.66 Addressed in this fashion, the blessed and auspicious Goddess Durgā,
By whom this universe is supported, spoke melodiously with a deep inner smile. [116]

The Goddess said: [117]

5.67 "What you say is true; there is no falsehood in what you have uttered.

Śumbha is lord of the triple world, and Niśumbha is his equal. [118]

5.68 But how can I go back on my word?
Let me tell you of the promise I once dim-wittedly made: [119]

5.69 He who conquers me in battle, he who overcomes my pride,
He whose strength is comparable to mine in the world, just he will be my husband. [120]

5.70 Therefore let Śumbha come here, or the great Asura Niśumbha.
Having conquered me, he will (then) readily take my hand in marriage. Why delay?" [121]

The messenger said: [122]

5.71 "You are a haughty one, O Goddess! You should not speak in this fashion in front of me!
What man is there in the triple world who can stand in front of Śumbha and Niśumbha? [123]

5.72 Even the gods cannot stand in battle with the other demons,
O Goddess. How much less can you, a single woman? [124]

5.73 All the gods, led by Indra, were no match in battle
For this Śumbha and the others. How can you, a woman, go into battle with them? [125]

5.74 You should go to Śumbha and Niśumbha, just as I said.
Let it not come to pass that you are brought into their presence being dragged by the hair, losing your dignity!" [126]

The Goddess said: [127]

5.75 "So it must be. Śumbha is a mighty one, and Niśumbha exceedingly brave,
But what can I do, since this rash promise was made long ago? [128]

5.76 Go along now. Everything that I have said,
You relate that properly to the lord of the Asuras, and let him do what is appropriate." [129]

****

The seer said: [1]

6.1 Having heard these words of the Goddess, the messenger was filled with indignation.
Returning to the king of the demons, he recounted everything in detail. [2]

6.2 Having given ear to the words of the messenger, the king of the Asuras,
Filled with anger, spoke to the general of the Asuras named "Eyes of Smoke" (*dhūmralocana*). [3]

6.3 "All right, Smokey, enveloped by your army,
Forcibly bring that wicked woman here, upsetting her by dragging her by the hair. [4]

6.4 If another should rise up to rescue her,
He is to be slain, whether he be god or Yakṣa or Gandharva." [5]

The seer said: [6]

6.5 Commanded in this fashion by the demon-king, the Daitya Dhūmralocana
Speedily sallied forth, surrounded by sixty thousand Asuras. [7]

6.6 Seeing the Goddess standing on the snowy mount,
He bellowed in a loud voice: "Come into the presence of Śumbha and Niśumbha! [8]

6.7 If you do not come with delight to my master right now,
Then I will immediately take you by force, upsetting you by dragging you by the hair." [9]

The Goddess said: [10]

6.8 "Sent by the lord of demons, mighty, and surrounded by your army,
You take me by force. What can I do about it?" [11]

The seer said: [12]

6.9 Thus addressed, old Smokey-Eyes rushed at her.
Ambikā reduced him to ashes with the menacing sound of "Hmmmmmm!" [13]

6.10 Then Ambikā rained upon the great cruel army of Asuras
A shower of sharp arrows, spears and battle-axes. [14]

6.11 Shaking its mane, uttering a fearsome roar in anger,
The lion-mount of the Goddess then fell upon the Asura army. [15]

6.12 Some he slew with a blow of his paw, others with his jaws,
And still other great demons with the trampling of his hind legs. [16]

6.13 The lion tore open the bellies of some with his claws,
And beheaded others by cuffing them with his paws. [17]

6.14 Still others had their heads and arms broken by him,
And he drank the blood of others while tossing his mane. [18]

6.15 In an instant the entire army was brought to destruction by the noble,
Enraged lion-mount of the Goddess. [19]

6.16 Having heard that old Smokey-Eyes had been slain by the Goddess
And his entire army wasted by the Goddess's lion, [20]

6.17 The lord of the demons, Śumbha, became enraged. With his lower lip trembling,
He gave orders to the two great Asuras Caṇḍa and Muṇḍa: [21]

6.18 "Damn it, Caṇḍa! Damn it, Muṇḍa! You two
Go there, surrounded with many forces, and bring her here quickly, [22]

6.19 Seizing her by the hair or trussing her up. But if you have any doubt about being able to do this,
Then let her be assailed in battle by all the Asuras with their various weapons. [23]

6.20 When that wicked woman has been assaulted and her lion slain,
Then seizing and binding this Ambikā, let her be brought here!" [24]

****

The seer said: [1]

7.1 Directed in this fashion by him, the demons, arranged as a fourfold army
With Caṇḍa and Muṇḍa at their head, went forth with upraised weapons. [2]

7.2 Then they saw the Goddess, smiling slightly, mounted
On her lion on the great golden peak of the highest mountain. [3]

7.3 Having seen her, they made ready in their efforts to abduct her,
While others approached her with swords drawn and bows bent. [4]

7.4 Ambikā then uttered a great wrathful cry against them,
And her face became black as ink in anger. [5]

7.5 From the knitted brows of her forehead's surface immediately
Came forth Kālī, with her dreadful face, carrying sword and noose. [6]

7.6 She carried a strange skull-topped staff, and wore a garland of human heads;
She was shrouded in a tiger skin, and looked utterly gruesome with her emaciated skin, [7]

7.7 Her widely gaping mouth, terrifying with its lolling tongue,
With sunken, reddened eyes and a mouth that filled the directions with roars. [8]

7.8 She fell upon the great Asuras in that army, slaying them immediately.
She then devoured the forces of the enemies of the gods. [9]

7.9 Attacking both the front and rear guard, having seized the elephants
Together with their riders and bells, she hurled them into her mouth with a single hand. [10]

7.10 Likewise having flung the cavalry with its horses and the chariots with their charioteers
Into her mouth, she brutally pulverized them with her teeth. [11]

7.11 She seized one by the hair, and another by the throat.
Having attacked one with her foot, she crushed another against her breast. [12]

7.12 The weapons and missiles that were hurled by the demons
She seized with her mouth, and crunched them to bits with her teeth. [13]

7.13 The army of all those mighty and distinguished demons
She destroyed: she devoured some, and thrashed the others. [14]

7.14 Some were sliced by her sword, others pounded with her skull-topped staff.

Just in this way did the Asuras meet their destruction, ground up by the edges of her fangs. [15]

7.15 Immediately upon seeing the entire army of the Asuras slain,
Caṇḍa rushed at the incredibly fearsome Kālī. [16]

7.16 The great Asura enveloped the dread-eyed female with a horrendous great shower of arrows,
And Muṇḍa did the same with discuses hurled by the thousand. [17]

7.17 This stream of discuses entering her mouth
Resembled a multitude of suns entering into the middle of a black cloud. [18]

7.18 Then Kālī, her ugly teeth gleaming within her dreadful mouth,
Angrily cackled with terrible sounds. [19]

7.19 Mounting her great lion, the Goddess ran at Caṇḍa,
And having seized him by the hair, she cut off his head with her sword. [20]

7.20 On seeing Caṇḍa slain, Muṇḍa rushed at her.
She caused him to fall to the ground, wrathfully smitten with her sword. [21]

7.21 On seeing Caṇḍa slain, and also the valorous Muṇḍa,
What was left of the assaulted army was overcome with fear, and fled in all directions. [22]

7.22 Picking up the heads of Caṇḍa and Muṇḍa, Kālī
Approached Caṇḍikā and spoke words mixed with loud and cruel laughter: [23]

7.23 "Here, as a present from me to you, are Caṇḍa and Muṇḍa, two beasts
Slain in the sacrifice of battle. Now you yourself can slay Śumbha and Niśumbha!" [24]

The seer said: [25]

7.24 Seeing the two great Asuras brought there,
The beautiful Caṇḍikā spoke these playful words to Kālī: [26]

7.25 "Because you have seized Caṇḍa and Muṇḍa and brought them here,
You will henceforth be known in the world as the Goddess 'Cāmuṇḍā'." [27]

****

The seer said: [1]

8.1 When Caṇḍa had been killed and Muṇḍa slain,
And the extensive armies annihilated, the lord of demons [2]

8.2 Śumbha became incensed, his mind deranged with anger.
He ordered the marshaling of all the Daitya armies. [3]

8.3 "Now let the eighty-six Udāyudha demons with all their troops,
And the eighty-four Kambus surrounded with their own forces go forth. [4]

8.4 May the fifty families of Koṭivīrya demons,
And the one hundred families of Dhūmra proceed at my command. [5]

8.5 Similarly the Kālaka, Daurhṛda, Maurya, and Kālakeya demons
Should proceed quickly, prepared for battle, at my command." [6]

8.6 Having issued these orders, Śumbha, lord of Asuras, whose directive is terrifying,
Sallied forth, surrounded by many thousands of magnificent troops. [7]

8.7 On seeing him approach with his army in fearsome fashion, Caṇḍikā
Filled the space between earth and sky with the twanging of her bowstring. [8]

8.8 Then her lion let loose a monstrous roar, O king,
And Ambikā elaborated this noise still further with the sound of her bell. [9]

8.9 Kālī, her mouth agape and filling the directions with snarls,
Drowned out even the noise of the bowstring, lion, and bell with her gruesome sounds. [10]

8.10 On hearing this din, the enraged Daitya armies
Surrounded the Goddess, her lion, and Kālī on all four sides. [11]

8.11 At that very moment, O king, in order to destroy the enemies of the gods,
And for the sake of the well-being of the supreme gods, very valorous and powerful [12]

8.12 *Śakti*s, having sprung forth from the bodies of Brahmā, Śiva, Skanda,
Viṣṇu, and Indra, and having the form of each, approached Caṇḍikā. [13]

8.13 Whatever form, ornament, and mount a particular god possessed,
With that very form did his *śakti* go forth to fight the Asuras. [14]

8.14 In a heavenly conveyance drawn by swans, with rosary and waterpot,
Came forth the *śakti* of Brahmā: she is known as Brahmāṇī. [15]

8.15 Māheśvarī sallied forth, mounted on a bull, bearing the best of tridents,
With great serpents for bracelets, adorned with the crescent of the moon. [16]

8.16 Ambikā having the form of Guha (Skanda), as Kaumārī went forth to fight the demons,
With spear in hand, having the best of peacocks as her mount. [17]

8.17 Then the *śakti* known as Vaiṣṇavī went forth, mounted on Garuda,
With conch, discus, club, bow and sword in hand. [18]

8.18 The *śakti* of Hari who has the matchless form of a sacrificial boar
Then came forth, bearing the body of a sow. [19]

8.19 Nārasiṃhī, having a form like the man-lion,
Then went forth, with many a constellation cast down by the tossing of her mane. [20]

8.20 Then Aindrī, with thunderbolt in hand, mounted upon the lord of elephants,
Went forth; she had a thousand eyes, just like Indra. [21]

8.21 Then Śiva, surrounded by these *śakti*s of the gods,
Said to Caṇḍikā: "May the demons now be quickly slain by you in order to please me." [22]

8.22 Then from the body of the Goddess came forth the very frightening
Śakti of Caṇḍikā herself, gruesome and yelping like a hundred jackals. [23]

8.23 And she, the invincible one, spoke to Śiva, of smokey, matted locks:
"You yourself become my messenger to Śumbha and Niśumbha. [24]

8.24 Say to those two arrogant creatures
And to all the other demons who have assembled there for battle: [25]

8.25 'If you wish to live, then Indra must get back the triple world,

The gods should have their proper portions of the sacrifice returned, and you should go back to the nether world. [26]

8.26 If, on the other hand, you are desirous of battle because of ill-begotten arrogance about your strength,

Then come along: let my jackals satiate themselves on your flesh!'" [27]

8.27 Since Śiva himself was sent by her as a messenger,

She has become known throughout the world as Śivadūtī ("She who has Śiva as messenger"). [28]

8.28 Upon hearing the words of the Goddess that were conveyed by Śiva, the great Asuras

Filled with pride went to where Kātyāyanī stood. [29]

8.29 Then at the very beginning of the battle, the enemies of the gods,

Puffed up with pride, showered the Goddess with torrents of arrows, lancces, and spears. [30]

8.30 She playfully broke the arrows, spears, lances, and axes that were hurled

With great arrows released from her twanging bow. [31]

8.31 Then right in front of him (Śiva?) Kālī roamed about, ripping open some with strokes of her spear,

And crushing others with her skull-topped staff. [32]

8.32 Wherever Brahmāṇī ran, she destroyed the prowess of the enemies,

Quenching their valor by dousing them with water from her waterpot. [33]

8.33 Māheśvarī with her trident, Vaiṣṇavī with discus,

And Kaumārī with her most dreadful spear then slew the demons. [34]

8.34 At the blow of Aindrī's thunderbolt, Daityas and Danavas fell

By the hundreds; torn open, they showered the ground with torrents of blood. [35]

8.35 Others fell ripped by the blow of Vārāhī's snout, their chests sundered

By the tips of her tusks, chopped up by her discus. [36]

8.36 Nārasiṃhī devoured still other great demons; tearing them with her claws,

She roamed about the battlefield, filling the sky with her snorts. [37]

8.37 The demons who were shattered by the cruel laughter of Śivadūtī
Fell broken to the ground, and she gobbled them up. [38]

8.38 The leaders of the enemies of the gods, on seeing the great demons
Being pulverized by the band of Mothers with their respective weapons, ran for their lives. [39]

8.39 When he saw the demons fleeing, tormented by the band of Mothers,
The great cruel Raktabīja went forth to do battle. [40]

8.40 Whenever a drop of blood fell from his body to the earth,
Then out of it would rise up from the earth a great demon that was just like him. [41]

8.41 With club in hand, the great demon fought with Indra's *śakti,*
And Aindrī smote Raktabīja with her thunderbolt. [42]

8.42 Blood immediately gushed forth from the one who was struck with the shaft.
From it there rose up mighty soldiers with the very same form. [43]

8.43 However many drops of blood fell from his body,
So many men were born, comparable in valor, strength, and might. [44]

8.44 And those men born of blood fought there
With the Mothers still more terribly, hurling their wicked weapons. [45]

8.45 When his head was smashed again by a blow from her thunderbolt,
Blood flowed yet again, and from it men were born by the thousands. [46]

8.46 Vaiṣṇavī assailed him with her discus in battle,
And Aindrī beat the lord of demons with her club. [47]

8.47 The world was filled with great Asuras just like him,
Born by the thousands from the blood that flowed when he was cut by Vaiṣṇavī's discus. [48]

8.48 Kaumārī wounded him with her spear, and Vārāhī with her sword,
And Māheśvarī wounded the great demon Raktabīja with her trident. [49]

8.49 The great demon Raktabīja, filled with rage, struck
Each and every one of the Mothers with his club. [50]

8.50 From the flow of blood that fell in torrents to the earth
From the one who was wounded by the spear, lance, and so forth, demons were born by the hundreds. [51]

8.51 By those demons born from the blood of this one demon, the entire world
Was pervaded; then the gods became utterly terrified. [52]

8.52 On seeing the gods quaking, Caṇḍikā immediately laughed aloud.
She spoke to Kālī: "O Cāmuṇḍā, open wide your mouth. [53]

8.53 With this mouth of yours, quickly take in the drops of blood produced by the fall of my weapons
And the great demons who are born from that blood. [54]

8.54 Roam about on the battlefield, consuming the great demons who are born from him.
Thus will this demon, his blood dried up, meet his destruction. [55]

8.55 In this way, these terrible ones will be consumed by you, and no more will be born."
Having spoken thus, the Goddess then gored him with her spear. [56]

8.56 With her mouth Kālī seized upon the blood of Raktabīja.
The latter then struck Caṇḍikā with his club. [57]

8.57 But the blow of the club did not cause her even the slightest pain,
While much blood flowed from his body when struck. [58]

8.58 Cāmuṇḍā took it all into her mouth, from every direction,
And also into her mouth entered the great demons who were born from his blood. [59]

8.59 Cāmuṇḍā chewed them up, and drank his blood.
With spear, thunderbolt, arrows, swords, and lances the Goddess [60]

8.60 Wounded Raktabīja, whose blood was being drunk by Cāmuṇḍā.
Mortally wounded by that constellation of weapons, the great demon Raktabīja [61]

8.61 Fell to the earth bloodless, O king!
And then, O king, the gods entered into boundless joy. [62]

8.62 When he was slain, the band of Mothers danced about, intoxicated by his blood. [63]

****

The king said: [1]

9.1 "It is simply wonderful that you, O blessed one, have told me
This *Māhātmya* of the Goddess's activity connected with the slaying of Raktabīja. [2]

9.2 I want to hear more, about what Śumbha and the outraged Niśumbha
Did when Raktabīja was killed." [3]

The seer said: [4]

9.3 When Raktabīja was killed, and the others slain in battle,
Śumbha and Niśumbha entered into an unparalleled frenzy. [5]

9.4 On seeing the great army being wasted, blustering with outrage,
Niśumbha rushed forward, with the very best of the demonic army. [6]

9.5 In front of him, behind him, and on both sides were great Asuras;
Angry and biting their lips they rushed forth to slay the Goddess. [7]

9.6 On came the great soldier Śumbha, too, surrounded by his own army,
To do battle with the Mothers and then angrily to slay Caṇḍikā. [8]

9.7 Thereupon there broke out a titanic struggle between the Goddess and Śumbha and Niśumbha,
Who were like two great thunderclouds releasing the most dreadful torrent of arrows. [9]

9.8 Caṇḍikā shattered those arrows with her own volley of arrows.
She beat the two demon lords on their arms and legs with her streams of weapons. [10]

9.9 Picking up his sharpened sword and his radiant shield, Niśumbha
Struck the wonderful lion mount of the Goddess on the head. [11]

9.10 When her mount was assailed, the Goddess immediately broke Niśumbha's great sword
With a double-edged arrow, and likewise his shield that had the lustre of eight moons. [12]

9.11 When his sword and shield were broken, the great demon unleashed his spear:
She broke it in two with her discus, even as it came toward her. [13]

9.12 Trumpeting with rage, the demon Niśumbha then seized his lance:

The Goddess crushed it in midflight with a blow of her hand. [14]

9.13 Laying ahold of his club, he hurled it at Caṇḍikā:
It was broken, reduced to ashes, by the Goddess's trident. [15]

9.14 Then, having struck the leader of the demons who was rushing on, axe in hand,
The Goddess drove him to the ground with showers of arrows. [16]

9.15 When he saw his brother Niśumbha, of fearsome valor, thus slain on the earth,
The furious Śumbha went out to engage Ambikā in battle. [17]

9.16 Mounted on his chariot, with his magnificent weapons raised on high
By his eight arms without equal, he shone forth, appearing to fill the entire sky. [18]

9.17 Having seen him coming forth, the Goddess caused her conch to resound,
And the twanging of her bowstring made a ghastly noise. [19]

9.18 She filled the directions with the sound of her own bell,
Which destroyed the radiance of all the demon armies. [20]

9.19 Then her lion filled the heaven, the earth, and the ten intermediate directions
With massive roars that sapped the rut of great elephants. [21]

9.20 Kālī, too, springing up into the sky, pounded the earth
With her hands, and all the previous sounds were drowned out by the din. [22]

9.21 Śivadūtī made an inauspicious cackling sound.
These noises terrified the demons, and Śumbha went into a rage. [23]

9.22 When Ambikā demanded, "Stop! Stop, you wicked one!"
Then cries of "Victory!" were uttered by the gods from their places in the sky. [24]

9.23 The spear that was released by Śumbha as he approached, terrible with its flames,
Coming on like a great fire mass, that spear she hurled down with her firebrand. [25]

9.24 The entire interval between the three worlds was filled up by Śumbha's lionesque roar,

But it was drowned out by the dreadful sound of the Goddess's whirlwind. [26]

9.25 The Goddess broke the arrows released by Śumbha, and he shattered hers in retaliation
With hundreds and thousands of terrible arrows of his own. [27]

9.26 Then Caṇḍikā, enraged, gored him with her lance.
Wounded, he passed out and fell to the ground. [28]

9.27 Then Niśumbha, regaining consciousness and picking up his bow,
Assailed the Goddess, Kālī, and her lion with arrows. [29]

9.28 Having made himself ten-thousand-armed, the lord of demons,
This son of Diti, blanketed Caṇḍikā with ten thousand discuses. [30]

9.29 Then the blessed, angry Durgā, who destroys adversity and suffering,
Shattered those discuses and arrows with her own arrows. [31]

9.30 Thereupon Niśumbha, taking up his club, ran at Caṇḍikā,
Surrounded by the demon army, in order to slay her. [32]

9.31 Caṇḍikā instantly split the club of the onrushing one
With her sharp-edged sword, and he took up his spear. [33]

9.32 As Niśumbha came on with spear in hand, Caṇḍikā pierced
That tormentor of the gods in the heart with a swiftly thrown pike. [34]

9.33 From the heart of the one who was run through by the pike came forth
Another mighty, valorous person crying, "Stop!" [35]

9.34 Laughing boisterously, the Goddess cut off the head
Of the one who came forth with her sword, and he fell to the ground. [36]

9.35 Then her lion chewed up some of the demons whose necks he had broken with his dreadful jaws,
And Kālī and Śivadūtī did the same to others. [37]

9.36 Some great demons perished, shattered by Kaumārī's spear.
Others were engulfed in water that Brahmāṇī had purified with *mantras*. [38]

9.37 Some fell impaled by Māheśvarī's trident,
Others were ground to dust on the earth with blows from the snout of Vārāhī. [39]

9.38 Some demons were quartered by Vaiṣṇavī's discus,
And others by the thunderbolt released from the tips of Aindrī's fingers. [40]

9.39 Some demons perished, others fled from the great battle,
And still others were devoured by Kālī, Śivadūtī, and the lion. [41]

****

The seer said: [1]

10.1 On seeing his brother, dear to him as his own life, slain
And his army slaughtered, the enraged Śumbha spoke these words: [2]

10.2 "O Durgā, puffed up with misplaced pride in your own strength of arms, don't be so haughty!
It is by relying on the strength of others that you fight, with this inflated sense of your own importance!" [3]

The Goddess said: [4]

10.3 "I alone exist here in the world; what second, other than I, is there?
O wicked one, behold these my manifestations of power entering back into me!" [5]

10.4 Thereupon, all the goddesses, led by Brahmāṇī,
Went to their resting-place in the body of the Goddess; then there was just Ambikā, alone. [6]

The Goddess said: [7]

10.5 "When I was established here in many forms, it was by means of my extraordinary power.
That has now been withdrawn by me. I stand utterly alone. May you be resolute in combat!" [8]

The seer said: [9]

10.6 A terrible struggle then ensued between just the two of them, the Goddess and Śumbha,
While the gods and demons looked on. [10]

10.7 With showers of arrows, sharp weapons, and dread missiles

Did the battle take place, once again arousing fear throughout the entire world. [11]

10.8 The heavenly weapons that Ambikā unleashed by the hundreds,
Those the lord of demons broke with his own counterstrikes. [12]

10.9 And the gleaming missiles that he hurled, those the supreme queen
Playfully broke with dread utterances of "Hmmmmmm!" and the like. [13]

10.10 Then the demon enveloped the Goddess with showers of arrows.
Enraged at this, the Goddess shattered his bow with her arrows. [14]

10.11 When his bow was broken, the lord of demons took up his spear.
The Goddess broke it with her discus, even as it rested in his hand. [15]

10.12 Then raising up his luminous sword, adorned with a hundred moons,
The lord of demons rushed at the Goddess. [16]

10.13 Caṇḍikā instantly broke the sword of her assailant
And also his shield that was as spotless as sunbeams, with sharp arrows shot from her bow. [17]

10.14 Then, with his horse slain, his bow broken, and without a charioteer, the demon
Picked up a fearsome club in his effort to slay Ambikā. [18]

10.15 She shattered the club of the onrushing one with sharpened arrows.
Immediately he fell upon her with upraised fist. [19]

10.16 The leader of the demons brought his fist down upon the Goddess's heart,
And she walloped him on the chest with her palm. [20]

10.17 The blow of her palm knocked the demon king to the ground,
But he immediately got up again. [21]

10.18 Springing up and seizing the Goddess, he climbed high into the sky.
Caṇḍikā did battle with him there without any support. [22]

10.19 There in the sky the demon and the Goddess warred with one another,
An unprecendented struggle that filled the sages with wonder. [23]

10.20 Then having grappled with him for a long time, Ambikā,
Springing up, whirled him around and hurled him to the earth's surface. [24]

10.21 On striking the earth, he who had been hurled instantly raised up his fist.
Desirous of destroying Caṇḍikā, he ran at her. [25]

10.22 The Goddess then knocked to the ground the lord of all demonic worlds, even as he ran,
Having broken open his chest with a spear. [26]

10.23 With his life breath gone, pierced by the tip of the Goddess's spear, he fell to the ground,
Causing the entire earth, with its oceans, islands, and mountains, to tremble. [27]

10.24 The flaming clouds of portent that formerly had gathered became tranquil,
And rivers once again flowed within their banks, when he was slain. [29][19]

10.25 When that wicked one was dead, the whole universe became soothed,
Regaining its natural condition once more, and the sky became spotless. [28]

10.26 Then the minds of all the throngs of gods were overcome with joy.
When the wicked one was slain, Gandharvas sang with gay abandon, [30]

10.27 Others caused their instruments to resound, and groups of Apsarases danced about.
Favorable winds began to blow, and the sun shone brilliantly. [31]

10.28 The sacred fires blazed peacefully, and the sounds that had been produced throughout the quarters died away. [32]

****

The seer said: [1]

11.1 When the great lord of demons was slain there by the Goddess, Indra and the other gods, led by Agni,
Praised Kātyāyanī, because their wishes had been fulfilled, their faces radiant, their desires made manifest. [2]

11.2 "O Goddess, who takes away the sufferings of those who take refuge in you, be gracious; be gracious, O mother of the entire world.

Be gracious, O queen of all, protect all; you are the queen, O Goddess, of all that does and does not move. [3]

11.3 You have become the sole support of the world, for you abide in the form of the earth.

By you who exist in the form of water, all this universe is filled up, O one of inviolable valor. [4]

11.4 You are the power of Viṣṇu, of boundless valor; you are the seed of all, the supreme illusion.

Deluded, O Goddess, is this entire universe; you, when resorted to, are the cause of release right here on earth. [5]

11.5 All the various knowledges, O Goddess, are portions of you, as is each and every woman in the various worlds.

By you alone as mother has this world been filled up; what praise can suffice for you who are beyond praise, the ultimate utterance? [6]

11.6 When you, the Goddess who has become everything, granting heaven and ultimate freedom,

Are praised, what fine words could suffice for the eulogy? [7]

11.7 O you who abide in the heart of every individual in the form of intelligence,

Granting heaven and ultimate freedom, Goddess Nārāyaṇī, praise be to you! [8]

11.8 O you who bring about the process of change, in the form of minutes, moments, and so forth,

The very power manifest at the destruction of the cosmos, O Nārāyaṇī, praise be to you! [9]

11.9 O you who are blessed with every felicity, auspicious, accomplishing every intent,

O protectress, three-eyed Gaurī, O Nārāyaṇī, praise be to you! [10]

11.10 O you, the eternal, who become the power of creation, sustenance, and destruction,

Abiding in the qualities of primordial matter, actually consisting of those qualities, O Nārāyaṇī, praise be to you! [11]

11.11 O you who are intent upon rescuing those who suffer and are downcast and who take refuge in you,

O you who take away the suffering of all, O Nārāyaṇī, praise be to you! [12]

11.12 O you who are mounted upon a chariot yoked to swans, having the form of Brahmāṇī,

Sprinkling water in which *kuśa* grass has steeped, Goddess Nārāyaṇī, praise be to you! [13]

11.13 O you who carry a trident, moon, and snake, having as your mount a massive bull,

Having the form of Māheśvarī, O Nārāyaṇī, praise be to you! [14]

11.14 O you who are surrounded by peacocks and cocks, faultless, and carrying an enormous spear,

Having the form of Kaumārī, O Nārāyaṇī, praise be to you! [15]

11.15 O you who have taken up the best of weapons, conch and discus, club and bow,

Be gracious, O one with Vaiṣṇavī's form; O Nārāyaṇī, praise be to you! [16]

11.16 O you who have seized a great terrible discus, by whom the earth was upraised with your tusks,

Auspicious and having the form of a boar, O Nārāyaṇī, praise be to you! [17]

11.17 O you who set out to slay the demons, having the dreadful man-lion form,

In conjunction with the rescue of the triple world, O Nārāyaṇī, praise be to you! [18]

11.18 O you who are crowned and have a great thunderbolt, flaming with a thousand eyes,

Aindrī, the destroyer of Vṛtra's life breath, O Nārāyaṇī, praise be to you! [19]

11.19 O you who slew the mighty army of demons, having the form of Śivadūtī,

Of fearful form, of mighty roar, O Nārāyaṇī, praise be to you! [20]

11.20 O you whose mouth is terrifying with its teeth, who are ornamented with a garland of skulls,

O Cāmuṇḍā, crusher of Muṇḍa, O Nārāyaṇī, praise be to you! [21]

11.21 O Lakṣmī, modesty, great knowledge, faith, prosperity, Svadhā, firm one,

O great night, O great illusion, O Nārāyaṇī, praise be to you! [22]

11.22 O wisdom, Sarasvatī, choicest one, well-being, Bābhravī, the dark one,

O restrained one, be gracious, O queen; O Nārāyaṇī, praise be to you! [23]

11.23 O you who have the very form of all, queen of all, endowed with the power of all,

Protect us from dangers, O Goddess; O Goddess Durgā, praise be to you! [24]

11.24 May this gentle face of yours, adorned with three eyes,

Protect us from all ghosts; O Kātyāyanī, praise be to you! [25]

11.25 That fearsome trident, terrible with flames, laying waste the Asuras without remainder,

May that trident protect us from danger; O Bhadrakālī, praise be to you! [26]

11.26 That bell that destroys demonic splendors, having filled the world with its sound,

May that bell, O Goddess, protect us from evils as if we were children. [27]

11.27 That sword of yours, smeared with mud and the blood and fat of Asuras, gleaming with rays,

May that sword be for our welfare; O Caṇḍikā, we are bowed down to you! [28]

11.28 When delighted, you destroy all afflictions, but when angered, you destroy all longed for desires.

No accident befalls men who have resorted to you, for those who resort to you have truly entered a refuge. [29]

11.29 This destruction of great *dharma*-hating Asuras, which you have now accomplished, O Goddess,

Having multiplied your own body into many forms—O Ambikā, what other goddess can do that? [30]

11.30 In the various knowledges, in the scriptures requiring the lamp of discrimination, and in the primordial sayings, who other than you

Causes this world to whirl around so much, in this pit of egoism, this pitch black darkness? [31]

11.31 Where there are demons and serpents of terrible poison, where there are enemies, where armies of villains,

Also where the forest fire rages in the middle of the ocean, abiding there, you protect all. [32]

11.32 O queen of all, you protect all; having all for your very soul, you are said to support all.
You are worthy of praise by all who exercise power; those who bow down in devotion to you, they become the refuge of all. [33]

11.33 O Goddess, be gracious: protect us always from the fear of enemies, just as you have now promptly saved us from bondage by the Asuras.
Quickly may you bring the sins of all the worlds to tranquillity, and the calamities born of the ripening of portents. [34]

11.34 Be gracious, O Goddess, to those who bow down, O you who take away the afflictions of all.
O you who are worthy of praise by all who dwell in the triple world, be a boon giver to the worlds." [35]

The Goddess said: [36]

11.35 "I am indeed a boon giver, O you gods; the boon that you crave with your mind,
Choose that: I grant benefaction to the worlds." [37]

The gods said: [38]

11.36 "The pacification of all miseries in the triple world,
Let just that, and the destruction of our enemies, be accomplished by you." [39]

The Goddess said: [40]

11.37 "When the twenty-eighth *yuga* in the Vaivasvata Manu-interval has arrived,
Two more great Asuras, also named Śumbha and Niśumbha, will arise. [41]

11.38 Then born in the house of the cowherd Nanda, taking birth from the womb of Yaśodā,
Dwelling on Vindhya mountain, I will then slay these two. [42]

11.39 On another occasion descending to earth with a most dreadful form,
I will slay the Vaipracitta demons. [43]

11.40 Devouring these great terrible Vaipracitta demons,
My teeth will become red like the flower of the pomegranate. [44]

11.41 Then the gods in heaven, and human beings in this world of mortals,
Always praising me, will call me 'Red-tooth' (*raktadantikā*). [45][20]

11.42 Once again, when there has been no rain, no water, on earth for a hundred years,
Then, remembered by sages, I will come into being without being born from a womb. [46]

11.43 Since I will look at the sages with a hundred eyes,
Human beings will then praise me as 'Hundred-eyes' (*śat-akṣī*). [47]

11.44 Then I shall support the entire world with life sustaining vegetables,
Produced from my own body, until the rains come, O gods. [48]

11.45 In this way, I will attain fame on earth under the name 'She-who-supports-with-vegetables' (*śākaṃbharī*). [49]
There I will slay the great Asura named Durgama.

11.46 Thus, my name will come to be renowned as 'the Goddess Durgā.' [50]
And when I have again taken on fearsome form in the Himālayas,

11.47 I will destroy demons for the sake of protecting sages. [51]
Then all the sages will lower their bodies to me in praise.

11.48 My name will become famous as 'the fearsome goddess' (*bhīmādevī*). [52]
When a demon named Aruṇa shall do a lot of killing in the three worlds,

11.49 Then I, taking on bee-form, consisting of innumerable bees, [53]
Will slay the great demon for the well-being of the triple world.

11.50 Then people everywhere will praise me as 'Queen-bee' (*bhrāmarī*). [54]
In this way, whenever there is trouble produced by demons,

11.51 Then taking on bodily form, I will bring about the destruction of enemies." [55]

****

The Goddess said: [1]

12.1 "He who, with composed mind, will always praise me with these hymns,
For him I will destroy all misfortunes; of this, there is no doubt. [2]

12.2 Those who proclaim (*kīrtayiṣyanti*)[21] the destruction of Madhu and Kaiṭabha, and the slaying of the Asura Mahiṣa,
And likewise the demise of Śumbha and Niśumbha, [3]

12.3 On the eighth, fourteenth, and ninth days of the lunar fortnight with singleness of mind,
And those who will recite (*śroṣyanti:* "cause to be heard") my supreme *Māhātmya* with devotion, [4]

12.4 To them nothing bad will happen, nor any misfortunes arising from wrongdoing.
For them there will be no poverty, nor any separation from loved ones. [5]

12.5 For this person there will be no danger from enemy, villain, or king,
Nor from weapon, fire, or flood at any time. [6]

12.6 Therefore this my *Māhātmya* is to be recited (*paṭhitavyam*) by those who are mentally composed,
And it is always to be heard (*śrotavyam:* "caused to be heard") with devotion: it is a great conduit to the highest well-being. [7]

12.7 May this my *Māhātmya* quell all misfortunes born of great illnesses,
And also the three kinds of natural calamity. [8]

12.8 Where it is always properly recited (*paṭhyate*) in my sanctuary,
That place I will never abandon; my presence is established there. [9]

12.9 In the offering of oblations, at worship, in the fire ceremony, at the great festival,
All these doings (*caritam*) of mine are to be proclaimed (*uccāryam*) and heard (*śrāvyam*). [10]

12.10 When oblation and worship are done, either with or without knowledge,
I have regard for it, and also for the fire offering that is performed. [11]

12.11 A man who is filled with devotion, having heard (*śrutvā*) this my *Māhātmya*

At the great annual worship that is performed during the autumn, [12]

12.12 Becomes released from all afflictions, endowed with wealth, grain, and children
Through my grace; of this, there is no doubt. [13]

12.13 On giving ear (*śrutvā*) to this my *Māhātmya* and to my auspicious epiphanies,
And to my valor in battles, a man becomes fearless. [14]

12.14 His enemies perish, well-being prevails,
And his family rejoices for a man who hears (*śṛṇvatām*) this my *Māhātmya.* [15]

12.15 One should listen to (*śṛṇuyāt*) this my *Māhātmya* everywhere, at the propitiation ceremony,
On seeing a bad dream, and when there are terrible astrological portents. [16]

12.16 Calamities and dreadful celestial omens are brought to an end,
And the nightmares that men see become good dreams. [17]

12.17 Children who have been seized by evil spirits become calm,
And where there has been a shattering of union, there comes to be the highest friendship between men. [18]

12.18 This *Māhātmya* is unexcelled at destroying the might of all evil-doers.
From its recitation (*paṭhanāt*) comes the destruction of demons, ghosts, and goblins. [19]

12.19 This entire *Māhātmya* brings one very close to me. [20]
The delight that I take in being worshipped with the finest animals, flowers, *argha*-offerings, incense, perfumes, and lights,

12.20 With the feeding of Brāhmaṇas, oblations, water offerings, [21]
And various other offerings and gifts, day and night, for a whole year,

12.21 That same delight is produced in me when (this *Māhātmya*) is uttered (*uccarite*) and heard (*śrute*) but once. [22]
When heard (*śrutam*), it destroys sins and leads one to perfect health.

12.22 The proclamation (*kīrtanam*) of my births grants protection from evil spirits, [23]

Since it deals with my conduct in battles, laying waste the wicked demons.

12.23 When it is heard (*śrute*), there will be no danger to human beings from their enemies. [24]

The praises that are uttered by you and by the seers of Brahmā,

12.24 And those which are made by Brahmā himself, these produce an auspicious mental state. [25]

He who is enveloped by forest fire, deep in the woods or on its outskirts,

12.25 Or is surrounded by villains in an isolated place, or seized by enemies, [26]

Or is pursued by lions and tigers, or by elephants in the jungle,

12.26 Or is sentenced to death by a cruel king, or is thrown into bondage, [27]

Or is buffeted by a great wind when sailing in a boat on the great ocean,

12.27 Or has weapons hurled at him in the most dreadful of battles, [28]

In all terrible afflictions, or tormented with pain,

12.28 The man who remembers (*smaran*) this work (*caritam*) of mine under such circumstances is released from his difficulty. [29]

By my power, lions and the like, villains and enemies

12.29 Flee far off, when one remembers this activity (*caritam*) of mine." [30]

The seer said: [31]

Having spoken thus, the blessed Caṇḍikā, of fearsome prowess,

12.30 Disappeared from in front of the onlooking gods. [32]

The gods, free from affliction, resumed their respective dominions, just as before,

12.31 All of them enjoying shares in the sacrifice, their enemies slain. [33]

When Śumbha, enemy of the gods, tormentor of the universe, was slain by the Goddess in battle,

12.32 And also the very terrible Niśumbha, whose valor was without equal [34]

And who was very brave, then the remaining demons returned to the nether world. [35]

12.33 Just in this fashion does the blessed Goddess, even though she is eternal,
Provide protection for the world, O king, by coming into being again and again. [36][22]

12.34 By her is all this universe deluded; she produces everything.
Propitiated, she grants knowledge; delighted, she bestows prosperity. [37]

12.35 O king, this whole egg of Brahmā is pervaded by her,
Who is Mahākālī at the end of time, having the form of the great pestilence. [38]

12.36 She herself is the great pestilence at one time; she herself, unborn, becomes the creation at another;
And she, the eternal, provides support for what is created at yet another time. [39]

12.37 In times of well-being, she is the good fortune of men, granting them prosperity in their homes.
In times of privation, she exists as ill-fortune, for the sake of destruction. [40]

12.38 Praised and worshipped with flowers, incense, perfumes, and the like,
She grants wealth, sons, an auspicious mind, the pathway to *dharma*. [41]

****

The seer said: [1]

13.1 Thus have I related to you, O king, the supreme *Devī-Māhātmya*. [2]
She is the Goddess, with this sort of power, by whom this universe is supported.

13.2 Just in this way is knowledge fashioned by her who is the illusory power of blessed Viṣṇu. [3]
By her are you, and this *vaiśya*, and other men of discrimination deluded;

13.3 So were others in the past, and so will still others be deluded in the future. [4]
O king, you should take refuge in her, the supreme queen,

13.4 The one who, when propitiated, grants men enjoyments, heaven, and ultimate release. [5]

Mārkaṇḍeya said: [6]

Upon hearing these words of his, king Suratha,

13.5 Having paid homage to the illustrious seer who practiced severe austerities, [7]

Despondent because of his excessive concern for himself, and because his kingdom had been taken away,

13.6 Immediately went forth to practice austerities himself, as did the *vaiśya*, O great sage. [8]

Settling down on the bank of a river, with the aim of obtaining a vision of the Mother,

13.7 He and the *vaiśya* practiced austerities, reciting the supreme *Devī-Sūkta* ("Hymn to the Goddess"), [9][23]

Having set up an image of the Goddess, fashioned of earth, on the riverbank.

13.8 The two of them worshipped her with flowers, incense, fire, and water, [10]

Sometimes fasting entirely, sometimes restricting their diet, with their minds on her, composed in thought.

13.9 They gave her offerings sprinkled with blood from their own limbs. [11]

When they had worshipped her with great self-restraint for three years,

13.10 The supportress of the universe, Caṇḍikā, spoke to them, delighted, in front of their very eyes. [12]

The Goddess said: [13]

"Whatever is desired by you, O king, and by you, O *vaiśya*,

13.11 May you receive all that from me; delighted, I give it now to you." [14]

Mārkaṇḍeya said: [15]

Then the king chose a kingdom that would not perish even in another lifetime,

13.12 And his own kingdom now, with the power of his enemies forcibly overthrown. [16]

And the wise *vaiśya*, his mind despairing of things of this world, chose knowledge

13.13 Which destroys attachment to the notions of "I" and "mine." [17]

The Goddess said: [18]

"In just a few days, O king, you will regain your own kingdom, [19]

13.14 Having slain your enemies; it will then be yours permanently. [20]
Upon death, receiving another birth from the god Vivasvan, [21]

13.15 You will be the Manu named Sāvarṇi here on earth. [22]
And the boon that you, O best of *vaiśya*s, have asked of us, [23]

13.16 That do I grant you: knowledge that is conducive to perfection will be yours." [24]

Mārkaṇḍeya said: [25]

Having given to the two of them the boon that each desired, [26]

13.17 She immediately disappeared, praised by them with devotion. [27]

Thus having received a boon from the Goddess, Suratha, the best of rulers, [28]

Upon receiving another birth from Sūrya, will become the Manu known as Sāvarṇi, will become the Manu known as Sāvarṇi. [29][24]

PART II

Encounters With the Goddess

4

The Legacy of a Text

Given that the *Devī-Māhātmya* crystallizes at a particular moment in time, more or less in the form that has been translated in the preceding chapter, what are the dynamics of its ongoing life in India? This is the question that will occupy us for this and the next three chapters. It in turn may be understood as the particular form of a more general question: How is it that a verbal composition lives on past the occasion of its original utterance or its first commitment to writing?

Such a question may appear curiously abstract and almost absurd in its simplicity. It seems obvious that people *read* texts, and that they *interpret* them in a variety of ways. The so-called Great Books of any civilization are simply those that have been most read over the course of time, because of the value of the ideas that they contain.

It is precisely this obviousness, however, that is being called into question by the revolution that was briefly described in our first chapter—the revolution in the way we think about the relationship between written documents and the religious life. We took note there of several ways in which this new awareness forces those of us who live in the twentieth century West to reexamine familiar assumptions about such matters, and about literacy in general. For those who would like to pursue these interesting topics further, William A. Graham's recent book, *Beyond the Written Word*, provides a marvelous point of entry.[1] The following brief excerpts are illustrative:

Silent, private reading appears to have become dominant only with

> the advent of widespread literacy in much of Western Europe, which was largely a nineteenth century phenomenon.
>
> . . . .
>
> We [in the modern West] stand on this side of the epochal transition accomplished to large degree by about 1800 in the urban culture of Western Europe, and now still in progress elsewhere, from a scribal or chirographic, and still significantly oral culture to a print-dominated or typographic, primarily visual culture. Our alphabetic "book culture", like our "book religion", is not even the same as the "book culture" (or "book religion") of sixteenth- or seventeenth-century Europe, let alone that of classical antiquity, the Medieval or Renaissance West, or the great literary civilizations of Asia past and present.[2]

The full implications of this new line of inquiry, with its attendant reorientation toward our familiar, written materials, will not be apparent for some time. In the interim, and as part of the reorientation process, it has seemed advisable to adopt the stance toward verbal composition and transmission that is struck in the first paragraph of this chapter. That stance might be developed more systematically along the following lines.

The focus of our inquiry is on a verbal *utterance*, an *oral* phenomenon. We make such an emphasis not just because of recent scholarly alertness to the importance of discriminating oral and literate modes of communication, but also because of the Indian preference —noted in our first chapter—for the oral medium over the written. Our goal is to understand how a particular verbal utterance lives over the course of time. Such an utterance may, of course, become reduced to writing, but such an event is part of that utterance's later history and should not be taken for granted.[3] The specific utterance in which we are interested, of course, is the *Devī-Māhātmya*, an utterance of some 579 verses. It may be simpler at this point, however, to imagine that we are interested in the history of a brief utterance, say, "Sāvarṇi, who is Sūrya's son, is said to be the eighth Manu."[4] If we think about the circumstances in which a speaker might use such a phrase, a number of possibilities come to mind. The phrase might occur merely as part of everyday conversation, a unique, casual utterance with no major emotional investment on the part of the speaker. It might also be that the words are a more considered response of the speaker to some circumstantial stimulus: On viewing an inspiring sculpture, or listening to emotionally evocative music, he or she utters appropriate words. Alternatively, the speaker might be reciting these words from memory, to which they were committed at some time in the past. Or perhaps he or she is reading them aloud, lifting them off the written or printed page over which the eye is moving. We can also imagine that the speaker might be an epic poet, a bard who cannot read but who has the keen ability to tell afresh a familiar story, often at great length, and to do so within the constraints of metre and rhyme.[5] The point that runs through these examples is simply that a given verbal utterance may be variously inspired and variously related to the circumstances of its utterance. Those circumstances may also include other media: iconic, graphic, musical, and so forth.[6]

Just as there is variety in the context that gives rise to a particular utterance, so, too, is there variety in what follows in its wake.[7] If it is an ephemeral utterance, it passes from the scene, gone forever. More durable phrases evoke a range of responses. If the *content* is experienced as edifying, it may be remembered verbatim, or its general sense may be retained and then rearticulated at a later time, without literal fidelity to the original. If it is the *form* of the phrase that is deemed powerful—as is the case with Indian *mantra*s—then it will be retained immutable in human memory, subsequently to be rearticulated or muttered in worship (*japa*), perhaps with an eye toward transforming one's consciousness, perhaps as an act of devotion. Someone may, of course, write the phrase down, translating the oral phenomenon into a written one, and in India we note that it may be written down in one of a variety of scripts. If this occurs, the previous options remain, though perhaps significantly transformed.[8] New possibilities also emerge, most notably the composition of commentaries on the verbal artifact. Retained in either oral or written mode, the words may become intertwined with other media, inspiring new sculpture, vivified in song, recited in ritual, dramatized in festival life. The variety of ways in which humans have engaged with words—particularly those that for one reason or another have been deemed sacred—is, in sum, simply enormous.

All of this has a very direct bearing on our inquiry into the legacy of the *Devī-Māhātmya.* At one time, I aspired to provide a comprehensive study of how the text has ramified for Hindu life in the centuries since its composition, but the scale of such an undertaking proved overwhelming. A comparable task in the study of the Christian tradition might be to ask how the passion story—a "verbal artifact" even briefer than our text—has been engaged with by Christians in different times and places. Simply to determine what constitutes the relevant evidence would be a daunting assignment. Correspondingly, I have radically limited the nature of the evidence we will consider, and in doing so I have sought to keep us close to the functional question that is central to our emerging self-consciousness about the fact of scripture: What is it that people *do* with their written documents? We shall therefore be paying attention here to the specific kinds of interpretive material that has gathered around the text—the *aṅga*s and commentaries—material that reflects at least one way in which Hindus have come to grips with this verbal artifact. There are, of course, other ways of engaging with this artifact and in our final chapter we shall glance at some contemporary encounters with the text, drawing on a range of sources.

As a final step in orienting ourselves to the task at hand, it may be useful to describe our approach as *a phenomenology of the text proper* —a description of the way the text as a whole functions—and then to contrast this approach with other possible inquiries into the legacy of the text. We shall consider three such possibilities.

We might, for instance, alight on the fact that there are numerous retellings of the myths of the *Devī-Māhātmya* in later Purāṇic literature, and it would doubtless prove fruitful to study these in relationship to one another. We would notice that there is a fairly complete account of our text's mythology in the *Śiva Purāṇa*, where the story is roughly half as long as it is in our text, and another complete version appears, at about five times the length, in the *Devī Bhāgavata Purāṇa*. If we were able to set these accounts in historical sequence and then to explore the many versions of individual myths, particularly the slaying of Mahiṣa, that have appeared in Purāṇic and later vernacular literature, we would have illuminated an important dimension of the later Goddess tradition in India. In this case, the lens through which we would be focusing our study—in contrast to our present effort to highlight the text proper—would be *the mythology of the Goddess*, some instances of which are found in the *Devī-Māhātmya* and some elsewhere. It is the brief work of Stietencron[9]—to which we shall return for different reasons in a moment—that comes closest to providing this kind of historical synopsis of the Goddess's mythology, but there are full studies of other myths that have demonstrated the utility of this kind of approach, for instance, Paul Hacker's study of the mythology of Prahlāda, Frank Whaling's of the Rāma cycle, and Clifford Hospital's of Bali.[10]

A somewhat different focus is obtained if we use as our lens not the mythology, but *the cult of the Goddess* and if we emphasize not Sanskrit, but *Tamil* sources. This is, in fact, what Alf Hiltebeitel is doing in his projected three-volume study, *The Cult of Draupadī*, the first volume of which has appeared recently.[11] It is Hiltebeitel's intent to examine one "singularly representative cult" of popular devotional Hinduism, the South Indian Draupadī cult, in such a way as to illuminate the dynamic relationship between regional religious life and the epic *Mahābhārata*.[12]

Relying primarily on the contemporary "street drama" (Terukkūttu) of northern Tamilnadu, he explores a stunning hypothesis: "Despite the fact that [as we noted in chapter 2] the classical *Mahābhārata* makes little direct reference to the goddess, the epic narrative would seem to be informed by the goddess's mythology."[13] The massive evidence that is provided by this "folk interpretation of the *Mahābhārata* that places the goddess at its center" teaches us a great deal about both the substance and the genres of popular religious practice, particularly as it involves goddesses. In terms of our specific concern, we should note that the Goddess's engagement with the buffalo demon is absolutely pervasive of the material with which Hiltebeitel is working. Instances of this and other ways in which discrete elements of the *Devī-Māhātmya* are found within the Draupadī cult include the following: some cult stories refer to a demon assuming various animal and human guises, as Mahiṣa does;[14] "humans and buffaloes are interchangeable as sacrifices to the goddess," recalling their convergence in the figure of Mahiṣa;[15] the laughter of Draupadī as she taunts Duryodhana is reminiscent of the Goddess's laughter at Mahiṣa prior to their battle;[16] the theme of the Goddess's adversary wanting to marry her is variously attested in both the Draupadī cult and the *Devī-Māhātmya*;[17] the sprouting of Draupadī's sons from the sowing of Bhīma's blood on the ground, and the regenerative demons who are lapped up by their vanquisher in the allied Renuka myth, seem inspired by our text's story of Raktabīja;[18] as the folk tradition tells of Draupadī dwelling in forest exile, she "is herself a multiform of Kālī, the dishevelled goddess linked with inauspiciousness and death";[19] the sacrifice of Aravaṉ in the Tamil epic tradition is linked to the South Indian practice of heroic self-mutilation, whose prototype is found in the *Devī-Māhātmya*'s account of the king and *vaiśya* worshipping the Goddess with blood from their own limbs;[20] and, finally, the birth from fire of Draupadī herself, as of her antagonist's weapons, is evocative of the Goddess's birth from the combined *tejas* of the gods in our text.[21] One need not subscribe entirely to Hiltebeitel's particular methodology to appreciate the way in which it illuminates the refracted trajectories that parts of our text have followed into the remote corners of cultic life. Hiltebeitel does not, however, deal with the text as a whole. Nor is that his intent. He has put the Draupadī cult, not the *Devī-Māhātmya*, at center stage. Moreover, he is asking a different kind of question, and the power of his synthesis—like that of structuralism generally—is that it arranges the "discrete elements" of text, image, and behavior in such a way as to identify underlying patterns. Our engagement with our text, by contrast, is concerned to examine it as an autonomous phenomenon with an integrity of its own. As we shall see shortly, our investigation will also involve us in ritual life. But it will be inquiry into the way in which a specific verbal artifact has been appropriated that leads us there, not the investigation of a particular cult.

Finally, it would be possible to inquire into the legacy of our text through consideration of *iconic representations of the Goddess* as slayer of the buffalo demon Mahiṣa (*mahiṣāsuramardinī*). Such an inquiry is one of the major contributions of the recent work of Steitencron.[22] The other, to which we referred just above, is his tracing of the Goddess-Mahiṣa myth through the Purāṇic literary corpus. Comparison of the evidence provided by these two kinds of graphic media shows expected similarities, but even more striking discontinuities, over which we need to pause here. Later textual accounts in the Purāṇas, notes Stietencron, build on the *Devī-Māhātmya* to explore the relationship between the Goddess and Mahiṣa in greater detail. One line of development emphasizes the Goddess's beauty and has Mahiṣa choosing union-in-death with the Goddess, since he cannot have union-in-love. The other inquires into the source of Mahiṣa's power. A typically great variety of answers is provided, at least one of which affirms that Mahiṣa is a partial incarnation of the Goddess's (sometime) consort Śiva. In both cases it is *bhakti*, loving devotion to the Goddess, that leads to the radical reconception of Mahiṣa, who in late sources ends up being the Goddess's model devotee.[23] Iconic representation of the Goddess-Mahiṣa encounter, however, is much more diverse. Stietencron identifies five types of sculptural representation, but only the last three are attested in texts. Figures 4.1-4.5 at the end of this chapter provide examples of these types, which Stietencron describes as follows: (1) goddess wrestling with a rearing-up buffalo, (2) goddess raising the buffalo up from behind, (3) goddess struggling with a buffalo headed human demon, (4) goddess standing on the head of a buffalo, and (5) Mahiṣa emerging in human form from the neck of his buffalo-shape.[24] Since it is possible to date sculpture with a good deal more precision than texts, Stietencron uses this evidence to reconstruct the history of the motif of Goddess-as-killer-of-buffalo-demon. Originally a local myth in north India in Kushan times (second-third centuries C.E.; types 1 and 2), it became enfolded into a cult that spread throughout the subcontinent, often under royal sponsorship, as part of the *bhakti* movement between the sixth and ninth centuries (type 3); subsequently it became refined in both art and text as part of the ongoing devotional movement (types 4 and 5). Throughout Indian history and up into modern times, Stietencron concludes, the myth has played an important role in "Hinduizing" tribal cults, linking the great Goddess to regional deities.[25] Such a brief summary scarcely does justice to the rich detail of Stietencron's study, but it is sufficient to indicate an impressive methodological alternative to our own approach. It raises important questions for considering the relationship between textual and sculptural representations of common subject matter. The *Devī-Māhātmya*'s textual account clearly portrays the Goddess in combat with a hybrid buffalo-human demon, corresponding to Stietencron's third type of iconographic representation. This suggests that the art and the cult of the buffalo-killing goddess, as reflected in types 1 and 2, are considerably older even than the *Devī-Māhātmya.* This in turn leads us to reflect more broadly on what should properly be considered the "carrier" of a religious tradition: its texts? its art? its ritual? its ritual specialists? perhaps its music? its political patrons? These are not questions we must answer here, but they will need attention in the near future, as part of our increased awareness of the *varied media* of religious life, and our emerging self-consciousness about which of these media we select for scholarly scrutiny.[26] In the interim, we now turn, in our next two chapters, to the accretions to, and the encounters with the *Devī-Māhātmya* that have occurred in writing, namely, the text's *aṅga*s and its commentaries.

Figure 4.1 Aihole, (Bijapur-Mysore), sandstone, late sixth century. Goddess breaking the buffalo's neck with her knee.

Figure 4.2 Bādāmi, (Bijapur-Mysore),sandstone, late sixth century. Four-armed Goddess raising the buffalo by his hindquarters.

Figure 4.3 Mahābalipuram, granite, second quarter of the seventh century. Buffalo-headed human Mahiṣa cringing before the Goddess.

Figure 4.4 Tiruvalañjali, granite, first half of the tenth century. Goddess standing on the head of the slain buffalo demon. (Courtesy, Tanjore Art Gallery)

Figure 4.5 Ālāmpur, red sandstone, eighth century. Goddess slaying Mahiṣa in human form as he emerges from his buffalo shape. (Courtesy, Ālāmpur Museum)

5

Encounter With the Text I—The Ritual and Philosophy of the Aṅgas

Introduction

We begin our examination of the material that has gathered around the *Devī-Māhātmya*, not with a study of its commentaries, but by looking at the "limbs" or "subsidiary texts" or "appendages" (*aṅgas*) that the text has acquired "fore and aft."[1] The reason for this is simple: The commentaries take for granted the existence of the *aṅgas*. The way in which the *aṅgas* figure in the tradition's encounter with the *Devī-Māhātmya*, however, is part of a larger pattern. Therefore, let me begin our exploration of the text's legacy by simply describing what one finds on inquiring into the "received text" of the *Devī-Māhātmya*. What happens to the "verbal artifact" of 579 verses that we met in chapter 3?[2]

If one examines the complete *Mārkaṇḍeya Purāṇa*, either in manuscript form or one of the several published editions, one sometimes finds that the *Devī-Māhātmya* is the only part of the text to have attracted commentarial attention.[3] More noteworthy, however, is that it is more common by far for the *Devī-Māhātmya* to circulate as an independent document. In this form, it exists in numerous editions and virtually innumerable manuscripts. When the text circulates in this independent fashion, the Purāṇic connection never entirely disappears from sight for there are recurrent references to the *Mārkaṇḍeya Purāṇa* in the colophons that come at the end of the chapters.[4] We shall have occasion shortly to examine whether our text's use of the term *māhātmya* in chapters 12 and 13 refers specifically to a *text*, but here we should note that when the *Devī-Māhātmya* circulates apart from its Purāṇic mooring, the alternative title of *Durgā-Saptaśatī*—"700 (Verses) to Durgā"—is used much more frequently. The text is also commonly divided into three unequal parts: the first consists of chapter 1, the second of chapters 2-4, and the third of chapters 5-13. At the beginning of each part a different presiding goddess (*devatā*), none of whom is mentioned by name in the text itself, is invoked. At the same junctures there is also specification of the seer (*ṛṣi*), deity (*devatā*), and metre (*chandas*) for that part of the text, a practice commonly followed with the hymns of the *Ṛg Veda*.[5] Also provided for each part are distinctions of Tantric origin: *śakti*, *bīja*, and *tattva*. As an independent text, moreover, the *Devī-Māhātmya* virtually *never* stands alone. Rather, it has gathered about it these subsidiary texts known as *aṅga*s. They are usually enumerated as six, three which precede the text of the *Devī-Māhātmya* itself—Kavaca ("the armor"), Argalā ("the stopper, the door-stop"),[6] Kīlaka ("the bolt")—and three which succeed it—Prādhānika Rahasya ("the chief secret, the secret pertaining to primary matter"), Vaikṛtika Rahasya ("the secret pertaining to changes or modifications"), and Mūrti Rahasya ("the secret pertaining to forms or images"). At either end of the *Devī-Māhātmya* itself, as a kind of buffer or "covering" (*sampuṭa*) between the text and the *aṅga*s, appears a hymn. The hymn preceding the text is usually known as the Rātri Sūkta ("Night Hymn") and the succeeding one is designated the Devī Sūkta ("Goddess Hymn"). There is a difference of opinion, however, as to whether these names refer to Vedic hymns (*Ṛg Veda* 10.127 and 10.125, respectively) or to the hymns found in the *Devī-Māhātmya* (in the first and fifth chapters, respectively). Finally, we should note that when the text circulates in this independent form, it usually has one or more of its many commentaries printed below the text. Often a translation or gloss in one of the modern vernaculars appears underneath the text and/or commentary, or on a facing page.

The threefold division of the text of the *Devī-Māhātmya* is a matter that is elucidated in the three *aṅga*s entitled Rahasyas, to which we shall turn shortly. It is this fact, combined with the above-noted observation that the commentaries take for granted the existence of the *aṅga*s, that prompts us to start our inquiry into the tradition's encounter with the text by considering these "appendages." In light of their importance, it would be enormously helpful if we had details on how the text came to be surrounded by these interpretive additions, but I have encountered nothing in my studies that would enable me to answer such a question.

The most that can be said at present is that (1) it is possible to date some of the commentaries to the eighteenth century, and those commentaries understand the 700-verse phenomenon on which they are commenting to be embedded in the *aṅga*s; and (2) artistic evidence suggests that the *aṅga*s have been associated with the text since the fourteenth century.[7] The most renowned of the commentaries, the *Guptavatī* of Bhāskararāya, extends over both the thirteen chapters of the *Devī-Māhātmya* and the subsidiary material. Indeed, so close is the connection between text and *aṅga*s that a modern commentator can maintain, in reference to the central struggle of the *Rāmāyaṇa*, that the real reason that Rāma slew Rāvaṇa was because the demon had recited the *Devī-Māhātmya* without the *aṅga*s![8] Even scholars, perhaps reflecting this traditional view, are sometimes prone to blur the distinction between text and *aṅga*, as in a recent article by Pratapaditya Pal, where the author imputes to the *Devī-Māhātmya* material that comes, in fact, from the Vaikṛtika Rahasya, an invocatory verse, and the Kavaca.[9]

What, then, are these *aṅga*s, and what do they tell us about the tradition's engagement with the core text? On the basis of reading and discussing the material with a number of contemporary Hindus, some of whom value the text in their own religious lives and some of whom do not, I believe the following to be reasonable observations.[10]

The *aṅga*s are chiefly concerned with the ritual use of the words of the *Devī-Māhātmya*. They assume that those words will be recited aloud, and that they will be uttered in the presence of images. The *aṅga*s that precede the "text" focus on the ritual preparation of the one who is to recite it and on maximizing its power. Those that follow it are concerned with the iconography of the images, and with the relationship between the several forms of the Goddess that are represented in the images, and in the text. This entails articulating a rudimentary philosophy of the Goddess, her activity, and her text. The *aṅga*s, in short, deal with the acts, the sounds, and the sights of worshipping the Goddess.

We are perhaps reminded at this juncture of Lawrence Babb's observation that "religion is a thing done, not a thing 'believed.'"[11] Though our modern, Western, literate sensitivity may suspect that the tradition has done something funny here, by superimposing a formal, ritual concern on a text that is manifestly important for its content, we should note that the *Devī-Māhātmya* itself invites this kind of treatment. Before proceeding to more detailed analysis of the *aṅga*s, therefore, we must glance briefly at what the *Devī-Māhātmya* has to say about ritual.

Apart from general references to "taking refuge" and to the practice of austerities, three specific instances of ritual activity are mentioned in the *Devī-Māhātmya*. The first is the recitation and hearing of the *māhātmya* itself, the merits of which are extolled in the first twenty-nine verses of chapter 12. The second is "the great annual festival that is performed in the autumn." [12.11], presumably Durgā Pūjā/Navarātra. This festival is identified as a particularly auspicious occasion for reciting the *māhātmya*, but no details are provided. Finally, there is reference in the last chapter to the king and *vaiśya* performing *pūjā* to an image of the Goddess, reciting the "Devī Sūkta," with offerings of flowers, incense, fire, and water that had been "sprinkled with blood from their own limbs" [13.7-9].

Given the fact that these references all appear in the last two chapters of the text, and that these same two chapters show a measure of self-consciousness about their own existence as a record of the Goddess's activity, the textual scholar is tempted to suggest that they are later additions. Indeed, in light of Stietencron's demonstration of the antiquity of the Goddess-buffalo myth, which we noted in chapter 4, the temptation to look for historical strata in the growth of the text is great: one might surmise that the original kernel was the story of Mahiṣa; to it were added first the Śumbha-Niśumbha myth, then the Madhu-Kaiṭabha story, with the whole being retouched when it was inserted into the *Mārkaṇḍeya Purāṇa*.[12] The subsequent addition of the *aṅga*s, particularly of the Rahasyas at the end of the text, would then simply be the next stage in the dynamic growth, in both form and content, of this account of the Goddess. Unfortunately, however, there is no written evidence to justify such stratification. So far as we can tell, the concluding frame story, with its ritual references, has always been part of this verbal artifact. While the text historian might hope that the forthcoming critical edition of the *Mārkaṇḍeya Purāṇa* will unearth an earlier version of the text, the functional analyst knows that the account that is normative for the later tradition includes the chapters with ritual references.

A closer look at some of the diction in these chapters may shed further light on the ritual life of the text. Let us therefore briefly consider one noun—*māhātmya*—and a cluster of verbs that describe what one should do with this *māhātmya*.

The word *māhātmya* is used once in our text prior to chapter 12, at 9.1, and it there possesses the rich ambiguity that also characterizes its later instances. The word is an abstract noun, from the compound adjective *mahā-ātma*, literally "one of great soul," but also (and much more commonly) simply "noble." The noun refers to the "distinctive greatness" of a particular person, place, object, and so forth. In light of India's proverbial glorying in diversity, it is not surprising to find many occasions on which the virtues of something are elaborated at great length. By extension, then, *māhātmya* comes to refer to the *verbal account* that enumerates or describes the distinctive greatness of a particular datum. It is a "glorification." It is precisely this tension between *māhātmya* as "distinctive greatness of the Goddess" and *māhātmya* as "verbal account of the distinctive greatness of the Goddess" that characterizes the *Devī-Māhātmya*'s use of the word. Indeed, the text heightens this tension by juxtaposing the word *māhātmya* more than once with a word for "activity" (*carita*). Correspondingly, a literal translation of 9.1 would be—"Wondrous [is] this narrated, by you to me, O blessed one / of the Goddess activity greatness dealing-with-the-slaying-of-Raktabīja"—where it is not unequivocally affirmed whether the greatness refers to the *activity* of the Goddess or to *what has been narrated.* On the nine occasions when the term is used in chapters 12 and 13,[13] there seems to be a preference for understanding *māhātmya* as "verbal account": chapter 12 begins by citing the virtues of praising the Goddess "with these hymns (*stava*)," and at 13.1 the seer speaks of "having related to you the *Devī-Māhātmya.*" Even this latter phrase, however, admits of being understood as "having told you of the greatness of the Goddess," and there are additional occasions where the word *carita* is used as virtually synonymous with *māhātmya* [12.28, 12.29]. The point is simply this: The language of the *Devī-Māhātmya* allows two understandings of what is most significant, one that emphasizes the *activity* of the Goddess, the other that emphasizes the *account* of that activity. In terms of our discussion in chapter 4 of the varied legacy that a verbal artifact may have, the logical consequence of emphasizing the Goddess's activity might well be to tell, or to sculpt, or to sing further about that activity. The consequence of emphasizing the account, however, would be to pay continued attention to matters of form, that is, to the kind of verbatim ritual recitation that we find emerging in the *aṅgas*. In any case, there is clearly precedent within the *Devī-Māhātmya* itself for prizing the distinctiveness of its particular phraseology.

If we grant then that, from at least one angle, the *Devī-Māhātmya* is an account of the Goddess's activity that is to be valued, the immediate question is: how do we do that? What do we do with this verbal artifact? The modern Western reader (*sic*) is tempted to say: We read it. The assumption is that we are dealing with a written document, and that this "text" should serve as the focus of our attention. There is indeed evidence that bookmaking has been understood as a devotional act in association with the Goddess, for the *Devī Purāṇa* provides detailed instructions for the physical constitution of a manuscript, and the *Nīlamata Purāṇa* even declares that "in the temple of Durgā, books (*pustaka*) should be worshipped."[14] Such instances may be understood as part of the emerging "cult of the book" that is attested in Purāṇic sources and that is characterized by a new positive evaluation of written words, which thereafter parallels the traditional Indian preference for their oral-aural, spoken and heard quality.[15] Be that as it may, however, when the *Devī-Māhātmya* speaks of how it is to be treated, it is as an oral-aural phenomenon, not as a written one. The evidence for this is not just the absence of words for writing, but the connotations of the four verbs that are used in chapter 12. Thus, the *māhātmya* is to be "proclaimed" or "declared" or "uttered" (*uccar*) [12.9, 12.21]. It is to be "told forth" (*kṛt*) [12.2, 12.22]. This account is something to be "recited" or "repeated aloud" (*paṭh*) [12.6, 12.8, 12.18]. Further, there is merit both in "hearing" the words oneself (*śru*) [12.9, 12.11, 12.13, 12.14, 12.15, 12.21, 12.23] and in "causing [someone else] to hear" them [12.3, 12.6]. One might, of course, argue that a physical document could actually be present as the starting point for proclamation and recitation, to be read aloud. But the fact remains that it is only in their utterance that the words reach their full potential, that the merit promised to one who engages with the *māhātmya* is fully realized. We should note, finally, that the language of our text has already begun to discriminate between different ritual activities, all of which are consequences of its orality-aurality: It is a good thing to *recite* the words; it is also a good thing to *hear* them; but it is also beneficial to *cause others to hear* them, presumably by sponsoring public recitation, where we may imagine the reciter to be someone who knows the text by heart.

While it may therefore be surprising to modern Western sensibilities to find the growth of ritual supplements around a core text that is arresting for its content—its vision of the Goddess—such growth is not inconsistent with certain cues that are found within the text itself. What the *aṅga*s do is to develop those cues in greater detail. We turn now to their further consideration.

The Armor, the Stopper, the Bolt: Kavaca, Argalā, and Kīlaka

As we now attend to the content of the individual *aṅga*s, we should not lose sight of two of their general features: their assimilation to the Purāṇic corpus and, beyond that, to the Vedas. We commented earlier on the dynamic and encyclopedic quality of the Purāṇas, which has meant they can serve as the (alleged) repository of all manner of popular material. (When once I pressed one of my *paṇḍit*s for the source of a charming story he had just told me, he said, with a wave of his hand and a twinkle in his eye, "It's in the Purāṇas. . . .") This material, however, is understood to be coherent, a "confirming elaboration" (*upabṛṃhana*) of the Vedic revelation, a translation of the more rarified and arcane tradition into popular terms.[16] It is a "revelation of mysteries" left unexplicated by the Vedas.[17] We take note of this fact here because one of the views of the status of the *aṅga*s is that they come from the Purāṇas, particularly (but not only) from the *Mārkaṇḍeya.* This is the identification that is made in the colophons that come at the end of some of the *aṅga*s.[18] That the *aṅga*s are not actually found in those Purāṇas is essentially beside the point: If we would know how the tradition has viewed them, it is enough to note that they are *understood* to be woven of Purāṇic fabric.

The broader Vedic resonance of the *aṅga*s is also suggested by other considerations, beyond what is implied in viewing the *aṅga*s as Purāṇic. We have already seen, for instance, that the practice of specifying the deity, metre, and seer (*devatā, chandas, ṛṣi*) for each portion of the text has its precedent in the way the tradition deals with the hymns of the *Ṛg Veda.* We noted, in addition, that one interpretation of the Rātri and Devī Sūktas that appear between the text of the *Devī-Māhātmya* and the other appendages is that they are the Ṛg Vedic hymns that go by these names. Finally, it is surely significant that there is one other verbal composition in India that has known this kind of growth of "limbs," also called *aṅga*s, around a supremely sacred nucleus. That is the *Ṛg Veda.* The hymns themselves date from perhaps 1200-1000 B.C.E., and around them grew, sometime between the eighth and fourth centuries B.C.E., a series of subsidiary compositions known as Vedāṅgas ("appendages to the Veda"). Individually they dealt with phonetics, metrics, grammar, etymology, ritual practice, and astronomy, and their overall purpose was "to promote a better reciting and understanding of the Vedic texts and their proper ritual employment."[19] When we come to consider the *Devī-Māhātmya*'s commentaries in the next chapter, we shall see that their interpretation is rooted in the Vedic tradition, particularly in their treatment of the text's verses as *mantra*s. That discovery will hardly be surprising, for at this juncture we can already say that the entire interpretative apparatus that has gathered around the text has to it a Vedic aura.

Unlike the three Rahasyas, the three preliminary *aṅga*s are not systematically related to one another. The interlocutors vary, and each gives evidence in its closing verses of being a separate composition, to be recited along with the *Devī-Māhātmya.* Together they amount to nearly ninety verses, but since some of them are extremely repetitious, I will here summarize and comment upon the individual *aṅga*s, while providing complete translations in the appendix to this study.

The crux of the Kavaca, "the armor," is the invocation of seventy-nine feminine divine forces for protection. It is, by extension, "the protective utterance." The spirit is similar to that found in the *Devī-Māhātmya*'s hymn at the end of chapter 4, where protection is sought in specific directions, employing particular weapons of the Goddess. The Kavaca goes much further, however, in a number of respects. The proliferation of specific, distinct, nameable forces is much greater: We recognize the "Seven Little Mothers"[20] described in verses 8-13, and some of the so-called nine Durgās in verses 2-5,[21] but most of the forces discriminated in the invocations of verses 14-37 accumulate rapidly, with only the briefest of characterizations. Significant, too, is the localization of each of these in a part of the reciter's body. This is clearly a manifestation of the Tantric "quest for salvation or for spiritual excellence by realizing and fostering the . . . divinity within one's own body"[22] with a specific practice known as *bhutaśuddhi*, "purification of the elements."[23] What the devotee is doing, in popular parlance, is protecting himself from the slings and arrows of the world by putting on the armor (*kavaca*) of the Goddess—the armor that *is* the Goddess. This basic conceptualization is made apparent by the easy interchangeability of two grammatical constructions: (1) seeking protection for a particular organ (in the accusative) and (2) invoking a particular deity in her organic dwelling place (in the locative). By invoking the indwelling goddess, the reciter's individual organs are deified, thus protected. (The reciter is understood to be male, for the protection of penis and semen is sought in verses 28 and 33, but this is not surprising.)

The Kavaca appears to be a composite document: verses 6-8 (which resemble *Devī-Māhātmya* 12.24-29 in their citation of circumstances from which the Goddess provides rescue) interrupt a process of specifying divine names, and verses 38-55 (like chapter 12 of the *Devī-Māhātmya*) provide a *phalaśruti*, a roster of the benefits of relying on the foregoing verbal composition. This fact is, however, unnoticed in the text itself, and in any case it pales in significance beside the clear sense of purpose with which the text concludes: "Having first done (*kṛtvā*) the Kavaca, one should recite the *Caṇḍī* of 700 verses." The Kavaca thus serves as a preliminary recitation in which the reciter, through a process of ritually protecting his entire being, prepares himself for the recitation of the *Devī-Māhātmya* that is to follow.

The Argalā, "the stopper,"[24] resembles the Kavaca in two respects. It is basically a series of invocations, and it concludes by linking its recitation to that of the *Devī-Māhātmya*, in the following fashion: "Having recited this hymn, a man should then recite the great hymn / Well-fashioned in verses, seven-hundred in number; (then) he obtains (all) good things." The terms that are employed, however, are virtually all names and descriptions that are familiar from the *Devī-Māhātmya*, and one senses that these are epithets of the supreme Goddess, rather than distinct forms. The fact that she is addressed as "four-armed" [15] reinforces this impression, as will become clear after we have examined the Rahasyas. The assistance of the Goddess is sought for either the destruction of enemies or the acquisition of some positive good. A common refrain, half a verse in length, appears in twenty of the twenty-three verses: "Give the form (or beauty: *rūpa*), give the victory, give the fame, kill the enemies." This is clearly a *dhāraṇī*, a specifically Tantric kind of *mantra* that "most often consists of an introductory formula paying honour to some deity, followed by an invocation of some power which is requested to protect the speaker and to destroy all evils that beset him. Its most lively element is the use of a chain of imperatives. . . ."[25] As we shall see later, one of the reasons that individuals recite the *Devī-Māhātmya* is to obtain particular mundane goals—in this respect not unlike the king in the *Devī-Māhātmya*—and perhaps the most famous of the Argalā's verses specifies one such goal. Ostensibly chauvinistic, it elicited a wry smile or humorous comment from everyone (all of them males) with whom I discussed the Argalā: "Grant me a wife, pleasing to the mind, who follows my inclinations / Born of a good family, who helps in crossing this difficult ocean of existence" [22].

Although the Kīlaka, "the bolt," is the briefest of the preliminary *aṅga*s, it is also the most problematical. Some of the difficulty is of a textual sort, a function of several ungrammatical or puzzling readings. Beyond this, however, the Kīlaka introduces us into a discussion of the efficacy of ritual action, but the issues are not fully explained in the written record. Extended discussion of the text and its commentaries with contemporary *paṇḍit*s suggests the following exegesis.

The basic concerns of the Kīlaka are how the fruits of reciting the *Devī-Māhātmya* compare with those of other ritual activity, and how to derive maximum benefit from its recitation. The interlocutor is simply "the seer," who describes action taken by lord Śiva on these matters. It is affirmed that Śiva created a conundrum: All ritual action that is undertaken in order to attain a particular end is deemed to be effective, but so is recitation of the *Devī-Māhātmya* (3-5). Because the fruits of reciting the *Devī-Māhātmya* were proving to be infinite, however, Śiva found it necessary to lay down certain conditions for reaping the rewards of its recitation.[26] This made the hymn hidden (*guhya*) [6], placed on it a restraint (*niyantranā*) [6], locked it up with a bolt (*kīlaka*) [8].[27] Those conditions pertain, first, to the *time* of recitation—one should recite with concentration on the eighth and fourteenth days of the dark fortnight of the moon (as also directed at *Devī-Māhātmya* 12.3)—and, second, to the *attitude* of the devotee—one should offer all one's belongings to the Goddess for her enjoyment, and she will then give them back, as gifts of grace [7]. All manner of benefits are affirmed to accrue to one who recites the *Devī-Māhātmya* with its bolt removed (*niṣkīla*) [9]. Knowing this, one should get on with proper ritual action, for without such action comes death, while with it comes *mokṣa* [10-11]. All good things come about through the grace (*prasāda*) of the Goddess, and even the soft recitation of her hymn brings results [12-14].

If this is a reasonably accurate reconstruction of the thrust of the Kīlaka, then three comments are in order. First, there is a quiet affirmation that the *Devī-Māhātmya* is a ritual text. It requires action, not of an ethical but a ritual sort, probably recitation. It is not simply to be kept in one's heart, or (assuming a written document) read silently to oneself, or studied. "Without action, one perishes" [11]. Second, the Kīlaka affirms that there are both objective and subjective conditions for proper recitation: It should occur on particular days, and the worshipper should be in a particular frame of mind. The *aṅga* makes clear that devotion is directed to the Goddess, and that the *Devī-Māhātmya* is her vehicle, though in some measure its recitation appears to be intrinsically effective, *ex opere operato*. Finally, we should note an apparent shift in the understanding of what constitutes the constraint that has been placed on recitation of the *Devī-Māhātmya*. Within the Kīlaka itself, the limits pertain to the occasion and the attitude of reciting the entire *Saptaśatī*. But in the way that the tradition now presents the *Saptaśatī* and its *aṅga*s, the limit or bolt has come to be understood as the words of the Kīlaka itself. The other limitations may, of course, still pertain, but the Kīlaka itself is now understood as "the bolt." It stands immediately in front of the *Saptaśatī*, as a preliminary verbal-composition-to-be-recited, and the efficacy of reciting *that* text is understood to hinge on the prior recitation of the Kīlaka.

The preliminary *aṅga*s thus have as their primary agenda the ritual preparation of the reciter of the *Devī-Māhātmya*. Recitation of the Kavaca, Argalā, and Kīlaka has armored the individual's body with the Goddess, assured him or her of victory and the acquisition of well-being, and made accessible the full power of the *Saptaśatī*. In chapter 7 we shall examine some of the details of recitation as performed, but for the moment we simply note the way in which the written record testifies to the ritual nature of engagement with this verbal artifact.

The Secrets Pertaining to Primordial Matters, Subsequent Modifications, and Forms: The Prādhānika, Vaikṛtika, and Mūrti Rahasyas

If we understand the preliminary *aṅga*s as emphasizing the auditory dimension of ritual and preparing the devotee for recitation, then the succeeding *aṅga*s may be seen as addressing the visual dimension of ritual and providing systematic linkage between images, text, and Goddess. To be sure, they, too, are to be recited, after recitation of the *Devī-Māhātmya*, but their subject matter is noticeably different from, yet complementary to, the Kavaca, Argalā, and Kīlaka.

The three Rahasyas ("secrets") form more of a unity than do the preliminary *aṅga*s, and they are consistently more engaged with the specific content of the *Saptaśatī* itself. They present themselves as a continuation of that text's dialogue between king and seer, and their point of departure resembles the king's request at the beginning of the *Devī-Māhātmya* to know of the Goddess's nature, her origin, and her own form (*svarūpa*) [1.46]. Now in the first verses of the Prādhānika Rahasya the king asks to be informed about the material nature (*pradhāna*) of the now familiar *avatāra*s of Caṇḍikā, and also about the *svarūpa* of Caṇḍikā herself, the one that is to be worshipped. The seer's answer extends over all three Rahasyas and provides, in roughly ninety verses, what has been called the "earliest systematic statement of Śākta philosophy."[28] In significant measure the Rahasyas are more like what Western sensibilities would consider a "commentary" than are the actual commentaries on the text. The first secret presents what we might call the internal life of the godhead, or more properly the "Goddess-head." The second secret describes how the forms of the Goddess-head become manifest and are related to various divisions of the text of the *Devī-Māhātmya*. The third secret provides detailed descriptions of the future forms (*mūrti*) of the Goddess that are briefly alluded to in chapter 11 of the *Devī-Māhātmya*. Let us now look at each of these in greater detail.[29]

The Prādhānika Rahasya is an account of the ultimate reality in the universe, the unmanifest (*avyākṛta*) form of deity, here understood to have the name Mahālakṣmī. Because the entire discussion takes place at the level of the unmanifest, it forms a sort of philosophical backdrop to the manifest (*vikṛti*) textual phenomenon that is the *Saptaśatī*. The connection between the two will only be made apparent subsequently, in the Vaikṛtika Rahasya. The concern of the Prādhānika is to describe the self-contained life of the divine, its nature and internal distinctions. It is therefore perhaps comparable in intent to Gauḍīya Vaiṣṇava exploration of the nuanced relationship between Rādhā and Krishna, or to what St. Augustine undertakes in *De Trinitate.* The view that it presents is not, to my knowledge, particular to any one school of Indian thought and, as we shall see in the next chapter, it can be made intelligible from the point of view of both Advaita Vedānta (by Nāgoji Bhaṭṭa) and Śrīvidyā (by Bhāskararāya). Having said that, however, we should note three ways in which the Prādhānika reflects broader Indian conceptualizations.

The first is in its employment of terminology associated with the Sāṃkhya school, particularly its notion of the three *guṇa*s, qualities or constituent strands. We have already seen that the *Devī-Māhātmya* itself adverts to such a concept,[30] but this is scarcely surprising as it is virtually pervasive of Indian thinking about cosmogonic matters from at least the time of the *Bhagavad Gītā.* A. N. Jani puts the basic issue this way:

> From the experience of the feelings of pleasure, pain and indifference through the various objects of the world they [the Sāṃkhya] have postulated the theory of three *guṇas* (constituents) called *sattva, rajas* and *tamas* which are respectively responsible for the experience of the above three feelings. The element in which these three constituents are found is called *Prakṛti* by them [sometimes also *pradhāna*]. These three *guṇa*s are generally in a state of equilibrium in the *Prakṛti.* But due to its contact with the sentient *Puruṣa* the *Prakṛti* gets agitated. The equilibrium is, therefore, lost and the disturbance of the three constituents takes place [resulting in the evolution out of *prakṛti* of the manifest world].[31]

We note here in passing that Sāṃkhya presents a philosophical dualism, of *puruṣa* and *prakṛti,* but this is not its principal legacy to the later tradition. The legacy is the notion of a dynamic, three-stranded evolution of the universe.

The second point of conceptual contact with the larger Indian tradition occurs in the discrimination of two levels of a single reality, or two ways of knowing that one reality. The basic concept is as old as the Upaniṣadic distinction between *nirguṇa* and *saguṇa* Brahman, and its later manifestations pervade both Buddhist and Vedic traditions. What we need to note here is the particular way in which the distinction appears in the Prādhānika Rahasya. We note, first, that even though the Prādhānika employs the language of Sāṃkhya's *prakṛti/pradhāna* to talk about distinctions within Mahālakṣmī, this does *not* imply that there is some sentient reality, some *puruṣa*, other than her. The Rahasyas present us with a monistic view of the universe, and none of the forms that they describe compromises the fundamental unity of the Goddess.[32] Where the discrimination between "ultimate" reality and "not-so-ultimate" reality occurs in the Prādhānika is at the end [27], where the text turns from describing the inner life of the Goddess-head to the functions that each of its different forms will play in the manifest world. It is here that the specific word *pradhāna*, "material nature," appears for the first time, and it is this theme that is then picked up in the next Rahasya, the Vaikṛtika.

The third feature of the Prādhānika Rahasya that is characteristically Indian is its overtly iconic, visual, and graphic account of the divine. This may bc particularly puzzling to Western sensibilities because, as we have just seen, virtually the whole of the Prādhānika is concerned with the unmanifest form of Mahālakṣmī, and yet the very first characterization that is offered by the seer is drenched in specific, visualizable detail:

> The foremost of all is Mahālakṣmī, constituted of the three qualities (*guṇa*s), the supreme queen. Her very own form (*svarūpa*) is both with and without characteristic marks; she abides, having pervaded everything. She carries a citron, club, shield, and drinking vessel. On her head, O king, she wears a snake, *liṅga*, and *yoni*. She shines with the color of burned gold, with ornaments of the same golden hue [4-6].

We notice, of course, that Mahālakṣmī's own form is affirmed to lack characteristic marks, as well as to possess them. But the text moves immediately to specify the characteristic marks, and says no more about the alternative. Our puzzlement may be somewhat reduced by realizing that we are here brought face-to-face with the Hindu propensity for wanting to *see* the divine, about which Diana Eck has written so incisively.[33] In lieu of our inheritance of an Hebraic antipathy to images and a Greek distrust of the senses stands India's prizing of *darśan*, "seeing." In the narrowest sense, this specifies what happens "when Hindus go to the temple, [and] their eyes meet the powerful, eternal gaze of the eyes [of the image] of God." But it implies, at a more philosophical level, reciprocal eye contact between human and divine as the avenue of mutual knowledge.[34] In this context, an interpretative translation of the king's opening question in the Prādhānika would be: "How can I know the Goddess if I don't know what she looks like?" Narrative of the Goddess's activity, already provided in the *Devī-Māhātmya* itself, therefore moves immediately to visual description of the divine appearance here in the Rahasyas.[35]

We turn now to the Prādhānika Rahasya's characterization of the unmanifest life of Mahālakṣmī. It may be verbally portrayed as follows, but in order to visualize the relationships more readily, I have also diagramed them in figure 5.1. The primal Mahālakṣmī, whom we have seen to be constituted of all three *guṇa*s, on seeing that the entire world was empty, took on (literally, "bore": *babhāra*) another form, employing the *guṇa* of *tamas* (dark mass-stuff) alone.[36] To this four-armed form, she gave the name Mahākālī, along with other names and characteristic actions [8-12]. Mahālakṣmī then assumed (*dadhāra*) another of her own forms (*svarūpa*) by means of the *guṇa* of *sattva* (pure intelligence-stuff). The primary name of this form was Mahāsarasvatī, and she, too, received additional names and qualities (13-15). Each of these forms was instructed to produce a set of twins, which she did, as did Mahālakṣmī herself. Mahālakṣmī produced a man, whom she called Brahmā, and a woman, called Lakṣmī. Mahākālī gave birth to the male Rudra and the female Sarasvatī, while Mahāsarasvatī bore Viṣṇu and Gaurī. "Thus did the two young females in a flash come to partake of maleness (*puruṣatva*)" [16-24]. Three marriages were then arranged by Mahālakṣmī: Sarasvatī uniting with Brahmā, Rudra with Gaurī, and Viṣṇu with Lakṣmī. The first of these couples produced an egg. The second broke it open, and out poured *pradhāna*, the material stuff of the universe. The third couple nourished and protected it.[37] "This indeed is Mahālakṣmī, O king, the mother, the queen of all who have power. She is both formless and possessed of form, carrying various designations. She can be described by other names, but by no other name (can she be fully described)" [25-29].

Three points may be made about this account. First, all of these differentiations should be understood as occurring within the Goddess herself. Nothing described here is extrinsic to her. Although she takes on different forms, they are all, both individually and collectively, her "own form" (*svarūpa*). Mahālakṣmī is the designation of both a particular form and the aggregate of all these forms.[38] Second, in the correlation of divine forms with the *guṇa*s, Mahālakṣmī is said to be constituted of all three *guṇa*s, but when *tamas* and *sattva guṇa*s are allocated to Mahākālī and Mahāsarasvatī respectively, there is an implicit predominance in Mahālakṣmī of the remaining *guṇa* of *rajas* (ruddy energy-stuff), though she remains characterized as "possessing three *guṇa*s." The significance of this parallelism will become apparent when we come to look at the *Saptaśatī*'s commentaries. Finally, we ought not to confuse the familiar goddesses Sarasvatī, Lakṣmī, and Kālī with Mahāsarasvatī,

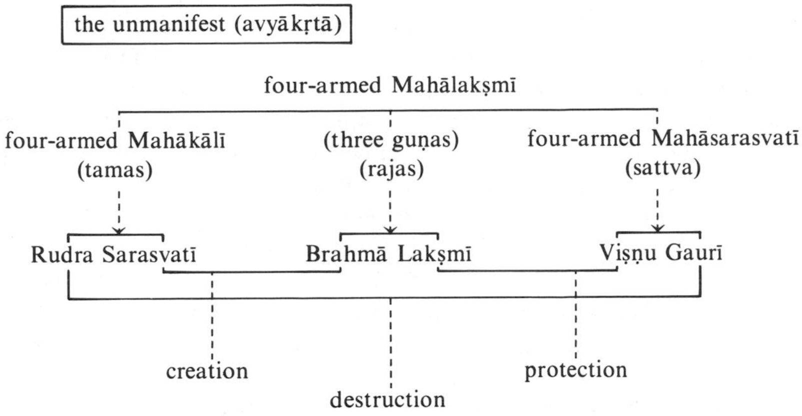

Figure 5.1 Diagram of relationships in the Prādhānika Rahasya

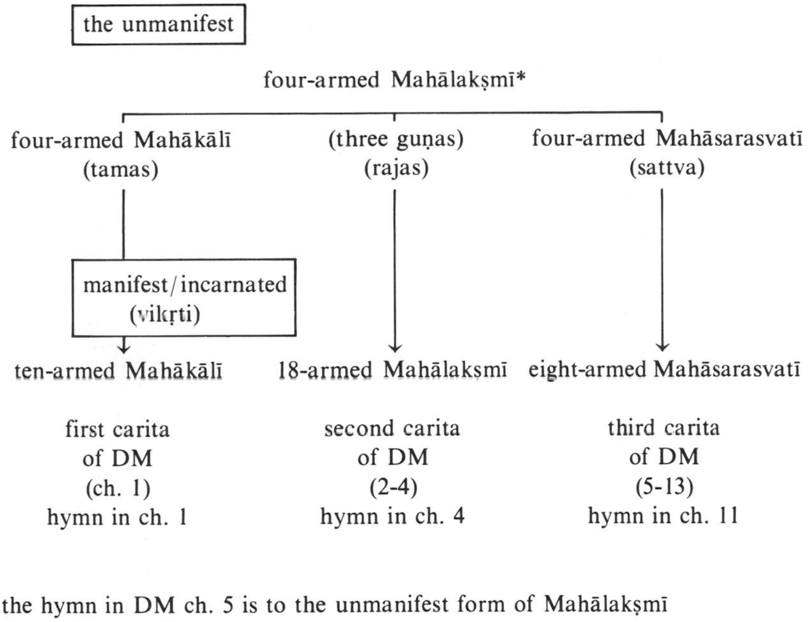

Figure 5.2 Diagram of relationships in the Vaikṛtika Rahasya

Mahālakṣmī, and Mahākālī. The former are divine forms of a second order, as it were, and it is they who are commonly known through their respective roles in the creation, protection, and destruction of the universe. The latter, however, in spite of their partial iconographic resemblance to the lower forms, are unmanifest, or we might say transcendent, elements of the Goddess-head.

The Vaikṛtika Rahasya, the secret dealing with subsequent modifications, takes its name from its concern with the manifestation or incarnation (*vikṛti*) of Mahālakṣmī. It does not explicitly state that each of the four-armed unmanifest forms produces a manifest form with the same name. It simply starts from the statement that she who is three-*guṇa*-ed, tamasic, and sattvic has three forms [1]. It then goes on to describe each of the three [2-16]. The names of these manifest forms are identical with the names of the unmanifest forms—Mahākālī, Mahālakṣmī, and Mahāsarasvatī—but their iconography is different. Each of these manifest forms, moreover, is identified with one of the three myths of the *Devī-Māhātmya*, according to a pattern that I have diagramed in figure 5.2. The iconography of these forms is much fuller than that provided in the Prādhānika Rahasya, for these are images to be employed in *pūjā*. The qualities ascribed to the incarnate Mahākālī include having ten faces and arms, and the *guṇa* of *tamas*. Mahālakṣmī is characterized as possessing all three *guṇa*s and, among other features, eighteen arms. Mahāsarasvatī has eight arms and the single *guṇa* of *sattva*. The Vaikṛtika then goes on to describe the configuration of the tableau for worship [17-23]. The crucial features (also apparent in the *yantra* that we shall discuss later on: see figure 5.3)[39] are that Mahālakṣmī is in the front row in the middle, with Mahākālī to the left and Mahāsarasvatī to the right. Behind them in the second row stand the three married couples from the Prādhānika Rahasya, from left to right, Rudra-Gaurī, Brahmā-Sarasvatī, Viṣṇu-Lakṣmī.[40] The Vaikṛtika now proceeds to link the most important of these forms with the different hymns of the *Devī-Māhātmya* [23-24]. Mahālakṣmī, in what we should understand to be her unmanifest four-armed form, is to be worshipped with the hymn that is found in chapter 5 of the *Saptaśatī*, while her three incarnate forms (*avatāra*s) are to be worshipped with the *mantra*s of the other hymns. The details of what this means are not obvious, but the Vaikṛtika—in addition to associating a particular incarnate form with each myth—also divides the *Saptaśatī* into three episodes, which it calls *carita*s [32], and at this point Bhāskararāya elaborates that the hymn in chapter 1 belongs to Mahākālī, that in chapter 4 belongs to Mahālakṣmī, and that in chapter 11 to Mahāsarasvatī. In this explanation, the commentator is reflecting the widespread understanding that each of the three episodes of the *Saptaśatī*

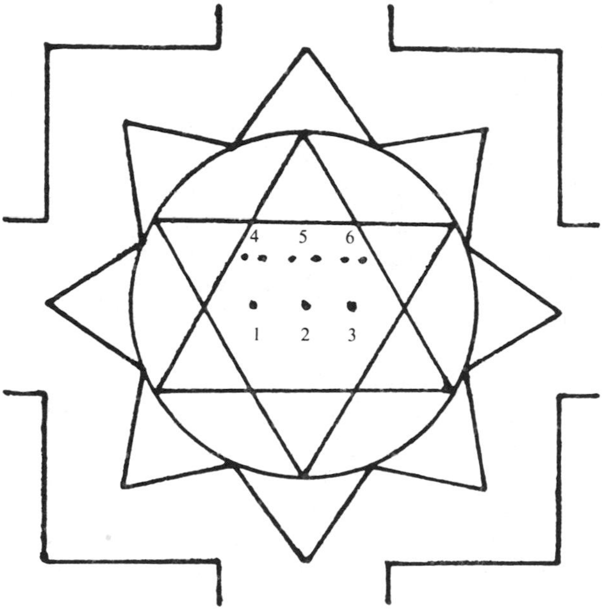

1. Ten-armed Mahākālī
2. Eighteen-armed Mahālakṣmī
3. Eight-armed Mahāsarasvatī
4. Rudra-Gaurī
5. Brahma-Sarasvatī
6. Viṣṇu-Lakṣmī

Figure 5.3 The *Devī-Māhātmya/Saptaśatī* Caṇḍī *yantra*

has one of these incarnate forms as its presiding deity, a matter that we can see to be implicit in the Vaikṛtika itself, and to which we shall return later. Finally, this Rahasya provides details on the kinds of materials that should be offered in *pūjā* to the 18-armed Mahālakṣmī, foremost of the incarnate forms, and it concludes with counsel on recitation of the *Devī-Māhātmya*: If one cannot recite the entire composition, one should do the middle episode alone, or the hymnic verses in chapter 5, and one should never recite only half an episode, for that would create a chink (*chidra*) in the armor [27-35].

The Mūrti Rahasya is the briefest of the three secrets, and it adds the least to our understanding of the way in which the *Devī-Māhātmya* has been appropriated. Its basic concern is to provide further information about the future *avatāra*s of the Goddess that are alluded to at the end of chapter 11 of our text. This consists primarily of fuller description of their appearance, and citation of the benefits of worshipping certain of them. It is not clear in the *Devī-Māhātmya* precisely how many future forms are being enumerated, and the Mūrti Rahasya is only somewhat more certain. There would appear to be five—the blessed daughter of Nanda, Red-tooth, Śākaṃbharī, Bhimā, and the Queen-bee—but other names also gather around these figures, and two of them (Hundred-eyes and Durgā) are also distinctive of the eleventh chapter of the *Saptaśatī*. Noteworthy, perhaps, is a new interest in the maternal qualities of these figures, manifest in the attention that is paid to the goddesses' breasts and in the characterization of the Goddess as "mother of the universe" [22]. This contrasts strikingly with the preferred martial imagery of the *Devī-Māhātmya*, and may suggest the role of Bengal in this particular elaboration of the *aṅga*s.[41]

The Mūrti Rahasya concludes with emphases that are characteristic of the *aṅga*s as a whole:

> You ought to learn this explanation of heavenly forms by heart.
>
> ....
>
> By means of reciting the *mantra*s one is released from all sins.
>
> ....
>
> Meditation on the Goddess is proclaimed by me to be the greatest secret of all.
> By exerting yourself in this way, you will be granted the fruit of your every desire [23-25].

The encounter with the Goddess to which the *aṅga*s attest thus places ritual recitation of the verbal artifact at center stage. The

Goddess's presence is understood to permeate the very structure of the text. Recitation is affirmed to have certain extrinsic effects, to reap certain fruits, but there is also a sense in which, by the act of recitation itself, when it is accompanied by appropriate visualization of her forms, the reciter participates in the very reality of the Goddess.

6

Encounter With the Text II—The Commentaries

Introduction

As we have seen in chapter 4, the variety of material that can be considered commentary on any given verbal artifact is vast. Sculpture, ritual activity, dance, and narrative reworking, to cite only some possibilities, may all be seen as part of the way in which humans appropriate and comment on words that they have found to be in some way significant. As we turn now to consider the commentary on the *Devī-Māhātmya* in the narrower and more conventional sense—verbal exegesis that is inscribed on the written page underneath the text that is being commented upon—we should remind ourselves that, in principle, there will be much that will escape the net of our inquiry. In our final chapter, we will inquire more expansively into the range of interpretive leverage that has been sought on our text. In the present chapter, however, we must ask what it is that has been going on in the written commentaries that have been composed upon the *Devī-Māhātmya.*

Within this more restricted scope, three additional caveats are in order.

First, as suggested earlier, one of the striking features of the contemporary exploration of scripture as a global phenomenon is the discovery of major alternatives to modern Western assumptions about the nature and function of religious texts. Not everything is as the post-

Reformation, post-Gutenberg, post-Enlightenment and now post-modern world would have it. Scripture, we are discovering, is an unanticipatedly rich and nuanced category of human expression. So, too, it would appear, is the notion of "commentary," which at first glance seems comparably straightforward. *Of course*, we say, people write commentaries on the verbal compositions that they value, whether they be literary classics, or religious scriptures, or legal constitutions. And yet once the comparative task begins in earnest, even the nonspecialist quickly recognizes that Jews and Christians have done very different things in commenting on their respective Bibles, producing such contrasting phenomena as the *Talmud* and *The Interpreter's Bible*, where the contrasts are not just in content, but also in form and intent. To expand the comparison into Confucian commentary on the Classics, or Islamic on the *Qur'ān*, is to become aware of even greater diversity. Traditions seemingly compose commentaries for very different reasons, and a great deal more study appears necessary before we can conclude that the prima facie category of commentary will stand up as a valid unit of comparison.

Second, even within just the Hindu tradition an extraordinary range of activity seems to have occurred in the literary phenomenon we call "commentary." Certain tendencies are, of course, in evidence. By virtue of the extraordinarily disciplined way in which Sanskrit grammar was classically taught and learned, commentators across all genres are fascinated with syntax and etymology.[1] Within philosophical and dramatic literature, the accompanying commentary regularly embodies the five characteristics of a *bhāṣya* given in the *Nyāyakośa: padaccheda* or word division, *padārthokti* or paraphrasing, *vigraha* or analysis of compounds, *vākyayojanā* or construing of sentences, and *ākṣepa-samādhāna* or answering of objections.[2] Within the aphoristic or *sūtra* literature, we necessarily find expansive commentaries by virtue of the premium that the authors of the original *sūtra*s placed on brevity: It is said that the author of such a text would sell his grandson in order to save a single syllable. It is a commonplace to see the schools of Pūrva and Uttara Mīmāṃsā, otherwise known respectively as Mīmāṃsā and Vedānta, as offering different kinds of commentary on the Vedic corpus, the former focusing on ritual injunction, the latter on soteriological insight. It is also well-known that an authoritative teacher of Vedānta was expected to compose commentaries on the so-called *prasthāna-traya* of the *Bhagavad Gītā*, the Upaniṣads, and the *Brahma Sūtra*s. All of these patterns notwithstanding, a host of unanswered questions makes it clearly premature to generalize about the nature of Hindu Sanskrit commentary. Why, for instance, does the *Ṛg Veda* virtually escape systematic commentary for over two thousand years, until the great fourteenth-century work of Sāyaṇa?[3] Why, for instance, should the devotion that is enkindled by the tenth Book of the *Bhāgavata Purāṇa* produce such a welter of commentaries when the rest of the Purāṇas, long understood as intimately intertwined with the *bhakti* movement, attract almost none?[4] Why, by contrast, should the commentaries on the *Devī-Māhātmya*, also a Purāṇic text, be so abstract and distanced from the fervor of *bhakti* (as we shall see)? Are there not different motives for composing commentaries on different kinds of literature? One suspects that the many Sanskrit terms for "commentary"—*kaumudī, candrikā, ṭīkā, darpaṇa, dīpakā, dīpanī, nibandha, nirūpaṇa, nirṇaya, parīkṣaṇa, prakāśa, prakāśikā, pradīpa, bhāṣya, vivaraṇa, vṛtti, vyākhyā*[5]—may reflect a series of distinctions of which we are at present only dimly aware. Be that as it may, our examination here of commentaries on the *Devī-Māhātmya* will tell us something about the encounter that the later tradition has had with this text. But we must be careful about drawing from this examination broader conclusions about the nature of Hindu commentary.

Finally, it will be recalled from our first chapter that the number of commentaries on the *Devī-Māhātmya* is enormous. I have cited the number sixty-seven, based on Theodore Aufrecht's *Catalogus Catalogorum* and other indices. Clearly a comprehensive study of them would be a massive undertaking. Even with a more modest aspiration, access to the material is exceedingly difficult. My own search for commentaries began a decade ago and produced only one in North American libraries, that of Nāgoji Bhaṭṭa. Continuing the process in India has been more fruitful, chiefly because of the kindness of the Mahārāja of Benares in lending me his father's personal copy of the Harikṛṣṇaśarma edition, published with seven commentaries by Veṅtakeśvara Press in 1916.[6] In 1981-1982 this was a rare find, a fact perhaps masked by its subsequent republication by Buṭalā and Co. I have no doubt that merely locating additional commentaries would be a long and tedious process. Nor, I think, is it necessary for my purposes. To inquire into the legacy of the text and to give some sense of how the text has been encountered in the interval since its composition, a representative sampling of the commentarial material is sufficient. Correspondingly, since I have been told repeatedly that in both north and south India the two most important commentaries are those of Bhāskararāya and Nāgoji Bhaṭṭa (Nāgeśa), it is on these two that I have focused my study, while consulting half a dozen others. It is primarily on these two commentaries that I shall draw in the balance of this chapter. There are important differences in religious orientation between them, and together they provide what I think is a fair sense of the way commentators "handle" the text.

Some would argue that biographical material is irrelevant to introducing our two commentators. This would be part of a larger structuralist argument against the historical separation of text, commentary, and contemporary religious life, an argument that it is necessary "to telescope the centuries" because "when texts, no matter how old and abstract, are commented on by Brahmin savants, they show the flesh and blood of contemporary observation."[7] The "meaning" of texts is here understood to transcend the perspective of any individual commentator. Even those who are persuaded that commentaries provide us with valuable historical perspectives on texts admit that their utility "is considerably diminished by the fact that we know next to nothing about these commentators themselves."[8] Without presuming to resolve the underlying methodological issues here,[9] I provide remarks on the two commentators and their work in the next section, then turn to an overview of Bhāskararāya's commentary on the *Devī-Māhātmya*, and conclude with some comparative remarks on Bhāskararāya's and Nāgoji Bhaṭṭa's engagement with the text.

Bhāskararāya and Nāgoji Bhaṭṭa

Our two commentators were contemporaries. Although dates for both retain an element of uncertainty, Bhāskararāya "may be taken to have flourished between the last quarter of the 17th and the second half of the 18th centuries," perhaps as late as 1768,[10] while Nāgoji Bhaṭṭa's career is said to have spanned the years 1688-1755.[11] Bhāskararāya may be somewhat younger, for on at least two occasions he quotes works by Nāgoji Bhaṭṭa, including the latter's commentary on the *Durgā-Saptaśatī*.[12] Since we know that Bhāskararāya's commentary on the *Devī-Māhātmya*, known as the *Guptavatī* ("Containing What Is Hidden"), was completed at Cidambaram toward the end of his career, probably in 1741,[13] Nāgoji Bhaṭṭa's commentary would appear to have been composed somewhat earlier.

Bhāskararāya has been called "the foremost intellectual authority among the adherents of the Śrīvidyā system" of Śākta Tantrism and "a scholar of vast erudition in the classical Indian sense."[14] According to an account of his life and literary works composed by one of his disciples,[15] he was a South Indian *Ṛg Veda* Brahman of the Viśvāmitra-gotra, born in the Maharashtra village of Thanuja, raised in the town of Bhāgā, then educated at his father's instance in Varanasi. A gifted student, he soon became known for his dialectical agility. Initiated into Śrīvidyā by Śivadatta Śukla at Surat, he traveled widely throughout the subcontinent, undertaking various pilgrimages, initiating important figures into Śrīvidyā, engaging in philosophical debate, constructing and renovating temples. Eventually he settled near Tanjore in a village that took his name, a gift from the ruler of Tanjore, where he continued teaching and writing until his death.

At least forty-two titles are ascribed to Bhāskararāya, though manscripts exist for only eighteen.[16] Their range is enormous, running from Vedānta, Mīmāṃsā, grammar, prosody, poetry, and logic to an independent treatise on Śrīvidyā, the *Varivasyā-Rahasya* ("The Secret of Worship"), and commentaries on the *Lalitā-Sahasranāma*, the *Yoginīhṛdaya*, various Śākta Upaniṣads, and, of course, the *Devī-Māhātmya*. A few of these works have been translated into English, but like most Tantric material, they remain inaccessible to all but the most determined student, and in significant measure opaque to those not initiated into Śrīvidyā. Fortunately, our understanding of Bhāskararāya and Śrīvidyā, as well as of Tantra more generally, is about to advance dramatically, thanks to the recent and forthcoming work of Douglas R. Brooks.[17] In anticipation of the dissemination of this work, and with a keen sense of the summary nature of the following discussion, it will be useful here to say a word about Tantra, "Śākta", and Śrīvidyā in order to understand the views that Bhāskararāya brings to writing his commentary on the *Durgā-Saptaśatī*.

The word "Tantra" has been fraught with misunderstanding and controversy from virtually the beginning of scholarly efforts to understand the phenomenon. Some of this difficulty derives from the esoteric nature of Tantra, some from the sheer complexity of the historical data, some from the alleged immoral aura that surrounds it. Aware of the morass of opinion and interpretation, André Padoux has recently maintained that it is nevertheless legitimate to

> admit Tantrism as a category of its own and [to] define it generally as a practical path to supernatural powers and to liberation, consisting in the use of specific *practices and techniques*—ritual, bodily, mental—that are always associated with a particular *doctrine*. These practices are intrinsically grounded in the doctrine that gives them their aim and meaning and organizes them into a pattern. Elements of the doctrine as well as of practices may also be found elsewhere in Indian religions, but when both are associated and welded into a practical worldview, Tantrism is there.[18]

Specifically with regard to Hindu Tantrism, Padoux then offers the following point of entry:

> Tantrism may be briefly characterized as a practical way to attain supernatural powers and liberation in this life through the use of specific and complex techniques based on a particular ideology, that of a cosmic reintegration by means of which the adept is established in a position of power, freed from worldly fetters, while remaining in this world and dominating it by union with (or proximity to) a godhead who is the supreme power itself. All practices and notions constituting the Tantric way correspond to a particular conception of the deity, polarized as masculine and feminine, and of the universe and man, both imbued with this divine power [*śakti*]. Thus it may be said that, for a Tantric adept, the quest for liberation and the acquisition of supernatural powers result from a tapping, a manipulating of this ubiquitous power.[19]

To the broad strokes of this portrait Goudriaan adds detail by identifying the "constituents" of Tantrism, which it may be useful to list here:[20]

1. A practical, individual road to salvation provides an alternative to the Vedic one.
2. Mundane aims are valued as well as spiritual emancipation.
3. A special form of yoga transforms animal instincts by rousing bodily energy upward through yogic centers.
4. A mystic physiology identifies the microcosm of the body with the macrocosm of the universe.
5. An assumed parallel between material phenomena and sounds is explored through speculation on the mystic nature of speech.
6. Certain verbal formulas (*mantra*s) are ritually invested with power.
7. Concrete devices like formulas, geometrical designs (*maṇḍala, yantra, cakra*) are employed to express metaphysical principles.
8. The supernatural world is realized through specific methods of meditation often involving the creation of mental images.
9. Reality is unitary, but characterized by complementary opposites at both divine and human levels.

10. Female manifestations called *śakti*s are important.
11. Realization of the double-sided nature of reality is accomplished through intentional, regulated contact with socially disapproved persons and entities.
12. Initiation by a qualified teacher is essential.
13. A complete set of ritual practices beside the Vedic is developed.
14. Reality is elaborately categorized, especially in number and speech symbolism.
15. Speculation begun in Brahmanical circles is further articulated.
16. The distinctive form of *yoga* is often related to alchemy and body culture.
17. A special religious geography is developed.
18. Special terminology and "code language" require special forms of exegesis.

Given the "soft" boundaries of Tantrism, some of these items will be found broadly distributed in Hindu life, for "no one feature alone is sufficient to distinguish Tantrics from non-Tantrics."[21] However, for our purposes, such items may be understood as Tantric if their context conforms to Padoux's insistence that it be shaped by an integrated concern for doctrine and practice.

Such a definition allows Tantrism to be understood as a "style" of human religiousness that is attested in the worship of a variety of deities, not all of them Hindu, and not all of them female.[22] It can therefore be partially discriminated from Śaktism, which "may be characterized as the worship of Śakti . . . , i.e. the universal and all-embracing dynamis which manifests itself in human experience as a female divinity, [to whom is] . . . inseparably connected . . . an inactive male power as whose power of action and movement the Śakti functions."[23] Tantrism and Śāktism may therefore be understood as "'two intersecting but not coinciding circles,'"[24] the former referring to a specifically characterized, integral convergence of doctrine and practice, the latter to worship of the central power (*śakti*) of the universe as female deity.

Śrīvidyā, then, can be understood as one of the premier instances of Hindu Śākta Tantrism. Specifically, it is the tradition (*saṃpradāya*) which deals with the worship of Tripurasundarī, "the most important Tantric form of Śrī/Lakṣmī, [who is] . . . the most benign, beautiful and youthful, yet motherly manifestation of the Supreme Śakti."[25] As an independent school, Śrīvidyā may date back to the fourth or fifth century, and is certainly older than its first systematic literary formulation in the eleventh and twelfth centuries.[26] Śrīvidyā gives distinctive formulation to the common Tantric view that the ultimate manifests itself in three degrees—gross (*sthūla*), subtle (*sūkṣma*) and supreme (*para*)[27]—in its affirmation that the ultimate appears in the respective forms of (1) the anthropomorphic image of Lalitā Tripurasundarī, (2) the *mantra* known as the Śrīvidyā *mantra*, and (3) the *yantra* known as the Śrīcakra.[28] The first of these is readily intelligible to the outsider, referring as it does to the image that is employed in *pūjā* or worship.[29] The latter two, however, are not only likely to strike the non-Indian neophyte as arcane, but they are also precisely the features of the tradition that receive the most scrupulous attention from Bhāskararāya. It is difficult to generalize about *mantra*, for the word has had a broad, imprecise meaning for a very long time, and its "exact force and meaning can be determined only through an exegesis that is text and tradition specific."[30] We may, however, note that Śrīvidyā and Bhāskararāya share the larger Indian sense that the primordial Brahman,[31] the fundament of the universe, has sound-form and that this sound-form devolves in various ways. One such way is into the mundane sounds of ordinary language. Another, affirms Śrīvidyā, is as *mantra*s, particularly concentrated and powerful manifestations of the goddess Tripurā, which are accessible only to initiates through a *guru*. Of these sound-forms, the fifteen- or sixteen-syllabled Śrīvidyā *mantra* is paramount. Employed in a ritual context, it is integral to the fulfillment of an initiate's meditative experience.[32] The visual counterpart to the Śrīvidyā *mantra* is the Śrīcakra *yantra*, consisting of nine intersecting triangles, four pointing upwards, representing Śiva or male, and five pointing downwards, representing Śakti or female. (See figure 6.1) Śakti herself is the presiding deity of the Śrīcakra, which thus represents the "conjugal union that created the universe."[33] Correspondingly, she is the *bindu* or dot at the very center of the *yantra*. Precisely how she became manifest as the Śrīcakra, how the material universe, properly seen, is itself a Śrīcakra, how the adept ritually reverses this process so that "he eventually comes to see creation from the vantage point of the creator"[34]—all this, as well as much more, is the burden of Bhāskararāya's writing on Śrīvidyā.

Finally, a brief word about the *philosophy* that Bhāskararāya brings to his commentary on the *Devī-Māhātmya* will be helpful. There is, of course, a certain artificiality in removing such a topic from the Tantric integration of doctrine and ritual that we noted above. Moreover, one of the striking features of the Śākta tradition is its *absence* from the traditional arena of Hindu philosophical discourse, from what is

Figure 6.1 The Śrīcakra *yantra*. (Courtesy, University of Chicago Press)

classically known as *darśana*.[35] Nonetheless, such a discussion will allow us later to avoid a certain puzzlement in Bhāskararāya's commentary on the *Devī-Māhātmya*, as well as to anticipate comparison with Nāgoji Bhaṭṭa.

One of the major points of contention in Indian philosophy, crisply dividing the major schools, pertains to theories of causation.[36] Some have affirmed that effects exist independent of their causes, that when something "new" is created, it is ontologically distinct from its causes. Known as *asatkāryavāda* ("the view of non-(pre)existing effects"), it is the view held by Buddhists and the schools of Mīmāṃsā and Nyāya-Vaiśeṣika. Against this is the position, most often associated with the schools of Sāṃkhya and Advaita, which affirms that effects preexist in their cause, that "an effect . . . is nothing but the cause itself, albeit seen in a different form or state."[37] This is known as *satkāryavāda*, "the view of (pre)existing effects." Among the proponents of such a view, there is a crucial further distinction, between (1) those who see effect as an actual *transformation* (*pariṇāma*) of an underlying substratum, and (2) those who see it as a mere *appearance* (*vivarta*), a superimposition on an underlying substratum. The former of these sees creation as a process of evolution or unfolding or exfoliation, as in Sāṃkhya's understanding of the evolution of the primordial *prakṛti*. The other position, usually associated with Śaṅkara's non-dual (*advaita*) Vedānta, affirms that the one reality of Brahman may be looked at from two different points of view: (1) from the empirical perspective, where it looks as if Brahman (with attributes: *saguṇa*) undergoes evolution into diversity, and (2) from the higher, mystically intuitive perspective where only Brahman (without attributes: *nirguṇa*) exists. The empirical perspective is here characterized by *māyā*, "illusion," by distinction of subject from object, a distinction that is superimposed on the (ultimately) true state of affairs. The empirical perspective, however, is not permanent, for the experience of mystical union—what Deutsch calls "the Brahman experience"[38]—overcomes or sublates all differentiation. Ultimately, and knowledgeably seen, only Brahman exists.

All of this has a very direct bearing on the philosophical perspective we encounter in Bhāskararāya. Like most Tantrics, he is a non-dualist: There is but one reality in the universe, and human beatitude consists in coming to know that reality experientially. He therefore shares a great deal with the Advaitin Śaṅkara. He refers to Śaṅkara throughout his works[39] and, in fact, pays homage to him in the second line of his commentary on the *Devī-Māhātmya*. But at the same time Bhāskararāya is a proponent of the *pariṇāma* view of the relation between cause and effect: There is ontological continuity between ultimate reality and ordinary experience, in all of the latter's sensuality and materiality. In this respect his thinking resembles that of Sāṃkhya and breaks sharply with Advaita.

To see precisely how Bhāskararāya defends this position would take us too far afield. It would also make him more of a pure philosopher than is appropriate. In significant measure his defense of this position is not a philosophical one—we recall the absence of the Śākta perspective from discussions in classical *darśana*—but a ritual one. It is as if he affirms that reality is one, that it is ontologically accessible through matter, and that such access is provided by the private ritual tutelage of a *guru*, rather than through the public discourse of philosophers.[40]

Having said this, we may note that when Bhāskararāya does describe the evolution of the original, undifferentiated reality of Brahman/Śakti into the manifest diversity of the world, he does so with two different emphases. One underscores the *binary* division that Brahman undergoes, into male or Śiva and female or Śakti.

> . . . by Its own conscious will (*icchā-*), act (*kriyā-*), and knowledge (*jñānaśakti*) as well as for Its own pleasure (*ānanda*) and for the pleasure of the beings it created, the Absolute Brahman took the form of binary divinity. Through the Deity's bifurcation into masculine and feminine aspects the multifarious names and forms of the Universe gradually devolve.[41]

The other perspective emphasizes the *triadic* nature of this creative process. It takes note of the threefold appearance of Śakti as desire (*icchā*), action (*kriyā/kṛti*), and knowledge (*jñāna*), hence the appropriateness of the name Tripurā ("Three Cities") to name the goddess. It goes on to correlate this trifurcation with various anthropomorphic forms and with the triangular structure of the Śrīcakra.[42] In neither the dyadic nor the triadic case, we may note, is the gender of deity a matter of critical importance. Although, for Bhāskararāya, it is the feminine principle that actualizes the divine impulse to creative self-manifestation, he is not primarily concerned to argue this point, for "the form in which she is worshipped is a matter of one's [own] tradition."[43] What is critical is the immediate access to ultimacy that is provided to human beings by the ontological continuum, whose agent and (from another angle) whose material substance is Śakti.

Against this backdrop, our introduction to Nāgoji Bhaṭṭa and his perspective can be briefer. The dates for him cited earlier, 1688-1755, are based on a number of inferences and, in general, biographical information is scanty. He appears to have been a Maharashtra Brahman, who was patronized by the ruler of a city on the Ganges somewhere above Allahabad, under whose patronage he wrote, among other things, a commentary on the *Rāmāyaṇa*.[44] We know something of his intellectual lineage, and Kane describes his learning as "of an encyclopaedic character."[45] Some forty-seven works have been ascribed to him, and they include commentaries on works of Sāṃkhya and Yoga, as well as independent treatises dealing with poetics, various branches of Dharma Śāstra, and grammar (*vyākaraṇa*).[46] It is the last of these that was his forte, reflecting the major emphasis in his training, and for which he achieved his renown. In other words, Nāgoji Bhaṭṭa is chiefly a grammarian. He is not an advocate for a particular school or religious sect. Rather, he became a master of the discipline that was the starting-point for entry into the world of Brahmanical learning, namely, the study of language itself.[47] Such mastery, coupled with a supple intellect, would easily have put him in a position to write broadly on the significant texts of his day.

If we thus identify Nāgoji Bhaṭṭa generally as a man of letters, an eighteenth century intellectual with no distinctive sectarian orientation and no particular axe to grind, we might then speculate about the philosophical orientation that would be found in his writings. He would be, one may legitimately suspect, an Advaita Vedāntin, not in any dogmatic sense, but in the sense that Śaṅkara's "asceticism and mysticism have been, for many centuries . . . , to the respectable Indian classes what art has been for the last century and a half to the bourgeoisie of Western Europe: something for which most of the majority has no talent, or dares not try, but which many of them feel somehow justifies their own dull and unimportant lives."[48] The intellectual climate in which Nāgoji Bhaṭṭa lived we may expect to have been Advaitin, just as we might say that, generally speaking, the intellectual climate of medieval Europe was Aristotelian. Such an expectation is, in fact, born out by Nāgoji Bhaṭṭa's commentary on the *Devī-Māhātmya*, as we shall see. There appears to be comparable testimony elsewhere in his writing. One of the knowledgeable Hindu scholars with whom I have discussed the *Devī-Māhātmya*'s commentaries reported seeing Nāgoji Bhaṭṭa opt in his grammatical work for an Advaitin interpretation when there was no necessity to do so, and when there were other possible interpretations.[49] We might therefore understand Nāgoji Bhaṭṭa as a kind of "cultural Advaitin."

What this means for the philosophical assumptions that Nāgoji Bhaṭṭa brings to his commentary on the *Devī-Māhātmya* is implicit in our earlier discussion of Indian theories of causation.[50] He, like Bhāskararāya, is a non-dualist: only Brahman exists. But where Bhāskararāya sees this Brahman/Śakti as having undergone transformation (*pariṇāma*) into the manifold universe, Nāgoji Bhaṭṭa sees diversity as mere appearance (*vivarta*), which has been ignorantly superimposed on the substratum of Brahman. Nāgoji Bhaṭṭa is therefore committed to the dual epistemology associated with Advaita Vedānta: The world as it is conventionally known (*vyāvahārika*) has only a provisional reality, for there is a higher perspective (*pāramārthika*) that overcomes ordinary discriminations of subject and object. We may, of course, talk in the Advaitin context about Brahman having qualities (*guṇa*), about different deities, their actions and their appropriate worship, and one may do so at great length. But all such talk is limited to the realm of provisional reality, *māyā*. Ultimately, only the non-dual Brahman is true.

Bhāskararāya's Guptavatī: *"Containing What Is Hidden"*

For one who approaches Bhāskararāya's commentary on the *Devī-Māhātmya* with Western, particularly perhaps with Protestant, notions of commentary, not just the content, but the structure of the commentary may appear puzzling. To expect some sort of remark on every verse, for instance, is to invite disappointment, for out of the 579 verses in the Harikṛṣṇaśarma edition that we met in chapter 3, Bhāskararāya offers comment on only 234, or about 40 percent of the total. Even this is misleading, however, for some of his comments are exceedingly brief, a mere gloss on a word, indication of a chapter ending, and the like. Oftentimes a textual passage will seem to cry out for comment—and Bhāskararāya will say nothing. One senses immediately that, rather than systematic exegesis of the text, something else is afoot here. We are put in mind of what Wilfred Smith has written about another effort to understand scripture cross-culturally:

> Muslims do not read the Qur'ān and conclude that it is divine; rather, they believe that it is divine, and then they read it. This makes a great deal of difference, and I urge upon Christian or secular students of the Qur'ān that if they wish to understand it as a religious document, they must approach it in this spirit. If an outsider picks up the book and goes through it even asking himself, What is there here that has led Muslims to suppose this from God? he will miss the reverberating impact. If, on the other hand, he picks up the book and asks himself, What would these sentences convey to me if I believed them to be God's word? he can much more effectively understand what has been happening these many centuries in the Muslim world.[51]

The issue is admittedly somewhat different in the case at hand, not least because we have here to do with Goddess rather than God. Allowing for such differences, however, the point remains well taken: What *do* these sentences convey to Bhāskararāya? Why does he comment so selectively on the *Devī-Māhātmya*'s verses? Just what is afoot here in his commentary?

At the end of this chapter, I shall offer a reflection on our commentators' motives for commenting on the *Durgā-Saptaśatī*, but let us begin exploring an answer to these questions based on the prima facie evidence that Bhāskararāya provides us. If the structure of his commentary is puzzling, it is also revealing, and that in a number of ways. For instance, if we calculate for each chapter the percentage of verses on which Bhāskararāya offers a comment, we find that the five most commented upon chapters are, in order of frequency, chapters 5, 4, 12, 11, and 1.[52] These are the four chapters in which the text's hymns appear, plus the chapter in which the Goddess provides instructions for the recitation of the *Devī-Māhātmya*. We may then recall that the Vaikṛtika Rahasya established a correspondence between the three manifest (*vikṛti*) forms of Mahālakṣmī and the hymns in chapters 1, 4, and 11, and that it understood the hymn in chapter 5 to be addressed to Mahālakṣmī in her unmanifest (*avyākṛta*) form. We begin to see an interconnection between *aṅga*s, text, and commentary. Another pattern emerges if we look at the substance of what Bhāskararāya says on the verses of the text proper. His remarks are not expansive, running only to some 400 lines, and yet, of the commentaries I have seen, only that of the grammarian Śantanu is of comparable length. This, in turn, might serve to remind us of the oral-aural, *guru-śiṣya* interaction that brings these comments to life: The written word is no more than a startingpoint for relational discourse, and without that discourse these words—any words—are dead. The words themselves point to the context in which they function.[53] Further, this pattern might be seen as a reflection of the ecumenical spirit that characterizes Bhāskararāya's work.[54] He need not write exhaustively on every worthy point, knowing that his readers or interpreters would elaborate as necessary. Rather, he need comment only where the possibility of *misunderstanding* arises, where his responsibility is to head off the occasion for clearly erroneous views. This same pattern is most telling, however, for its overt substance. Of the roughly 400 lines of commentary, some 250 of them are devoted to the question of how the verses should be enumerated and divided, so as to arrive at the requisite "700 (verses) to Durgā" (*Durgā-Saptaśatī*). Moreover, these are not understood to be mere "verses," that is, Purāṇic *śloka*s of eight syllables per quarter with a chiefly narrative function.

Rather they are *mantras*, verbal manifestations of the Goddess herself. What undergirds Bhāskararāya's concern with the constitution of the text, therefore, is not the pedantic concern of a text editor, but the acutely existential concern of a theologian and ritual specialist. One final structural feature of Bhāskararāya's commentary calls for our attention. In addition to commenting on the text proper and, as we might expect, on the *aṅgas*, Bhāskararāya provides a lengthy introduction. In the Harikṛṣṇaśarma edition this runs to some eight pages of dense, closely printed text, amounting to roughly 350 lines. Some of this material shows the same concern for proper division of *mantras* that predominates in his commentary on the text proper, but a number of other topics are brought under consideration as well. In fact, we learn at least as much about Bhāskararāya's encounter with the text from this introductory portion of his commentary as we do from his serial remarks on the verses of the text. Let us therefore consider the issues that Bhāskararāya addresses in his introduction as a way of focusing and summarizing the overall concerns of his commentary.

As noted earlier, Bhāskararāya begins with salutations to Śaṅkarācārya, after which he declares his intent. It is to make clear the meanings (*artha*) that are hidden (*gupta*) in nineteen chapters, thirteen from the *Mārkaṇḍeya Purāṇa*, plus Kavaca, Argalā, and Kīlaka, and the three Rahasyas. The *Saptaśatī* is noted to be exceedingly effective (*aptavatī*), but the proper method of engaging with it having been lost, it now "sort of suffers" (*iva taptavatī*). Acknowledging that other commentaries have been composed on the text, Bhāskararāya observes that they all focus on one of four topics—poetry (*kāvya*), grammar, logic (*nyāya*) or Vedānta—but they are of no use for one who wishes to know how to worship Caṇḍī. His hope is to fill that void. Thereafter follow fourteen *ślokas* that indicate the general topics of the commentary as a whole—from introduction through Mūrti Rahasya—after which prose discussion begins. Let us consider these topics under five analytical headings, following the order in which they appear in the text.

Śākta Philosophy. Bhāskararāya begins his substantive remarks with a vivid declaration. Its importance is underscored by the fact that both the declaration and the forty-odd lines of its explication are repeated virtually verbatim just prior to verse 1.1 of the *Devī-Māhātmya* proper.[55] That declaration is: "The deity named Caṇḍī is the highest Brahman, the queen through whom the crown is inherited." The latter part of this characterization is familiar, for verse 98 of the famous *Saundaryalaharī* has used the same language to characterize the Goddess who is there "equivalent to the neuter brahman of advaita thought."[56]

Bhāskararāya thus establishes immediately that the Goddess of the *Durgā-Saptaśatī* is this very same non-dual reality.

Bhāskararāya elaborates on this declaration in a number of ways, some of them very technical. First, he explores the meaning of the word *caṇḍī* as "the angry, terrible or passionate one," and notes how such language is conventionally used to talk about that which overwhelms, such as the terrible summer sun. He goes on to suggest that anger is awe-inspiring, can be productive, and he cites well-known classical passages: (1) the opening lines from the *Rāmāyaṇa*, where Vālmīki asks, "Is there a man in the world today . . ., Who, when his fury is aroused in battle, is feared even by the gods?";[57] (2) the opening line from the *Yajur Veda*'s Śatarudrīya litany, "Homage to thy wrath, O Rudra . . .";[58] (3) *Taittirīya Upaniṣad* 2.8.1, where it is said of Brahman: "From fear thereof the wind blows, from fear thereof the sun shines; from fear of this one Agni and Indra, with Death as fifth, run along."

Second, Bhāskararāya quotes from the *Ratna-traya-parīkṣā*, by the Śrīkaṇṭha Śaivite philosopher Appayya Dīkṣita, to establish how

> the one attributeless Brahman assumed two forms by Its own inherent power of Māyā. These two forms are styled respectively *Dharma* and *Dharmin*. The form *Dharma* divided itself into male and female. The female form is the consort (Devī) of the Supreme Śiva (*Dharmin*). The male form, Viṣṇu, became the material cause (*upādāna*) of the universe. These three forms together constitute the unconditioned Absolute.[59]

He then explores this evolutionary process from different angles. Turning to the Upaniṣads, Bhāskararāya cites several of the "great sayings" (*mahāvākyāni*) to establish that there is inherent dynamism within Brahman. Thus, *Chāndogya Upaniṣad* 6.2.3 indicates that at the first moment of creation *sat* (being) "reflected, 'May I become manifold, let me procreate,'" while *Bṛhadāraṇyaka Upaniṣad* 1.2.4 says that "He desired,"[60] and 1.2.6 that "He practiced austerities (*tapas*)."[61] Bhāskararāya understands such passages to be testimony to the threefold *śakti* of Brahman—knowledge (*jñāna*), desire (*icchā*), and action (*kriyā*). All three forms are specifically evidenced in his citation from *Śvetāśvatara Upaniṣad* 6.8. The Lord's "supreme *śakti* is said to be various, having as its very nature knowledge, power, and activity." Bhāskararāya then cites the opening line of Jaimini's *Pūrva-Mīmāṃsā-Sūtra*—"Now, then, the inquiry into Dharma"[62]—and proceeds to argue that what is meant here by *dharma* is not an external or behavioral phenomenon, but an internal one, like a throbbing pulse. It refers, in fact, to the Goddess, *cit-śakti*, the luminous power of thought, who is the agent of the five essential actions in the universe: creation, maintenance, destruction, obstruction, and grace-giving. What looks like the activity of others is, in fact, her work: She is the pure crystal that takes on the color of whatever is in proximity to it. She is called *cit*, luminous consciousness, not because it exhausts her nature, but because otherwise the absolute would have no name and we would have no inkling of what Brahman is like. Because of her, "Brahman sort of goes to 'thinkability.'"[63] Bhāskararāya uses the word *vṛtti*, whose range of meanings includes "existence" and "movement," to make a point about both ontology and soteriology. The ontological point is that the existence of particular things is a result of the Goddess/*cit-śakti*'s work. It is only through the repeated use of individual words for particular objects that we obscure the origin of those particular things in Brahman. The corresponding point in non-dual soteriology is that individuals paradoxically prefer their own individual existence to recognition of their *real* existence, namely, identity with the non-dual Brahman. For human beings there is thus a kind of dialectic between forgetting and remembering the true nature of reality.

Finally, Bhāskararāya links this discussion with terminology we have met in our examination of the Rahasyas. As we have just seen, the pure Brahman, whose nature is Dharma, whose aggregate (*samaṣṭi*) form (*vṛtti*) is named *cit*, also has three separate forms (*vyaṣṭi*s), namely, the three *śakti*s known as *icchā, jñāna*, and *kriyā*, which are understood to be "non-different" (*abhinna*) from Brahman itself. In other contexts, notes Bhāskararāya, these *vyaṣṭi*s are given other names and forms. When it is a question of distinctions in conduct, for instance, they have the names Mahāsarasvatī, Mahālakṣmī, and Mahākālī. In that context the customary name for their aggregate (*samaṣṭi*) form is Caṇḍī. Throughout the rest of his commentary, Bhāskararāya follows the view of the Vaikṛtika Rahasya, which understands the *vyaṣṭi* forms of the Goddess with these three names to preside over the three episodes (*carita*s) of the *Devī-Māhātmya*. (See figure 5.2.) Bhāskararāya then goes on to identify triads of names that correspond with the three *vyaṣṭi*s in other contexts: Brahmā, Viṣṇu, and Rudra in the Purāṇas (with Brahman as the *samaṣṭi* designation); Paśyantī, Madhyamā, Vaikharī in the stages of phonic emanation from the primordial Brahman, and so forth.[64] Bhāskararāya brings this portion of his commentary to a close by quoting *Saundaryalaharī* 98 in its entirety. Like most Hindus, he ascribes that text to Śaṅkara, though it now appears not to be from his hand.[65] The cited verse forms part of the concluding section in which the author prays "that he may receive Devī's grace, have the vision of her supernal form, achieve self-realization, and savor the sweetness of supreme brahman (parabrahman, neuter), which she is":[66]

> The knowers of the Scripture (āgama) speak of Druhiṇa's (Brahmā's) wife (Sarasvatī), the goddess of speech, [as you,]
> Padmā (Lakṣmī), the wife of Hari (Viṣṇu), [as you,] the mountain's daughter (Pārvatī), Hara's (Śiva's) mate, [as you,]
> you are an ineffable fourth [beyond these three], hard to reach, with power unbounded [by space, time, cause and effect, substance],
> O great power of creation (mahāmāyā), O wife of the supreme brahman (Sadāśiva), you put the universe through its revolution of appearances.[67]

The Navārṇa mantra. Bhāskararāya next undertakes to explain the phrase "without characteristic marks (*alakṣya*)," which occurs in the fourth verse of the Prādhānika Rahasya: "She has a form of her own that is both with and without characteristic marks." He begins by noting that among the many *mantras* applied to the worship of Brahman cum *śakti* with attributes, two are preeminent: the Navārṇa *mantra* and the *Saptaśatī*, which is here understood as constituting one very long *mantra*. Then ensues a lengthy explanation of the Navārṇa *mantra* and its relationship to the *Saptaśatī*. The discussion is exceedingly technical and detailed, resembling the kind of "mystic linguistics" found in the Jewish Kabbala.[68] The following points of general interest may be noted.

The Navārṇa *mantra* consists of the following syllables: *aim hrīṃ klīṃ cāmuṇḍāyai vicce*. Like many Tantric *mantras*, it does not "mean" anything in the conventional semantic sense.[69] It therefore invites symbolic interpretation. Bhāskararāya indicates that this *mantra* has been explained in one of the (late Śākta) Upaniṣads, the *Devī-Atharva-Śīrṣa-Upaniṣad*,[70] of which he quotes the first verse: "All the gods approached the Goddess (and asked), 'Who are you?' To this she replied (and Bhāskararāya quotes), 'I am of the very same form (*svarūpiṇī*) as Brahman,'" whereupon she provides a brief description of her *nirguṇa* and *saguṇa* forms. After this response, Bhāskararāya notes, the gods praise her initially with the first verse of the hymn found in the fifth chapter of the *Saptaśatī* [5.7]. This is the hymn which we have seen is understood to be addressed to the *samaṣṭi*, unmanifest form of Mahālakṣmī. (See figure 5.2.) Bhāskararāya goes on to describe the specific phonic constitution of the Navārṇa *mantra*, drawing on this same Upaniṣad [22-23], the Ḍāmara and other Tantras, making mention of Śrīvidyā. He then cites the classical threefold characterization of

Brahman as being (*sat*), awareness (*cit*), and bliss (*ānanda*), and correlates these qualities with the *vyaṣṭi* forms of the Goddess, Mahālakṣmī, Mahāsarasvatī, and Mahākālī, respectively. These in turn are identified with the first three syllables of the Navārṇa *mantra—aiṃ, hrīṃ, klīṃ*[71]—while the last two—*vicce*—are identified with the *samaṣṭi* form. Turning to the four remaining syllables, Bhāskararāya observes that they are the proper noun, Cāmuṇḍā, in dative case, with an implied "Hail to . . ." He notes that the etymology of the name is given at *Saptaśatī* 7.23-25, and affirms that, just as the name brings together the two demons Caṇḍa and Muṇḍa, so does Cāmuṇḍā herself bring together two kinds of knowledge, that of the world and that of Brahman. As the midpoint in the *mantra*, she links the *vyaṣṭi* and *samaṣṭi* forms. Bhāskararāya suggests an etymological link of the name Cāmuṇḍā, via the word *ādana* (food), with the Upaniṣadic notion of everything constituting food for Brahman,[72] but he also notes that regional and non-Sanskritic languages may bear on understanding this name.[73] In characteristic fashion, he finds no objection to any of these explanations. He finally offers a non-esoteric version of the *mantra* in verse form:

> Praise be to Kālī, Lakṣmī, Sarasvatī, to Caṇḍikā:
> Shattering the knot of ignorance that binds my heart, release me!

This teaches, he says, the fundamental non-difference of the individual soul from Brahman. One who would know more should take refuge at the feet of a guru.

Bhāskararāya then proceeds to show how the *Saptaśatī* is linked to the Navārṇa *mantra.* He starts with the statement in Prādhānika Rahasya 4 that "Mahālakṣmī is foremost of all." She is therefore the highest, "fourth" form of the deity, with a predominance of the quality of *rajas.* It is this same status, Bhāskararāya notes, that is recognized in the Navārṇa *mantra,* for the syllable *aim* is Mahālakṣmī, and the fact that it is the first syllable in the *mantra* is an indication of her primacy. He then proceeds, in a lengthy instance of mystical phonology, to show how the first verse of the *Saptaśatī* is an exoteric version of the same *mantra:* Properly understood, the *Saptaśatī* and the Navārṇa teach, indeed *are,* the same reality. This is substantiated by other citations from the *Saptaśatī,* focusing on passages that portray the Goddess in relation to the three primary male deities, or in her status as cosmic sound.[74] Bhāskararāya then grounds this discussion in ritual, by identifying the Vedic cum Tantric categories of deity, seer, metre, *śakti, bīja,* and *tattva* that we met at the beginning of the last chapter, and indicating that one should perform *nyāsa* to the first three of these. This consists of the ritual assignment of sounds and letters to different parts of the devotee's body.[75] In identifying the appropriate letters, Bhāskararāya again offers esoteric interpretation of certain verses from the *Saptaśatī*,[76] with the observation from Prādhānika Rahasya 24 that "those who have eyes will see this, but others will not."

Meditation (dhyāna) on the Three Vyaṣṭi Forms of the Goddess. Bhāskararāya now provides description of the visual appearance of the goddess who presides over each of the three *carita*s of the *Saptaśatī*. In popular editions of the text, these so-called meditation verses are often printed at the very beginning of chapters 1, 2, and 5, respectively, reflecting the impetus we noted in our discussion of the Prādhānika Rahasya: To know and worship the deity one must know what she looks like.[77] Here are the three verses cited by Bhāskararāya:

> The one who carries sword, discus, mace, arrow, bow, iron club, spear, missile, human-head, and conch in her (ten) hands, three-eyed, adorned with ornaments on all her limbs,
> Shining like a blue gem, with ten faces and feet, Mahākālī do I reverence, whom Brahmā praised while Viṣṇu slept, in order to slay Madhu and Kaiṭabha.
>
> . . . .
>
> She who wields rosary, battle-axe, mace, arrow, thunderbolt, lotus, bow, waterpot, club, spear and sword, shield, conch, bell, wine-cup,
> Trident, noose and splendid discus with her (eighteen) arms, who has the complexion of coral, Mahālakṣmī do I worship, slayer of Mahiṣa, enthroned on a lotus.
>
> . . . .
>
> She who bears bell, trident, plow, conch, pestle, discus, bow and arrows in her (eight) lotus-like hands, whose brilliance shines like the autumn moon,
> Born from the body of Gaurī, the substratum of the three worlds, the great (*mahā*) unequalled Sarasvatī I worship here, destroyer of Śumbha and other demons.

The Saptaśatī Caṇḍī Yantra. Having thus performed meditation *inwardly* by mentally imaging the deities, Bhāskararāya notes, one should now do so *outwardly*, by performing ritualized bodily identification (*nyāsa*) with the diagrammatic (*yantra*) form of Caṇḍī.[78] He briefly describes the *yantra* that we met in chapter 5 (figure 5.3) and its worship. The *yantra* shows in the front row, from left to right, the three manifest forms of the Goddess, who superintend the three *carita*s of the *Saptaśatī:* the ten-armed (and ten-faced) Mahākālī, the eighteen-armed Mahālakṣmī, and the eight-armed Mahāsarasvatī. Behind them in the second row are arranged the three couples from the Prādhānika and Vaikṛtika Rahasyas: Rudra-Gaurī, Brahmā-Sarasvatī, and Viṣṇu-Lakṣmī. In the private recitations of the *Devī-Māhātmya* that I have witnessed (of which I shall say more in the next chapter), a *yantra* with this configuration is painted on a piece of flat metal, using a mixture of red powder and water. It then serves as the focus of the devotee's attention throughout the recitation, both in *nyāsa* and in receiving other elements of the *pūjā* offering.

The Saptaśatī Mantra. Bhāskararāya understands all of the material under our first four headings to be fundamentally an exegesis of the Navārṇa *mantra*, for he now turns "secondly"[79] to a discussion of "the *mantra* whose form is a multitude of verses (*śloka*s), consisting of three episodes (*carita*s)," that is, the *Saptaśatī* itself. Noting that there are several accounts of these episodes in the *Vāmana*,[80] *Devī Bhāgavata*, and *Mārkaṇḍeya Purāṇa*s, the *Lakṣmī* and other Tantras, he affirms that the *Mārkaṇḍeya* account is paramount—because it is concerned with human fulfillment (*puruṣārtha*), because it provides the basic rules for its own recitation in chapter 12, and by general consensus.[81] He notes, however, that the title *Saptaśatī*, "Seven Hundred," is troubling, for he knows that the text amounts to somewhat fewer than 600 verses. He considers a number of interesting ways of explaining the title. One is to allow the non-difference (*abheda*) of the palatal sibilant *ś* and the dental sibilant *s*, in which case *Saptaśatī* becomes *Saptasatī*, or "Seven True Females." This may then be understood as referring to the seven forms mentioned in the Prādhānika Rahasya: the unmanifest *samaṣṭi* form of Mahālakṣmī, the three unmanifest *vyaṣṭi* forms, Mahākālī, Mahālakṣmī, Mahāsarasvatī, and the three females they produce, Sarasvatī, Lakṣmī, and Gaurī. Alternatively, the seven may be the forms of the Goddess identified in chapter 11 of the text: Nandajā, Raktadantī, Śatākṣī, Śākaṃbharī, Durgā, Bhīmā, and Bhrāmarī.[82] Bhāskararāya has no objection to either of these explanations. He then turns to possible ways of arriving at the title as it stands, as an apparent reference to 700 verses. We are immediately reminded of his distinctive way of engaging the text, for rather than comparing different manuscripts to see how many verses they contain as a text editor might do, he cites the testimony of different Tantras—the *Yāmala, Vārāhī*, and *Kātyāyanī*—on the length of the text. As modern hermeneutics knows, there is no interpretation apart from context, and for Bhāskararāya it is the Tantras that determine this context. That the testimony of these Tantras varies he attributes to their being different *śākhās* (branches, recensions) of the tradition, just as there are *śākhās* in transmission of Vedic tradition. He considers the possibility that the numerological puzzle might be solved by adding in the verses of the Kavaca, Argalā, and Kīlaka, but this, too, falls short of 700. Moreover, he notes, such a solution would fly in the face of two facts: the reference in the Kavaca itself (verse 49) to reciting the Kavaca prior to reciting the 700-versed Caṇḍī, and the tradition that, just as there are ritualized verbal keys of *bīja, śakti*, and *kīlaka* for each episode of the *Saptaśatī*, so do the Kavaca, Argalā, and Kīlaka serve as these keys for the *Saptaśatī* as a whole. These *aṅgas* are truly "subsidiary appendages," not part of the basic text. Failing such a solution, Bhāskararāya offers his way of dividing the text into 700 verses in a separate section entitled "division of *mantras*" that is inserted between his commentary on the preliminary *angas* and his commentary on 1.1. It is this division that is reflected in the apparatus to our translation in chapter 3.

Bhāskararāya brings his introduction to a close by considering aspects of its proper ritual recitation. Of these we may note his reference to Śiva's action in the Kīlaka as providing the great method for restraining and releasing the full power of the *Saptaśatī*. Beyond that, he identifies two other methods for removing curses that may have been placed on the text and limited its effectiveness: one is to recite the chapters in the special order—13, 1, 12, 2, 11, 3, 10, 4, 9, 5, 8, 6, and 7 twice; the other is to recite the middle episode first, then the first episode, then the third. Chapters should be read straight through without interruption, otherwise repeated. One should not read the words only mentally, that is, privately, but should utter them aloud. In reading, the book should be placed on a stand, rather than held in the hand. The Vedic and Tantric categories of seer, metre, *devatā*, and so forth should be identified for each episode, and the three episodes are noted to be conducive respectively to the three goals of human life: *dharma, artha*, and *kāma*. Bhāskararāya considers whether the Rātri and Devī Sūktas that we saw in chapter 5 to provide "stitching" (*sampuṭita*) between the six *aṅgas* and the *Saptaśatī* are the Vedic or Tantric (i.e., Saptaśatī) hymns by those names. He favors the former interpretation, and I have therefore included translation of the Vedic hymns in our Appendix on the *aṅgas*. Bhāskararāya does recognize that the hymns in the *Devī-Māhātmya* have a special status, which he characterizes here and in his comment on 12.23 as that of being "seen" (*dṛṣṭa*), rather than "made" (*kṛta*). This means that they are not-of-human-origin (*apauruṣeya*), but eternal like the Veda.[83] In support of this interpretation he cites the *Lakṣmī Tantra*,[84] a text of which we shall see more in the next section. Finally, he makes note of appropriate times for recitation, the kinds of offering (*bali*) that should accompany it, and of regional variations in recitation practice. Throughout he quotes liberally from various Tantras.

The substance of what Bhāskararāya says in his remarks on individual verses of the *Devī-Māhātmya* grows naturally out of what he has said in this introduction. We may note that he superimposes on top of the text's division into three *carita*s a structure of four *paṭala*s or sections, but this does materially affect his exegesis.[85] The way in which he interprets particular passages is best seen in a comparison with Nāgoji Bhaṭṭa, to which we now turn.

Comparative Considerations

Like Bhāskararāya, Nāgoji Bhaṭṭa offers a substantial introduction to his commentary. It is briefer and generally less penetrating, also less esoteric, than Bhāskararāya's.[86] It deals with, among other things, ritual use of the text, but since we are concerned here with presenting the way commentators have encountered the text in fairly broad strokes, not providing a study in comparative ritual, it seems preferable to focus on philosophical differences between the commentators. This will leave the detailed examination of ritual engagement with the text for future study,[87] while engaging here the traditional Western interest in the philosophical formulation of religious issues.

Both Bhāskararāya and Nāgoji Bhaṭṭa take for granted that the Rahasyas are integral to an understanding of the *Saptaśatī*, and they are the authorities most frequently cited by both commentators. The next most preferred source of citation is the *Lakṣmī Tantra*, a text from perhaps the tenth century that Sanjukta Gupta characterizes as distinctive for its "exclusive treatment of the Viṣṇuite mother-goddess Lakṣmī, the Śakti of Viṣṇu-Nārāyaṇa" and for the eclectic synthesis that it fashions "out of all the various concepts current in the Pāñcarātra and Tantric milieu," which enable it "to overcome sectarian boundaries."[88] No other text is cited more than a handful of times: such texts include the *Harivaṃśa*, and the *Vāmana, Vārāha, Śiva*, and *Devī-Bhāgavata Purāṇa*s. What the commentators share, therefore, is a common stock of sources, and what differentiates them is the way they apply this material to understanding the *Saptaśatī.*

The crucial point in that differentiation is the theories of causation, of the one and the many, that respectively inform Śrīvidyā and Advaita Vedānta, to which we gave preliminary consideration above. A synopsis of Bhāskararāya's views is found in his comments on 1.68-69 and 10.3. The latter is the dramatic passage where the Goddess resumes the varied female deities into herself, prior to the final combat with Śumbha. Bhāskararāya's explanation is a simple one: He cites the famous saying from *Chāndogya Upaniṣad* 6.2.1: "In the beginning, my dear, there was just being alone, one only, without a second." What we have at this point in the *Saptaśatī* then is simply a return to the state of primordial unity. This process is the mirror image, in Bhāskararāya's view, of the way in which the diversity of forms had unfolded at the very beginning of the text, where, in response to Brahmā's invocation, "the goddess of darkness (*tāmasī*), going forth from (Viṣṇu's) eyes, nose, arms, heart, and breast, presented herself in front of Brahmā" [1.68-69]. Bhāskararāya's comment at this point consists of the following "secret" (*rahasya*). Although she is intrinsically characterized by all three qualities (*guṇa*s), the Goddess here takes on a form dominated by *tamas* (dark mass-stuff) because of the nature of the killing that is required in this *carita*, the removal of delusion, where Mahākālī predominates. In the second episode, a different sort of killing is required, the impassioned overcoming of sheer power, and hence the form adopted has a predominance of *rajas* (ruddy energy-stuff), that is, Mahālakṣmī.[89] In the third *carita*, it is in her role as queen, where she bewitches with her beauty, that Mahāsarasvatī activates the role of *sattva guṇa* (pure intelligence-stuff).[90] In other words, the Goddess takes on form appropriate to the situation: Just as one would not use a screwdriver to drive nails, so must her particular form be appropriate to what is asked of her. Bhāskararāya understands that behind these three *vyaṣṭi* forms looms the *samaṣṭi* form of Caṇḍī, "the fourth" (*turīyā*), who is the supreme Brahman.[91] But by definition she does not act in the narrative. Overt textual references to her are rare, and she may thus appear to be nowhere in evidence. However, since all beings are derivative from her, every action that is accomplished by others is essentially her action,[92] and so, from another angle, she is everywhere.

It is in Bhāskararāya's brief, dense exegesis of the Prādhānika Rahasya that he provides the linkage between such serial comments on the verses of the *Saptaśatī* and the more abstract philosophy of his introduction. There are doubtless several reasons for this: The Rahasyas are more systematic than the *Saptaśatī*, they are more self-consciously monistic, and they provide readier evidence for the existence of Caṇḍī/ Caṇḍikā as "the fourth." The key points in his exegesis are these. (See figure 5.2 to ease comprehension of the issues.) Reminding his readers of his introductory description of how Brahman has the two forms of Dharma and Dharmin, Bhāskararāya indicates that the name Caṇḍikā is applied to both forms, but particularly to the aggregate (*samaṣṭi*) of forms into which Dharmin separates in order to be worshipped. Those separate forms are, of course, Mahākālī, Mahālakṣmī, and Mahāsarasvatī. "Caṇḍikā" is thus apparently a fourth designation, but as a reality she is not different (*abhinnā*) from the other three. Devoid of form (*nirākāra*), unseeable (*alakṣyā*), without specific qualities, yet characterized by the three *guṇa*s (*nirguṇa . . . triguṇa*), she pervades her three incarnations (*avatāra*s). Confusion may arise, Bhāskararāya acknowledges, because the designation "Mahālakṣmī" serves two purposes: as a name of Caṇḍikā, the highest Brahman, and as a name for one of her separate (*vyaṣṭi*) forms, but one should not be misled by this.[93] As Mahālakṣmī in *vyaṣṭi* form she still retains a preeminence over the other two *vyaṣṭi*s, for she is consistently said to be "characterized by (all) three *guṇa*s," while Mahākālī and Mahāsarasvatī are characterized by the individual *guṇa*s of *tamas* and *sattva*, respectively.[94] Bhāskararāya recognizes, however, that once she has "taken on" the *vyaṣṭi* forms of Mahākālī and Mahāsarasvatī with their corresponding *guṇa*s, what remains is an implicit predominance of *rajas guṇa* in the *vyaṣṭi* form of Mahālakṣmī.[95] This is important because it enables Bhāskararāya to affirm the systematic distribution of three *vyaṣṭi*s and three *guṇa*s across the three episodes of the *Saptaśatī* while still affirming, with Prādhānika Rahasya 4, that "Mahālakṣmī is foremost of all."

There are other important consequences of this interpretation. There is, of course, an easy correspondence between four forms of deity and four hymns of the *Saptaśatī*.[96] And Bhāskararāya's use of the word *turīyā* in characterizing Caṇḍikā as "the fourth" brings immediate association with Gauḍapāda's use of the word to characterize the highest Brahman in his famous Kārikā on the *Māṇḍūkya Upaniṣad*.[97] Of greatest significance, however, is the rich multivalence that now inheres in the name Mahālakṣmī. At one end of the spectrum, it identifies the unmanifest foundation of the universe. At the other end it refers to the particular deity whose activity is described, and whose praise is sung, in the second episode of the *Devī-Māhātmya*. The ontological accessibility of ultimate reality, which we earlier saw to be a feature of Tantric thinking in general,[98] is here vividly captured by the pregnant application of the deity's name: Mahālakṣmī, who cures our ailments and rids us of Mahiṣa, is also Mahālakṣmī, the primordial Brahman.[99] Nor should we overlook the way in which Bhāskararāya more specifically underscores the Rahasyas' monism. We earlier characterized the Prādhānika, for all of its attention to the proliferation of Mahālakṣmī's forms, as basically an account of the internal life of the Goddess-head. To this Bhāskararāya now adds the comment (verse 24) that, even when female deity takes on maleness, the differentiation is outweighed by what he calls "mutual permeation" (*vyāpya-vṛtti*), the quality that leads water in a dish to get hot when the dish itself is heated. Similarly, we saw in chapter 5 that it is when the Prādhānika turns from the evolution of the unmanifest Goddess-head to that of the manifest world that it first uses the word *pradhāna*, "material nature" [verse 27]. By way of explanation here, Bhāskararāya introduces the exact evolutionary terminology of Sāṃkhya, thus reminding us how Tantra sees effects as transformation (*pariṇāma*) of underlying substratum. For Bhāskararāya, then, reality is a virtually seamless web, and his reading of the *Saptaśatī* weaves individual verses into the larger pattern of Mahālakṣmī's activity.

For Nāgoji Bhaṭṭa there is no comparably clear articulation of Advaita Vedānta, but he provides lots of clues that suggest such a reading. For instance, where Bhāskararāya has equated the Goddess's resumption of forms into herself with the non-duality of Brahman, Nāgoji says that Ambikā then stood entirely alone "because of the lack of differentiation within the *mūla-śakti*" [10.4].[100] Elsewhere [4.6] he calls her the "*mūla-prakṛti*."[101] Similarly, it is in the form of ignorance that she causes *samsāra*, but in the form of knowledge (*vidyā*) that she brings it to an end [5.11]. *Māyā* itself is to be understood as ignorance (*avidyā*) [11.4]. Also, what makes the terribleness of the Goddess so great is that it cannot be "sublated" (*atirikta*) by anything other than knowledge of Brahman.[102] The technical terms that Nāgoji Bhaṭṭa is using here—especially *mūla-śakti*, "primal power," and *mūla-prakṛti*, "primordial matter"—can be variously interpreted, but the reference to "sublation" suggests a perspective that is specific to Advaita Vedānta.[103] That is, assuming a dualistic epistemology, this description of the Goddess applies only to the "lower" sphere of conventional knowledge (*vyāvahārika*), not to the realm of ultimate truth (*pāramārthika*). The former is overcome—or sublated—by the latter. Whatever is said about the Goddess therefore bears on an understanding of Brahman-with-qualities (*saguṇa*) or Īśvara, not the "transcendent" Brahman-without-qualities (*nirguṇa*).[104]

Given this point of entry, other of Nāgoji Bhaṭṭa's comments fall into a pattern. Where Bhāskararāya passes lightly over the text's statement that the Goddess "is born in many forms" [1.47], Nāgoji feels impelled to say that the Goddess has no chief birth, and any discussion of her having conventional "births" is of a secondary sort. Where Bhāskararāya can affirm that the unmanifest (*avyākṛtā*) Goddess who is *prakṛti* remains unchanged by the action of "name and form" that emerges out of her [4.6], Nāgoji Bhaṭṭa offers a characteristically Vedāntin gloss: The supreme non-dual Ātman or Brahman is regarded as *prakṛti* because of the "superimposition" (*adhyāsa*) on it of distinctions, particularly the distinction of separate selves.[105] Since in this context virtually all that can be said of the highest Brahman is that it is "being, awareness, bliss," any action that is predicated of the ultimate must be meant in a metaphorical sense. Thus, we find Nāgoji Bhaṭṭa making generous use of the particle *iva* ("as if") in interpreting the Goddess's activity, in order to protect the transcendence of *nirguṇa* Brahman: Whatever implies duality, such as action, can only apply to Brahman in a relative sense, and only to Brahman as conceived from a limited perspective.[106] The extreme case of such a hermeneutic is found at 8.57, where the blow of an antagonist's club is said to cause the Goddess "not even the slightest pain." Nāgoji Bhaṭṭa—in an instance of what one of my *paṇḍits* called "using a canon to kill a mosquito"—explains this as a function of her having the luminous, blissful *ātman* as her nature. For similar reasons we find Nāgoji taking pains to dissociate the anger implied by the name Caṇḍī/Caṇḍikā from the true nature of ultimate reality.[107] This, of course, contrasts strikingly with Bhāskararāya's bold identification of Caṇḍī with the highest Brahman, reflecting, in turn, the underlying contrast between Vedāntin and Tantric assessments of the senses and of sensual imagery.

For both Bhāskararāya and Nāgoji Bhaṭṭa, then, the *Saptaśatī* attests to a divine reality whose primary form lies "off canvas," as it were, from the text proper. For Bhāskararāya that reality is the non-dual Brahman, otherwise known as Mahālakṣmī, "the fourth." This reality is ontologically connected to the world, and to the text of the *Saptaśatī*, in an evolutionary process of transformation (*pariṇāma*) that is described in the Prādhānika and Vaikṛtika Rahasyas. Similarly, for Nāgoji Bhaṭṭa that reality is the non-dual Brahman, and he, too, characterizes it as "the fourth," drawing on Vedāntic exegesis of the syllable OM.[108] But for Nāgoji, that non-dual reality does not actually evolve into the world and/or the text, although it gives the appearance (*vivarta*) of doing so. What is involved in this appearance is a shift in the epistemological perspective of the knower of Brahman—from (ultimately) knowing Brahman as *nirguṇa* to (conventionally) knowing Brahman as *saguṇa*. Whatever characterization of Brahman Bhāskararāya may make (cataphatically) in the name of Mahālakṣmī, Nāgoji must finally deny (apophatically) in the name of Brahman who transcends all characterization.[109]

Given that both Bhāskararāya and Nāgoji Bhaṭṭa do a plausible job of making different kinds of "sense" of the Durgā-Saptaśatī—which is scarcely surprising in light of what hermeneutical theory has taught us about the interpretative process—it might be useful to close this chapter with brief speculation on the motives prompting these commentators (and others) to engage interpretatively with the *Devī-Māhātmya.* Such speculation is occasioned primarily by awareness of the intellectual "distance" between Bhāskararāya's primary home in Śrīvidyā (and Nāgoji Bhaṭṭa's in grammar) and the Purāṇic substance of the text as we met it in chapter 3. One manifestation of this distance is the fact that Bhāskararāya makes so little mention in the *Guptavatī* of his major works on Śrīvidyā and, conversely, refers so little to the *Guptavatī* in those other works.[110] Though Śrīvidyā and the *Devī-Māhātmya* admittedly both represent Śākta orientations, the former understands the Goddess as the benign Śrī, while the latter sees her as the horrific Caṇḍikā. How can this be? And why should a non-Śākta like Nāgoji Bhaṭṭa even bother with commenting on such a text?

An answer to such questions has, I believe, two parts.

The first is to recognize that already in the eighteenth century the *Devī-Māhātmya* was a well-known and very popular text. Bhāskararāya acknowledges that a good many commentaries already existed in his time, and the overwhelming number of surviving text manuscripts suggests that, although Bhāskararāya and Nāgoji Bhaṭṭa have doubtless added to the text's renown, they did not initiate it. How the *Devī-Māhātmya* came to be so popular by the eighteenth century is another question, and a difficult one. We saw earlier that the text has been associated with the *aṅgas*, as an illuminated manuscript, since at least the fourteenth century. Further research will surely add further details to the picture. Given the unlikelihood of ever having a full understanding of the text's historical career, however, it is worth pondering the reflections of a very thoughtful and learned contemporary devotee, A. N. Jani, of whom we shall hear more in the next chapter. In Jani's estimation,[111] the verses that comprise the *Devī-Māhātmya* were, in all likelihood, originally Purāṇic compositions. While they do constitute a kind of digression in the *Mārkaṇḍeya*'s account of Manu-intervals, raising the possibility of their prior independent existence, they clearly belong, both stylistically and substantively, to the Purāṇic genre. However, surmises Jani, over time these words were found to have—like lots of other words in India—a potency that transcended their semantic sense. They came to function as *mantra*, their power turned to a variety of ends, and so they came to have an independent life of their own, outside the Purāṇic context.[112] But the power that these verses had was dangerous and, given unfettered access to it, they began to be misused. It became necessary to contain their potency. What we have in the Kīlaka, Jani affirms, is the mythological residue of this historical process: the effort to place a ritual restraint on the efficacy of reciting the *Devī-Māhātmya*, which subsequently became understood as the ritual recitation of the Kīlaka itself, that is, the withdrawing of "the bolt," prior to recitation of the words of the *Devī-Māhātmya*. Finally, in Jani's view this effort to control the power of the *Saptaśatī mantra* reached its apex with the rise of Tantric ritual recitation. This was formal, stylized technique, designed for maximum realization of the power inherent in the words, like intensifying a beam of light that had previously been shining with less than full brightness. The fact of the matter is that between the sixth and eighteenth centuries the *Devī-Māhātmya* grew from being a verbal composition of unknown significance to an oral-aural and written phenomenon of great popularity, open to diverse interpretation. What Jani's reflections point toward—in anticipation of knowing more about the history of both Tantra and *mantra*—is, at least, a plausible understanding of this fact. They ask us to take seriously the presence of genuine power in the words of the text.

The second part of our rumination on our commentators' motives pertains to their attitude toward tradition, and to the remarkable breadth of their learning. Since we know more about Bhāskararāya than Nāgoji Bhaṭṭa, the issues are clearer in his case, but the principle seems generally applicable. On putting the question about the apparent "distance" between the Śrī of Śrīvidyā and the Caṇḍikā of the *Saptaśatī* to Bhāskararāya's able contemporary interpreter, Douglas Brooks, I received the following response.[113] It is not uncommon for the scholarly contributions of Śrīvidyā traditionalists to go well beyond their own particular *sādhanā*, or religious practice. Even at the level of practice, Śrīvidyā adepts often maintain several *sādhanā*s concurrently, even when they appear contradictory, and, writes Brooks, "virtually all of the adepts with whom I have had extensive contact 'keep' at least the *mantraśāstra* of three or four horrific Devīs that they have learned (often though not exclusively) from their Śrīvidyā gurus." Moreover (and we here anticipate our discussion in the next chapter), today "in the south among Śrīvidyā worshippers (both in public and private) the DSS [*Durgā-Saptaśatī*] is brought *within* the traditions of the benign Devī and the fact that it focuses on a *ghora* [horrific] aspect is down played or used as an example of the 'wholeness' of the goddess, or to emphasize the complementary nature of her aspects." Consequently, there would be nothing in principle that might keep Bhāskararāya from commenting on, or putting into practice, the *Saptaśatī*. Living in the south, but having studied in the north, he knew of the text's wide popularity. This knowledge, combined with his own encyclopedic learning and willingness to range into subjects beyond Śrīvidyā, made the *Saptaśatī* a natural object of his attention.[114] He was providing a service to the tradition by offering intelligent commentary, of both a theoretical and a practical sort, on a very well-known text. The context in which he encountered the *Saptaśatī* was therefore not defined in narrow sectarian terms by Śrīvidyā, but by the broad cultural and religious life of his day. The same, we may imagine, holds true for other commentators. While the description and explanation of the *Saptaśatī*'s ongoing popularity are tasks for future work—undertaken in a very preliminary way in our next chapter—we will not be far wrong in understanding the text as an integral part of the popular "Great Tradition" for at least the past several hundred years. As such, given the range of hermeneutical possibilities that it offers, it would beckon a wide range of learned commentators. And they have, we now see, responded accordingly.

7

Encounters in the Contemporary World

Introduction

As we come to the end of this study, it is appropriate to broaden our focus once again. In the past two chapters we have inquired into the legacy of the *Devī-Māhātmya* by concentrating specifically on the verbal material that has become attached to the text, its *aṅga*s and commentaries. We have surveyed some of the ways that this verbal artifact has been encountered, against the backdrop of having recognized in chapter 4 that it has also left a legacy—has also been encountered—in the media of myth, cult, and iconography. Our inquiry has been both selective and historical, examining some of the mechanisms of the text's life over the centuries since its composition. But the *Devī-Māhātmya* is far more than an antiquarian curiosity, and it would be misleading to suggest that India's encounter with these words has been chiefly a thing of the past. The text is among the handful of best known religious documents in contemporary India, and we must here attend to that fact.

In focusing on the contemporary scene, I am aware of leaping over a great many historical details that are both interesting and important for understanding our text's full legacy. From at least the fifteenth century, for example, the *Devī-Māhātmya* has been translated into the vernacular languages of India, and it has been reworked in a variety of ways.[1] A particularly fascinating instance of this is found in the *Caṇḍī dī Var*, composed in Punjabi by the activist tenth Guru of the Sikhs, Guru Gobind Singh (1666-1708).[2] The basic story there comes from the

Saptaśatī, which is embellished and allegorized. Mahiṣa is sent to humble the deities, who had egocentrically abandoned their duties. Having done so, he then fell into the same pattern of wicked behavior, abandoning his role as vessel of the divine will. The gods in despair implored Śakti, the divine power, to come to their rescue. The message to Sikhs of Guru Gobind Singh's time was clear:

> By their own fault the [Hindu] rulers of India were defeated by aggressive Muslim invaders, who are non-believers. But the Muslims did not follow the laws of justice and turned into great tyrants. The time was then ripe for the subjugated to rise and purge themselves of their immorality. Then in God's name, under divine tutelage as God's servants, with the active aid of God's divine Power, they would destroy the tyrants.[3]

If we juxtapose this episode with the way the *Devī-Māhātmya* is woven into the religious life of the contemporary Punjab,[4] or with the way recitation of the text is today sought by Sikhs and even by Muslims,[5] then there is clearly an enormous amount for us still to learn about how the text has been encountered both over time, and across the different religious communities of India. Further inquiry into historical particulars, however, I leave for another occasion.

Even our consideration of the contemporary scene must be selective, and I have chosen to exemplify the current life of our text by exploring three "moments" in the present chapter. These instances are, I think, representative, but they can only hint at the richness and complexity of the modern situation. This richness is a function not just of the variety of ways in which people encounter the *Devī-Māhātmya*—which is very great—but also of the lively contemporary debate about the nature of scripture, and about the nature of texts, to which we alluded in chapter 1. Methodology, in other words, rears its head, and raises fundamental questions about the nature of our inquiry. Brief consideration here of some of the issues may provide an appropriate prologue to discussion of our three examples.

Some fifteen years ago, in the course of summarizing his important study of popular religion in central India, Lawrence Babb distinguished between "the Goddess of the text" and "the Goddess of experience."[6] Noting that the *Durgā-Saptaśatī* was "the most important text of the goddess" in the village he was studying, Babb goes on to comment on how the text functions in Hindu life:

> It is important to realize that the *Saptashati*, like all Hindu texts, has two kinds of religious significance. It has, first of all, a kind of intrinsic potency as a collection of sacred utterances. The chanting of the *mantras* of which it is composed is a way of pleasing the goddess and tapping her great powers. But the *mantras* have meaning of another sort, for together they constitute one of the principal scriptural delineations of the goddess. The text is to be *understood* as well as *chanted*, and consequently in the editions available in the Raipur bazaar the Sanskrit stanzas are given together with their Hindi translation. The text explains the goddess, and provides a context for her in the pantheon as a whole.[7]

Although we know now that it is risky to generalize about the significance of "all Hindu texts,"[8] Babb's basic discrimination is a useful one. Moreover, it finds important corroboration in Mackenzie Brown's careful study of the emergence of the notion of the "holy book" in the Purāṇas.[9] During Vedic times, Brown notes, emphasis was placed on the sound (*śabda*) of words, rather than their meaning (*artha*). But in the Purāṇas one finds an increased emphasis on words' intelligibility, a subservience of "the *śabda* tradition" to "the *artha* tradition," and the two traditions have now coexisted, for perhaps a thousand years.[10] The convergence of Babb's and Brown's analyses suggests a typology—which we may here develop into the notion of a *spectrum*—of encounters with the *Devī-Māhātmya*: At one end lies emphasis on the form of the words, a concern chiefly with unlocking their power through recitation, while at the other end lies a primary concern with the words' meaning, which is articulated (as we shall see) in a variety of ways.

Such a scheme no doubt oversimplifies the reality of textual encounters. It does, however, allow us to do three things. First, it enables us to build on the "two kinds of significance" that Babb and Brown have noted, while acknowledging some recent research that indicates how complex the interplay between chanting (*śabda*) and understanding (*artha*) is. Second, it enables us to connect our discussion of "text" in the classical humanistic sense with the rather different sense of "text" that has characterized recent anthropological (and other) discourse. Finally, it allows us to impose at least a loose pattern on the enormous amount of material that bears on contemporary encounter with the *Devī-Māhātmya*.[11]

In light of what we have seen in the last two chapters, we might expect—and indeed we find—that the text is recited in a variety of situations, ranging from individual recitation in private, through recitation that is purchased by individuals from professional reciters, to the well attested public recitation during the festival of Durgā Pūjā/Navarātra.[12] Beyond this, however, there are significant possibilities for further nuance. The previously noted work in progress of Cynthia A. Humes, based on interviews with some 125 reciters from Uttar Pradesh, West Bengal, Madhya Pradesh, Rajasthan, and Bihar, will identify at least forty-three taxonomically distinct types of recitation of the *Saptaśatī*.[13] Some of these distinctions identify patterns of verse repetition, particularly with regard to the *sampuṭa* ("stitching, folding") of the verses of the *Saptaśatī* around a specific *mantra*, in order to obtain a particular goal. Others relate to the concept that the reciter has of the *Saptaśatī* as *mantra*, *tantra*, *māhātmya*, or *purāṇa*.[14] Humes' research also identifies special cases where recitation takes place without the *aṅga*s, for example, when it is recited "impersonally" (in temple worship) or for "offensive" purposes (inflicting injury on a third party). It pays attention, too, to innovations in ritual use occasioned by the technologies of tape recording, radio, and television. Such research indicates clearly that it is not sufficient simply to contrast recitation and understanding of the text, for the former takes many forms indeed. Others have also reported salient material, such as Kathleen M. Erndl's intriguing account of the young woman whose violent possession by the goddess Santoṣī Mā has been controlled by recitation of the *Devī-Māhātmya* on a daily basis for several hours at a time.[15] Then, too, there is evidence that recitation does not always entail recitation of the entire text, for the most popular paperback edition of the text is prefaced by the well-known "Saptaślokī Durgā," "Durgā of the Seven Verses," a selection of seven verses from the *Devī-Māhātmya* presenting the power of the text in condensed or abridged form.[16] What all of this evidence suggests is that recitation does indeed appear to be one of the major ways of encountering the Goddess through, or in, or as the words of the *Saptaśatī*, but such a conclusion must be seen as transitional to a fuller future understanding of what it means to "recite" a religious document.[17]

Just as it is necessary to expand Babb's implied typology in light of our increasing appreciation of how the *Devī-Māhātmya* functions when it is recited, so is it necessary to come to a larger sense of what it means to "understand" the text, to see it as "explaining" the Goddess.[18] The basic point here is that understanding the text does not necessarily mean attaining an intellectual mastery of its content. In fact, in the current context it does not mean that at all. When I asked my friend and colleague, A. N. Jani, who is intimately familiar with the text and from whom we shall hear more below, whether anyone ever *studied* the text, his immediate answer was "no." It is not the kind of verbal phenomenon over which the faithful pore. Encountering the *Saptaśatī* is therefore unlike the Protestant encounter with the Bible, unlike the Western encounter with the classics of Greece and Rome. All of this we saw in a preliminary way in chapter 1, by way of opening up the issues involved in thinking about scripture globally. Now, however, we must go further. It is not just that proper recitation takes precedence over cognitive mastery or substantive verbal exegesis. The text does, in fact, receive exposition, but it is of a very different sort: It takes place through the media of action and festival life, rather than in the words of teaching or preaching. What I primarily have in mind here is the relationship between the *Devī-Māhātmya* and the great celebrations of Durgā Pūjā/ Navarātra. We saw earlier that Veena Das has argued that contemporary healing rituals provide a kind of "exegesis" of the *Saptaśatī.*[19] What we need to note here is the remarkable analysis that another anthropologist, Ákos Östör, has provided of the Durgā Pūjā festival.

We observed just above that Durgā Pūjā is marked by public recitation of the *Devī-Māhātmya*, and we saw earlier that the text itself advocates recitation of the *māhātmya* on the occasion of the great autumnal festival [12.11]. The crucial point here, however, is that an enormous amount of festival activity occurs *other than* recitation of the text. That activity has been chronicled from a variety of perspectives and we need not describe it here.[20] We may note there are two annual Durgā Pūjās or Navarātras ("Nine Nights"), one in the month of Caitra (March-April) and the more major one in Aśvina (September-October).[21] Fertility motifs pervade the festival, and as currently celebrated it overlaps at the conclusion with the royal festivals of Rāmlīlā or Dassera.[22] It is an exuberant time, marked in one form or another by virtually every household. Neighborhood associations vie with one another in constructing images of Durgā slaying Mahiṣa, and the procession of these images to the riverbank, where they will be immersed at festival's end, is extraordinary. In Varanasi, for instance, hundreds of small groups accompany their respective images. Each Durgā is lavishly decorated, celebrated by musicians, from a single drummer to a Western style brass band. Smoke and smells are pervasive. Here is a dancer, there a juggler, there another dancer who drinks deeply from a bottle and blows across a torch, producing a five-foot flame that leaps upward into the night. The crowd that lines the narrow streets, estimated at 100 thousand people throughout the city, roars its approval. In broken English, through betel-stained teeth comes the inebriated question to the foreigner, "Aren't you *happy*?!" to which I impulsively reply, "Yes!" I realize in retrospect that, of course, I am and should be happy: We are celebrating here the victory of good over evil, the triumph of the Goddess.[23]

What does all this have to do with the *Devī-Māhātmya*? How shall we make sense of such situations? Östör's recent study, *The Play of the Gods*, suggests important answers to such questions, and we note them here as part of our "spectrum" of contemporary encounters with the text. Detailed consideration of Östör's work would take us far afield, but the following points are significant. At the most general level, Östör is interested in the problem of how ideas relate to action.[24] This puts him in the company of others who have of late explored the performative and ritual dimension of textual life.[25] His distinctive focus, however, is on festivals as forms of analysis, and the heart of his study is a comparison of the Durgā Pūjā and Śiva *gājan* festivals in a Bengali town. Like other comparativists, he is wary of imported categories of analysis and prefers to work inductively, employing thick description to arrive at indigenous experience and categories.[26] This means that written documents, in particular, are given no privileged position in Östör's study. They are simply part of the furniture of village life, like pots, water, and sunrise—to be elaborated only if indigenous experience indicates that it is appropriate to do so. On occasion Östör does juxtapose textual content and ritual behavior, where the text concerned is a manuscript of a lost Upapurāṇa that bears on conduct of the ritual.[27] But his general sense is that "the meanings discovered in textual studies cannot be assumed to be the same as those in the rites I have discussed," a position that is consistent with his preference for sociological over theological matters.[28] What gives Östör's work its importance for us is not that he summarizes the *Devī-Māhātmya* as part (but only part) of the mythic background of Durgā Pūjā.[29] It is rather that he finds the terminology of the *Devī-Māhātmya* (and the *aṅgas*) so applicable to the ordinary experience of villagers, to the extent that *its* categories of understanding are *their* categories. The point is worth citing in detail:[30]

> According to the Caṇḍī legend, there are three forms of the goddess, corresponding to the three gunas: Mahā Kālī or *tama guṇ*, Mahā Lakṣmī, or *raja guṇ*, and Mahā Sarasvatī, or *sattva guṇ*. These three forms issued from the goddess as her first creation; they also form the basis of the social order and of the people's participation in the pūjās. This classification differs from *jāti-bicār* (caste divisions) in that it refers to types and ways of worship (mat). There are different approaches to the gods, varying from one guṇ to another. The *sattvik mat* is the way of Vaiṣṇavas; most commonly this means worship without animal sacrifice, a purely devotional

> attitude in which the worshiper does not demand anything for himself. The *rajasik mat* is worship with pomp and great insistence on power, the ego (*ahaṃkār*), stressing the self, aiming to derive many benefits from the pūjā. *Tamasik mat* is the pūjā of the householder who wants all kinds of things from the deities in carrying out his everyday duties. . . . *Sattva*, *raja*, and *tama* are qualities (*guṇas*), types, and styles of life. . . . The first is truth, the way of the renouncer; the second is power, the way of the ruler; the third is the way of everyday life, the householder pressed by social burden. *Dharma*, *artha*, *kām*, *mokṣa* are categories of experience, in terms of which one ought to lead one's life. *Dharma* designates duties, *artha* the means of living, *mokṣa* the liberation from contingencies of living, and *kām* the desires of worldly life. Sattva is the way to mokṣa; dharma is primarily rajasik, the responsibility of rule; kām and artha are the units of everyday life—*tama*. . . . The goddess expresses the created world, and the three qualities define the whole of creation.

I do not wish to imply that the categories of villagers' experience are actually *derivative* from the *Saptaśatī* and its *aṅgas*. Rather, an interpretive scheme—that of the three *guṇas*—has been applied *both* to the text *and* to daily experience, with the result that there is a very tight *correspondence* between the two. Östör puts it this way, his fourth sentence being reminiscent of the philosophical concerns we met in the last two chapters:

> The divisions of Durgāpūjā designate dimensions of space, society, and ideology. . . . Specific pūjās celebrate the timeless, limitless dimensions of the goddess. . . . In all cases, however, the pūjās relate land, locality, and people to each other in a direct and particular way. Thus we are yielded unity and diversity in one stroke, without contradiction and without either substantive merging or separation. . . . The myths and legends of Durgāpūjā . . . are not just the property of Brahmanic or esoteric knowledge, . . . nor are they merely hidden in sacred texts. The great myths are common property and well known throughout the town. . . . The narratives of the Markandiya Purāṇ [*sic*] are selectively present in all Durgāpūjās of the town. . . . Here we no longer face a division or discontinuity between oral and written traditions. Nor can we oppose myth to ritual and recitation to performance in narrative. Durgā's return is *śāstra* [the order of things]: . . . the performance attests to the reality of the belief, and the belief is enacted in the performance.[31]

I have quoted Östör at some length because his analysis represents such an important perspective on the status of the *Devī-Māhātmya* in contemporary India. Even if one chooses to play down the role of texts, their substance turns out to be woven into the fabric of daily life. With or without his separation of textual analysis from sociological concerns, fieldwork will continue, and details of that fieldwork will doubtless add much to our ongoing inquiry into the Goddess and the media of her worship. In enfolding the results of such work into the basic understanding we have developed in the current study, we can continue to affirm Babb's ascription of two basic significances to the *Saptaśatī*, as *mantra* to be recited, and as story to be understood. We might even wish to go further and to suggest that recitation inclines toward emphasis on the text's form, while understanding inclines toward emphasis on its content. But we must then be prepared to follow Humes in recognizing that recitation admits of being variously done, and to different ends and purposes. And we must follow the anthropological evidence to acknowledge that the media through which *understanding* is achieved may be behavioral and unconscious, not just verbal and cognitive. It is the extreme breadth of the material that is relevant to comprehending how the *Devī-Māhātmya* is encountered today that has led me to suggest it be ranged along a spectrum, with the two fixed points of recitation and understanding. It is this same breadth that invites further exploration of how the text lives on today, beyond what is offered in the next three sections.

Scholar and Translator

In 1963, Vasudeva S. Agrawala published a translation of the *Devī-Māhātmya* under the title *The Glorification of the Great Goddess*.[32] This work came toward the end of a distinguished career as a scholar, during which he was affiliated with a number of institutions, with a wide-ranging interest in Indian cultural history.[33] His translation has been cited with some frequency since its publication. Along with the introduction and notes, it offers a perspective on the Goddess and her text that is found fairly regularly in casual conversations in India, and in popular writing in both Hindi and English.[34] The interpretation that Agrawala offers therefore seems an appropriate place to begin our consideration of contemporary encounters with the *Devī-Māhātmya*.

Agrawala's understanding of the *Devī-Māhātmya* is a function of his larger understanding of the place of the Purāṇas in Indian life. As editor of *Purāṇa* journal for many years, he often quoted a verse from the *Mahābhārata* [1.1.204] to the effect that Brahmanical learning entails expanding upon the Veda with historical and Purāṇic material. The latter is a confirming elaboration (*upabṛṃhaṇa*) of the former or, in Agrawala's words, "the metaphysical truth of the Veda is to be demonstrated in the Itihāsa-Purāṇa manner."[35] What Agrawala understands as Vedic truth is crucial to his approach. It is not a "system of dialectic philosophy, but a discipline of metaphysics," and "symbols are the language of metaphysics as words are of philosophy."[36] Correspondingly, Agrawala's perspective in Purāṇic studies is that of interpreting the symbols, and establishing the correspondences, which link the Purāṇic corpus with the Vedic. "Purāṇic stories are like exoteric envelopes concealing the mystical meanings of the Vedas which deal with cosmic truths."[37]

The central concern of Agrawala's translation and notes, therefore, is to expound the meaning of the text. Although he is familiar with some of the commentaries and knows that the text is recited at certain times,[38] he is not concerned with the text's ritual use. Rather, the *Devī-Māhātmya* is a text to be understood. Part of understanding it is to see it in its historical context, and Agrawala frequently calls attention to the cultural evidence found in the text, which places it in Gupta times.[39] But he maintains that the symbolic use the author makes of such material is of far greater importance.[40] The heart of his encounter with the text consists of unraveling its symbolism.

The basic truth that the *Devī-Māhātmya*, the Purāṇas, and the Vedas all teach is that ultimate reality is one, the self-existent Brahman. This reality may be spoken of "as the Eternal Man, but at the same time . . . as the Eternal Woman," as both God and Goddess.[41] In support of such an assertion, Agrawala quotes Carl Jung: "'Whether you call the principle of existence, God, Matter, Energy, or anything else you like, you have created nothing; you have simply changed a symbol.'"[42] He is also fond of a cryptic fragment from the *Atharva Veda* [10.8.27]: "Thou art woman, thou art man. . . ."[43] This one principle is understood to become two, male and female, "for the sake of creation." Reference to this is seen in the Ṛg Vedic description of heaven as father and earth as mother [1.164.8]. As the levels of creation unfold, male is the principle of stasis, the center of the circle, while female is the active principle, the circle's circumference.[44] Agrawala sometimes describes creation as occurring at two levels—mind and matter—sometimes at three—mind, life, and matter.[45] The primacy of mind leads him to affirm that, once the *Devī-Māhātmya* has identified the Goddess with consciousness (*cetanā*), "no other statement is necessary." It is, in fact, the verse making this identification [5.13] that he takes as the epigraph for his translation.[46] Regardless of which description of creation is adopted, tension is built into every level, for the "universe is in the visible form of . . . [the] conflict" between gods and demons (*asuras*). The demons are always the aggressors, and it is the Goddess's unique role—in part because she is the great demoness with jurisdiction over them (*mahāsurī*) [1.58], and in part because she is the principle of activity—to reestablish order, thereby reaffirming life and the creative process.[47] She is the redemptress of all levels of creation.

What we see in the *Devī-Māhātmya*, therefore, are fundamentally two things. First, there is testimony to the Goddess's Vedic roots, which are seen to lie directly in the Devī Sūkta [*Ṛg Veda* 10.125] and more obliquely in the famous Puruṣa Sūkta [*Ṛg Veda* 10.90], as well as in dozens of isolated references.[48] Second, the redemptive activity of the Goddess is shown to be operative throughout the created universe. In explaining this, Agrawala makes use of the three-*guṇa* scheme, but in a way that differs from what we have seen earlier:

> The plot of the Chaṇḍī has been conceived in three parts with a purpose, namely, the *pūrva* [first] *carita* corresponds to the plane of *sattva* or *manas* [mind], the *madhyama* [middle] *carita* to the plane of *rajas* or *prāṇa* [life], and the *uttara* [last] *carita* to the plane of *tamas* or *bhūtas* [matter]. The Asuric darkness exists in the Psychic Man, the Vital Man and the Physical Man. The conflict with Madhu-Kaiṭabha refers to the first, that with Mahisha to the second, and that with Śumbha-Niśumbha [,] etc. to the third.[49]

Agrawala pays most attention to the first episode, where the concentration of Vedic references is greatest.[50] Important linkage of the second episode to the *Ṛg Veda* is made (1) through Agrawala's reading of *Ṛg Veda* 10.189—a brief, difficult hymn that likens the morning sunlight to a bull (*mahiṣa*) approaching his mother (earth) and father (heaven)—as referring to Mahiṣa's assault on heaven; and (2) discussing the Goddess's constitution from the splendor of many gods in relation to the phrase, "Knowers of the truth say the one has many forms" [*Ṛg Veda* 1.164.46].[51] The third episode is seen to be the most significant for ordinary humans, for "the Physical body is the real arena of the battle, and victory for the divine powers must be decided in actual life on the plane of matter in which both *manas* and *prāṇa* take part with the physical sense-organs. . . . Mere thought is not enough."[52] This leads to a complex identification of the third *carita*'s demons with different levels of creation, and a corresponding analysis of the goddesses who defeat them.[53] Given this way of dealing with the text, it is not surprising that Agrawala also offers symbolic interpretation of the three humans who appear in the text's frame story. "They are veritable types of the human soul." The king exemplifies the man of action (*karma*), who is "overtaken by destiny." The *vaiśya* represents "the plight of gold, which . . . attracts round it the darkness of Asuric temptation." The seer "stands for balance between demands of the world and those of the Self, . . . the ideal Teacher which Indian . . . tradition has created. . . ."[54] In his exegesis of 1.35, Agrawala identifies the seer with those who "see equally well by day and by night," because he has knowledge of both Brahman and the world. He does not renounce either one for the sake of the other.[55]

What Agrawala offers us, then, is a contemporary exegetical encounter with the text of the Goddess. The significance of the text lies in the meaning of its words: what they teach us about Indian history, and, more importantly, how they re-present Vedic cosmogony and dramatize the central issue of life in this created universe, namely, the struggle between good and evil. For those who would learn from this teaching, the moral is clear:

> . . . man can never afford to sleep on his oars. He must put forth his best efforts in order to attain the spiritual victory which belongs to him as his birthright. The Asuric types are endless in time and place [,] manifesting as arrogant challenges to the moral and spiritual order. To meet them the Goddess has to incarnate as . . . the power that is produced from the physical, vital and spiritual sheaths of our own body. Pitted against her the demons go down.[56]

Pūjāri and Professor

It was my extreme good fortune in the fall of 1981 to make the acquaintance of Dr. A. N. Jani. Learning of my interest in the *Devī-Māhātmya* at a conference we both attended in Varanasi, he indicated that he used the text in his own religious life, and that he would be pleased to discuss it with me. Over the ensuing years, we have talked and corresponded at some length, including wonderful hours sitting outside the central shrine of the small Mahākālī temple in Baroda, where he serves in alternate months as chief officiant (*pūjāri*). With his kind permission, I include here in anecdotal fashion some of what I have learned about his engagement with the text, as a second instance of its contemporary life.

Jani "hails from the Trivedi family of priests of the *Mādhyandina Śākha* of the *Śukla-yajurveda* living for many generations at Ahmedabad," and moving to Baroda two generations ago.[57] Showing rare facility in language at an early age, he earned degrees up through the doctorate, studied for two substantial periods in Germany, then taught at Baroda and served as Director of the renowned Oriental Institute there. His academic achievements are impressive, earning him governmental recognition shortly after his retirement in 1981. He has also had a keen pastoral sensitivity, attested to by students and colleagues, that intersects with his scholarship. His Gujarati edition of the *Devī-Māhātmya*, for instance, which we used in chapter 3 to indicate how the text can be said to have "700 verses,"[58] is the third such edition, all of which have been underwritten by patrons and distributed gratis, so that interested individuals might have ready access to the Goddess and her text. There is about him a generosity of spirit and mischievous humor, as well as learning and piety.

Jani speaks fondly of his early days when, having expressed interest in carrying on the family tradition of serving as *pūjāri* at the Mahākālī temple, he found it a wonderful setting in which to study for his bachelor and master's degrees: The temple ministrations, attending the image and receiving *pūjā* offerings from those who came for *darśan*, were not terribly time-consuming, and the relative quiet made it an ideal place to prepare for his examinations. The tradition of reciting the *Devī-Māhātmya* at the temple (of which we shall see more below) was not a long-standing one, but was instituted by him in his youth. Apart from his religious interest in doing this, he had been influenced by an uncle who knew the text by heart and who would recite it for others for a fee. For a young man, particularly one with Jani's talents, this appeared to be a fairly simple way of making pocket money. Before he could hire out as a reciter of the text, however, Jani's *guru* required that he recite it one hundred times on his own. Having done so, he then began to serve as a professional reciter. It was scarcely a lucrative profession. The fee when he began was around seventy-five *paisa*, less than ten cents, and the fee for such services remains modest, between five and ten rupees in Jani's estimate, about seventy-five cents. Jani no longer recites the *Devī-Māhātmya* professionally for others, but refers those who are interested to other qualified reciters.

The interaction of Jani the reciter and Jani the budding Sanskritist occasioned one episode he recalled with delight. The normal time for reciting the *Devī-Māhātmya* with its accompanying ritual Jani found to be about two hours. While reciting the text, however, he would (not surprisingly) run across grammatical errors or misprints in the particular edition he had in front of him. The purist in him would then stop and write in the appropriate corrections. One day he began at 9:00 A.M., and at 2:00 P.M. that afternoon his father showed up and wanted to know what was going on. The family lunch had been delayed on his behalf, and when he failed to show up, people were concerned at what might have happened to him.

Current practice at the Mahākālī temple is for the *Devī-Māhātmya* to be ritually recited on the fourteenth (*caturdaśi*) day of the dark fortnight (*kṛṣṇapakṣa*) of the moon. Jani indicated that, upon his retirement, he had hoped to be able to recite the text daily, but the press of other activities has prevented him from being able to do so. If this were displeasing to the Goddess, she would be sure to let him know. Jani has a keen sense that whatever happens comes about because it is the will of the Goddess, as a manifestation of her grace. Similarly, although the text is capable of being turned to entrepreneurial ends, its power is incontrovertible and Jani speaks of it with awe. He and many, many others readily cite instances of its effectiveness in the lives of people they have known. In other words, the claims that the text makes for itself in chapter 12 are not just hearsay, but firsthand experience. A family feud was ended, an illness cured, an aspiration realized, an answer discovered. By way of underscoring this point, Jani related the following story that the great Tantric of Varanasi, Gopinath Kaviraj, told about his teacher, Viśuddhānanda. One day the teacher, a devotee of the *Devī-Māhātmya*, who was endowed with *sūrya-vijñāna*, the capacity to focus the light of the sun on a particular object and transform it into something else, was out traveling. As evening came, he told his cook, who was traveling with him, that he would be reciting the *Devī-Māhātmya* that night and should not be disturbed. Arising to relieve himself in the middle of the night, the cook forgot this admonition. He inadvertently opened Viśuddhānanda's door and was blinded by the light, just as the teacher was coming to the end of his recitation. Quickly shutting the door, he apologized the next morning, and was told that it was indeed fortunate that this had happened at the very end of the text. Had it occurred earlier, he would surely have been annihilated by the power that was present.[59]

The power manifested in this episode was a function, of course, not just of the words of the *Saptaśatī*, but also of the spiritual prowess of Viśuddhānanda. Jani is quite clear about this. Even though he sees himself as very much in the tradition of the Tantric Bhāskararāya, and is self-consciously indebted to him in the editorial and interpretive work he has done on the *Devī-Māhātmya*, he also speaks of "Tantrics" as individuals who have special occult powers. They have developed the *mantras*' potential in a particularly yogic direction and this leads people to respect them, and to fear them. Jani's remarks here are of a piece with Brooks' observation that the word "Tantra" in contemporary Indian vernaculars "conjures notions of effective black magic, illicit sexuality, and immoral behavior," but also refers to a positive kind of power, such as that specified in "a popular movement [which] . . . links the cure of 'sexual problems' experienced by married couples to specialists who openly call themselves 'Tantrics.'"[60] It is this multivalency of "Tantra" as concept and as phenomenon that makes it such a rich point of current inquiry, and we need not attempt to come to closure on that matter here.

As we saw at the end of the last chapter, part of Jani's engagement with the text consists of an effort to understand the historical process by which it has lived through the centuries. He suggests that the movement from Purāṇic to Tantric engagement with the text reflects the discovery of the mantric power of its words, the effort to restrict access to this power, and to maximize its realization through ritual means. Parallel with this, in Jani's opinion, occurred another development that explains the puzzling matter of how the *Devī-Māhātmya* came to be known as the *Durgā-Saptaśatī*. The common way of remunerating scribes in a scribal culture was by the number of verses (sometimes by the number of syllables) that they copied. The exact count was not always precise, and since there are "roughly" 700 verses (particularly if one throws in the *aṅga*s), it became known as "The 700." At first this practice was natural, and created no problem. But as the text's fame grew, as its mantric power became known, the question legitimately arose: "Why is this verbal artifact said to have *700* verses?" Providing an answer to this question has been part of the commentarial encounter with the text ever since.

Jani holds other interesting historical views—suggesting that it is the maternal, nurturing quality of Śāktism, as well as its ritual emphasis, that accounts for its absence from the debates of classical *darśana*; that over time Śāktism has become more monistic, also more dialectical; that Bhāskararāya is a key figure in both developments—but I shall leave these to one side in favor of his comparative remarks on the *Devī-Māhātmya* and the *Bhagavad Gītā*. The former, he noted, can be recited either for worldly gain or enjoyment (*bhoga*) or for final release (*mokṣa*), the point of differentiation being the intent (*saṃkalpa*) with which recitation is done. The text itself attests to both goals in the different aspirations of the king and the merchant, and the last chapter shows the maternal generosity of the Goddess on such matters, for she grants the king more than he asked for.[61] Nonetheless, most people—Jani estimated 90 percent—who recite the text, or have it recited for them, do so for mundane purposes. This contrasts strikingly, he suggested, with the

Bhagavad Gītā, which is also widely known and recited, but "as a *mokṣa* text." Both texts are *mahāmantras*, and the implied symbiosis between them extends to other matters: One is addressed to God, the other to Goddess; one is for Vaiṣṇavas, the other for Śāktas, and so on. He did indicate that the Vedic cum Tantric practice of specifying seer, metre, and so forth, which we have seen to be characteristic of ritually engaging the *Devī-Māhātmya*, also exists for the *Bhagavad Gītā*, as does the Tantric practice of associating particular words of the text with limbs of the body (*nyāsa*).[62] Whether Jani's pairing of these texts is common, and whether it is has anything to do with the historical convergence of Krishna, and of kingship, with the Goddess is a matter warranting further inquiry.[63]

We have referred often in the course of this study to the ritual recitation of the *Devī-Māhātmya*, and it is fitting therefore to conclude this "conversation" with Jani by providing an account of what transpires when he recites the text. In doing so, I make no claims for this being a typical recitation, for, as we have seen, Cynthia Humes has identified great variety in recitation styles.[64] This is simply a description of one such recitation, occurring in the Mahākālī temple in Baroda on *caturdaśi* day of *kṛṣṇapakṣa* of the month of Śravaṇa—in Western terms, August 23, 1987.[65] The ritual was based on the text with liturgical notes that Jani himself has edited. It began around 10:00 A.M. and lasted a little over two hours.[66]

The setting is the only room on the second floor of the temple, accessible by a narrow wooden stairway, located directly over the central shrine, *garbha gṛha* ("womb house") of Mahākālī. Jani is sitting cross-legged on the floor, facing east, the same direction that the image one floor below faces. I am seated to his right, also on the floor, facing north. We are alone except for a family friend who comes in part way through and sits quietly for the duration. At one point his son brings in freshly prepared fruit for the *pūjā*, then leaves. Immediately in front of Jani sits the open text on a low stand. Beyond the text is the ritual platform, perhaps eighteen inches wide and twelve inches deep, on which are: (*a*) in the center, a flat silver stand on which lies a metal disc on which the *Devī-Māhātmya yantra* (see figure 5.3) has been painted with red sandalwood paste; (*b*) at the right front, incense sticks; (*c*) at the left rear, a candle and a small red silk cloth that will be used to clothe the *yantra* after the deities have been installed. On the edge of the platform Jani has placed the microphone for my tape recorder; it records the entire ceremony except for three occasions when he momentarily turns it off during utterance of the Navārṇa *mantra*. Diagonally to Jani's left is a bowl of milk and some wax; to his right, a small pot of water, another of sandalwood paste, also a silver tray with flowers, flower petals, rice, and sweets, and a smaller tray into which offerings of flowers and water will be made.[67]

There are two basic foci to the ritual that precedes recitation of the text proper. One is the establishment of the divine presence in the *yantra*, with varied offerings to the deities who take up residence there: Mahākālī, Mahālakṣmī, Mahāsarasvatī, and the three couples who emanate from them. This idea of treating the deities like guests in one's home is characteristic of *pūjā* generally: "Lavishing attention on people about whom one cares profoundly" is Jani's way of putting it. The other focus is the ritual preparation and purification of the reciter of the text. Both ritual foci are developed with great precision and detail, which I here summarize as briefly as possible.[68]

The reciter begins by rinsing the mouth with water (*ācamana*), bringing the breath under control (*prāṇāyāma*), and declaring the intent of this particular recitation (*saṃkalpa*). The god of obstacles, Gaṇeśa, is called to mind (*gaṇapati-smaraṇa*), then one's teacher (*guru-smaraṇa*). The external environment is purified with appropriate invocations: first, the place of seating (*āsana-vidhi*) and the earth; then, malevolent spirits are driven away (*bhūtotsādana*) and the four quarters secured (*dig-bandhana*), constructing what Jani calls "a fire fortress" around the reciter. Next, the internal environment is prepared, purifying the elements (*bhūta-śuddhi*) and awakening the vital forces (*prāṇa-pratiṣṭha*). The letters of the Sanskrit language are serially assigned to parts of the reciter's body (*mātṛkā-nyāsa*), the candle flame established (*dīpa-sthāpana*), and the deities invoked into the *yantra* (*āvāhana*). There follows a sixteen step worship by which the deities are enabled to feel at home: offering of water for the feet, for drinking, offering of flowers, incense, and so forth (*ṣoḍaśopacāra*). Apology is sought for any ritual errors that might be committed, and the book from which we are reading is itself reverenced (*pustaka-pūjā*). The Kavaca, Argalā, and Kīlaka are then recited. The sense that pervades the ritual to this point is that of opening a doorway, a conduit perhaps, between properly installed deity and properly prepared reciter. Through this conduit the *mantra*s of the *Devī-Māhātmya* will be offered, and reciprocating power will in turn flow back upon the reciter.

Between recitation of the *aṅga*s and the text proper comes a series of ritual identifications that place sounds in the reciter's various limbs and relate them to the body of the deity (*nyāsa*).[69] Chronologically first is *nyāsa* of the Navārṇa *mantra*, followed—after a meditational verse—by that of the seers, metres, *devatā*s, *śakti*s, *bīja*s, and *tattva*s of the *Saptaśatī*, and then invocation of Mahākālī, Mahālakṣmī, and Mahāsarasvatī over the entire body. Recitation of the three meditational (*dhyāna*) verses to these forms of the Goddess is followed by the Rātri Sūkta, which in Jani's lineage is the non-Vedic version, that is, the hymn in chapter 1 of the *Devī-Māhātmya*.[70]

Jani then recites the verses of the *Saptaśatī*. He pauses at the end of each chapter and makes water offerings, ladling water from the pot into the adjacent tray. He places flowers daubed with sandalwood paste on the dish where the deities are in residence in the *yantra*. Periodically he replenishes the wax in the candle. Before beginning the next chapter, he makes an additional water offering.

On completing the *Devī-Māhātmya* proper, Jani recites the Devī Sūkta, performs a six-limbed *nyāsa* with various verses from the *Saptaśatī*, then utters a meditational verse and the Navārṇa *mantra*. The three Rahasyas are read, followed by an apology for omissions (*uttara-vidhi*), with reinforcement of the recitation's efficacy by reciting the ten-verse Kuñjikā Stotra. Offerings are made with the five elements of perfume, flower, incense, light, and the foods that have been assembled. The candle is circled slowly in front of the *yantra* (*ārati*), and flowers are showered upon it. The waterpot is banged like a bell, a summary dedication is offered, and the deities are dismissed (*visarjan*).

After the deities have departed, Jani distributes to his friend and to me the elements that remain as *prasāda* ("grace"): the water, which we rub on our heads, the milk, the fruit, and the sweets, from which the ants scurry away when Jani taps on the tray. Jani washes the *yantra* from the metal disc, and with the colored water marks our foreheads with the sign of the Goddess. As we make our way from the temple to Jani's house for lunch, the torrential monsoon rains of early morning have stopped. They are much needed in Gujarat this year. The sun shows signs of making it a hot and humid afternoon.

"Standing at the Feet of the Mother"

It is well-known that, of all the regions of India, with their varied linguistic and cultural life, none has been more drawn to worship of the Goddess than Bengal. As with so much else in the history of Śāktism, how this came to be is not clear. What is certain is that, for some time now, Bengalis have been distinguished for their adoration of "the Mother," as they know her. It is fitting therefore that our last example of contemporary encounters with the *Devī-Māhātmya* consider the views of a modern Bengali devotee. I shall call him C. R. Banerjea.[71]

Banerjea is a schoolteacher. He emigrated from Bengal to Bihar some twenty years ago in search of employment. His family came with him, and his sense of rootedness in Bengal—in diet, language, and religion—remains strong. He views recitation of the *Devī-Māhātmya* as relevant in the *pūjā* of all goddesses, with a particularly important role to play in Durgā Pūjā. Chiefly, however, he views the text not as a verbal artifact to be ritually employed, but as a document to be understood. What is important about the *Devī-Māhātmya* is what it teaches us about the Mother. Banerjea's understanding of what it teaches follows from his self-understanding as a *bhakti-vādi*, follower of the way of devotion. He speaks readily of how this bears on his engagement with the *Devī-Māhātmya*, as well as on religious life in general.

Most striking, in light of our earlier exploration, is Banerjea's outspoken hostility to the commentaries that have been composed on the text. When I asked him about a particular point in Bhāskararāya's *Guptavatī*, he replied that he never read Bhāskararāya, nor any of the other commentaries, "because they place bad implants in the mind." All of them are crypto-advaitins, he alleges, subordinating the Mother to Brahman, emphasizing knowledge at the expense of devotion. There is a measure of hypocrisy in such behavior, he says, for the commentators claim to worship the Goddess, saying, "Hello, Mother" and praising her beauty, but then proceeding to reduce her to mere thought (*cit*) and sound (*śabda*).[72] In doing this, they destroy her beauty. But they also destroy the necessary distinction between child and Mother, and the consequent opportunity for the child to provide service or worship (*seva*) to the Mother. A genuine devotee, claims Banerjea, would never write a commentary. If he or she had to write something, it would be less dessicated and analytical, more an ebullient expression of love—at most a practical expression of love in the form of a devotional manual. When I suggested that it sounded very much as if he would side with Rāmakrishna in the latter's homespun indictment of Śaṅkara for wanting to become sugar, rather than to taste it, Banerjea laughed in hearty agreement.[73]

Along with Banerjea's blanket indictment of commentators goes a specific wariness about those he calls "Tantrics." Part of this unease is related to his sense that Tantrics have smuggled a concern with knowledge (*jñāna*) into a devotional (*bhakti*) context. Invoking the *Bhagavad Gītā*, Banerjea insists that the two paths are different from each other, as well as from the path of action (*karma*). He acknowledges that the *Devī-Māhātmya* does indeed call the Goddess "the supreme, eternal knowledge (*vidyā*) that becomes the cause of release" [1.44]. But he is quick to point out that it also calls her "the great illusion" (*mahāmāyā*) [1.58], which he identifies with ignorance (*avidyā*). She is therefore something more, something larger than *jñāna*. She is the highest knowledge (*paravidyā*), beyond Brahman, "an affection that lies in your heart" and "grows a little day by day." Banerjea is also troubled by the reputed licentiousness of Tantrics. While he finds alleged social misconduct intrinsically disturbing, there is an underlying issue. The Goddess for him is, above all else, Mother. Anything that smacks of eroticism in relation to her is clearly wrongheaded, and potentially dangerous. The *Devī-Māhātmya* itself demonstrates this danger, Banerjea maintains, for the third episode teaches, among other things, that those who approach the Mother as consort or as lover must die. Correspondingly, he makes a sharp distinction between Śākta and Vaiṣṇava understandings of *bhakti*. The latter is famous for its elaboration of different emotional states (*bhāva*s) that the devotee can assume in relation to the divine: *śānta* (awe), *dāsya* (subservience), *vātsalya* (parental or fraternal affection), *sākhya* (friendship), and *mādhurya* (erotic love).[74] For the Śākta, Banerjea maintains, the last of these is particularly troubling, because of its passionate, sexual nature. The *bhāva* that comes closest to the spirit of Śākta *bhakti* is *vātsalya*, and even this must be further developed to draw out its maternal implications.[75] *Kalyāṇa* (auspicious beauty) is the word Banerjea applies to this quality, which he sees as inherent in females: latent in childhood, it flowers during puberty and reaches its fulfilment in the production of a son (*sic*) in marriage. The great and unique satisfaction that a woman takes in this event is of cosmic significance. It is what lies at the heart of the universe, for it is this same pleasure that the Mother takes in our existence, and in our well-being. We children cannot, of course, fully reciprocate, but we can honor the Mother appropriately—as each of us would our human mother.[76]

Banerjea sees the specific teaching of the *Devī-Māhātmya* as unfolding in six stages, what he calls six *sāṃmukhya*s, "presences," literally, "face-to-face-nesses."

The first *sāṃmukhya*, according to Banerjea, is *sattā sāṃmukhya*, "the way things are." It is the sense, apparent from the very beginning of the text, that there is something wrong with our conventional way of looking at things, that there is more going on than meets the eye, something beyond appearances. This is suggested by the large number of "and yets" (what Banerjea calls "the *api* word") running through the early verses: The king and *vaiśya* have been abused by worldly events, *and yet* their thoughts are drawn to their loved ones and former circumstances. They should be glad to be rid of their tormenters, *and yet*. . . . Worldly power seemingly does not avail, *and yet*. . . . The point of this *sāṃmukhya* is to demonstrate the reality of the Mother, a point that the king has particular trouble grasping because of his Vedic notion of deity as a limited entity, with a particular dominion. The Mother is not like this, says the seer, for although she does have "births," they do not detract from her eternality. This *sāṃmukhya* reaches its climax, and comes to an end, with the king's question at 1.33: "How does it happen that delusion falls even upon men of knowledge . . . ?"

The second *sāṃmukhya* extends from 1.34 through 1.44 and is called *vṛtti sāṃmukhya*, dealing with the Mother's "instinct" or "inclination." That instinct is delusion (*moha*), it is her very nature, and she drags the minds of even the most knowledgeable into ignorance. In the context of the Mother's life, which is without boundaries of any sort, the knowledge that any particular human being has is partial. What makes this particularly frustrating for individuals is that there is no way out of her influence.

The third *sāṃmukhya* is *tattva sāṃmukhya*, "the true state of affairs" and encompasses 1.47-48. At this juncture, says Banerjea, the seer could proceed in one of several ways, because the Mother has several forms and they appeal to different sensibilities. As *cit* (luminous thought), she is the movement within the heart that initiates worship. As *śabda* (sound), she is the secret *mantra* granted by a *guru*, whose power is realized through repetition. As playful activity (*līlā*), she is known through discursive accounts of that variegated activity (*kriyā*). No one form is complete by itself, but the seer's assessment of the two woebegones' spiritual condition is that they will be most receptive to the third form of the Mother. He proceeds accordingly.

The fourth *sāṃmukhya* is *līlā sāṃmukhya*, and it comprises most of the text, beginning at 1.49 and running through the end of chapter 12. It is the seer's extended narrative account of the Mother's cavorting in, and as, the universe (*līlā*).

Vidyā sāṃmukhya is the fifth *sāṃmukhya*, and consists of the seer's summary of the preceding exposition. Comprising the first four verses of chapter 13, it takes its name from the "knowledge" of the Mother that it conveys.

The final *sāṃmukhya* Banerjea calls the *svarūpa sāṃmukhya*, for it deals with the "own form" that the Mother reveals in 13.7-17. It presents the effort by the two new devotees to realize at first hand the truth they have had described to them. Banerjea emphasizes that it is in the act of worship (*seva*) that the Mother manifests herself to her devotees, but he also understands that the form in which she appears is an ineffable yogic apparition, not some anthropomorphic image such as one might reverence in *pūjā*.

The function of the *Devī-Māhātmya*, then, in Banerjea's view, is to instruct and arouse devotional sentiment in the heart of the hearer. It points the devotee toward a symbiotic and mutually satisfying relationship with the Mother. Banerjea is clear, however, that pure *bhakti* takes no thought for personal gain, but acts solely for the delight (*prīti*) of the Mother. Those who ask for mundane benefits have not yet seen the point, have not yet known and come to love the Mother. The goal of all this, says Banerjea, exceeds the conventional identification of five forms of *mokṣa*, which see the liberated soul in varying relationship to the ultimate—inhabiting the same world (*sālokya*), having the same form (*sārūpya*), existing in the same vicinity (*sāmīpya*), having the same sovereignty (*sārṣṭi*), and merging (*sāyujya*).[77] The goal of Śākta *bhakti* is something greater than all of these. The only way it can be described is with the phrase "standing at the feet of the Mother." The mysterious power of such a characterization is that it applies both to the goal of loving the Mother, and to the process that gets us there. Loving worship or *bhakti* is certainly that which draws us to the Mother. But in addition, says Banerjea, it gives us something to do when we are standing there at her feet.

Conclusion

Given the breadth of the material we have considered in this and the previous chapters, no easy summary is possible. Nor, I think, is it desirable, for to a considerable extent, the significance of what we have explored lies in the details: How a given phrase is translated in the *Devī-Māhātmya*, how a later interpretation engages in specific ways with the text's form and content, what sense a particular individual makes of this verbal artifact. Rather than attempt such a synopsis, it is more appropriate here to continue the historical momentum that has been implicit in the structure of our study. After first describing briefly the historical setting in which our text was composed, we then translated the text using language appropriate to the time of its composition, traced its legacy (in part) through subsequent centuries, and have in this chapter looked at some instances of its contemporary life. Where does this venture now appear headed? I can think of no better way to address such a question than to return to the three interests we discussed in chapter 1, the interests that first drew me to this study.

It is in pursuing the second of those interests—the emerging study of scripture as a self-conscious category of cross-cultural comparison—that we have made the most progress in this book. This is surely a function of the fact that the "revolution" in the way we think about such matters, which we sketched briefly in chapter 1, is of such recent origin. Much recent and current scholarship is, of course, of a very high order indeed.[78] But it seems likely that our documentation of the emphasis placed on recitation of the *Devī-Māhātmya*, often without understanding it, and of the extent to which the text is embedded in ritual of various sorts will add substance to efforts to develop a global taxonomy of what it is that people do religiously with their verbal artifacts. As is often the case in comparative study, we are also likely to be turned back upon familiar scriptural material in other contexts, asking of it questions that we might not have thought to ask prior to meeting Indian ways of encountering this text of the Goddess. In similar fashion, I suspect that questions about the media that are employed in religious life will continue to command attention. We have started here from the long-standing assumption of Western scholarship that written artifacts are significant, and that they are significant primarily for their content. We have seen how quickly this assumption gets called into question by the legacy of the *Devī-Māhātmya.* Not only is the "writtenness" of the artifact much less significant than its oral-aural quality, but the verbal medium, both written and spoken, also becomes intimately intertwined with the media of sculpture and gesture, of image and *yantra.* I have tried to suggest briefly in chapter 4 how very complex the situation is, and that suggestion has surely been reinforced by our subsequent attention to the data of Durgā Pūjā. Progress we are making, to be sure, in understanding both the *Devī-Māhātmya* and scripture generically. But since what is being investigated is the very medium through which contemporary scholarship expresses itself, and since the media of contemporary Western culture are themselves currently so much in flux,[79] it seems inevitable that this revolution will continue for some time to come.

On the third of the interests I expressed in chapter 1—that of injecting a note of historical method into the study of the Purāṇas, and into translation of the *Devī-Māhātmya*—our progress has been more modest. In part this is a function of the massive and impressive claim that those whom I have called "structuralists" have staked to the interpretation of Purāṇic materials. Little that I have said here erodes the credibility of such an approach, though I shall say more about method below. There is a good deal to be said, I believe, for now having available a translation of the *Devī-Māhātmya* which, having paid attention to historical factors, is reasonably reflective of the text's sense at the time of its composition, and is relatively unencumbered by the "baggage" that previous translations have often inadvertently carried. And I like to think that there is an intrinsic interest in seeing how later interpreters bring their heritage to life, in various ways, at various times. What it shows, at a minimum, is that history, and geography, make a difference—along, of course, with lots of other factors. With such an approach we learn a great deal, for instance, about Bhāskararāya, and about his eighteenth century way of being religious. And we come to see that this is quite different from the life and religion of, say, C. R. Banerjea, and that both are different from—yet both significantly engaged with—the words that were composed some fifteen hundred years ago.

I am also aware, however, of how fragmentary our historical inquiry has been, how much has been left unexplored and unsaid. It is, of course, obvious that there are lots of gaps still to fill. If nothing else, the current work may serve as a reference point in the ongoing process of understanding the nature and history of Goddess-worship in India. Beyond the obvious lacunae, however, I have also deliberately touched only in passing on two major issues in contemporary Indian studies, for fear that this book would grow beyond manageability. One is the issue of the relationship between Tantra and *bhakti*, the other the relationship between the Goddess and secular power.

On the former, Padoux writes: "Though the spirit of Tantrism is in many ways opposed to that of *bhakti*, both can be reconciled and are [sometimes] even promiscuously associated."[80] In this study, we have gained some sense of the potential for antagonism between Tantra and *bhakti*, chiefly revolving around whether one becomes (monistically) identified with the Goddess or (non-monistically) worships her. We have also seen in chapter 6 that *bhakti* and Tantra share many features, but that it is possible to distinguish between them, though not in a simple, linear fashion. This, in turn, has prepared us to understand how the same text might be simultaneously engaged by different individuals, from different perspectives, for different purposes. It is just such a situation that Madeleine Biardeau describes when she writes:

> Although in theory Tantra is very different from, indeed the reversal of, Brahmanic values, in actual fact and in most literature, there is no distinction. One finds Tantric themes in Purāṇas, and references to Purāṇas in Tantras. . . . The great Purāṇas are read in the temples, where the ritual is Tantric [but understood by "the masses" from the perspective of *bhakti*]. . . . Prayers and recitations serve both *bhakti* and Tantra, and it is in the temples that one sees the two come together.[81]

Pursuit of this line of thought would have required another cycle of fieldwork on my part, and I have thought it advisable to defer such an undertaking, particularly in light of the forthcoming work of Cynthia Humes.[82]

The interrelationship of kings and the Goddess has also consistently surfaced in our discussion. Historically, such a theme seems as old as the Indus Valley civilization.[83] We saw in chapter 2 that it runs through the literary sources that predate the *Devī-Māhātmya*, often in somewhat disguised form. The relationship between king and Goddess has an obvious centrality in the story that the *Devī-Māhātmya* tells, and earlier in this chapter it appeared as an important dimension of contemporary celebration of Durgā Pūjā. This theme has already attracted a considerable literature,[84] and I have been reluctant to leap from the relatively narrow focus I have adopted in this book into extended discussion of a subject that is so enormously consequential for the understanding of Indian culture as a whole. Others will surely be less reluctant, and I, for one, will welcome such ventures. Having here explored varied relationships between individuals and a text (albeit asking functional as well as content questions), I shall be interested to see how this information may be used to understand other dimensions of Indian life, past and present.

Finally, I note that the first interest that drew me to the study of the *Devī-Māhātmya* is also the one to which we have given the most modest attention in this study. That is my interest in the contemporary revolution in our ways of thinking about gender. We have noted in passing the male perspective that is assumed in such verses as Kavaca 28 and 33, and Argalā 22, asking for protection of penis and semen, and for acquisition of a good wife. We commented briefly on Bhāskararāya's views about the gender of ultimate reality. And we earlier saw C. R. Banerjea identify the birth of a son as the occasion for a woman's fulfillment. But for the most part, I have not sought to call attention to the gender implications of the material we have been studying. I have not done so for two reasons.

The first is that one of the clear early lessons emerging from feminist study is that one cannot assume that the existence of goddesses, or Goddess texts, in a given culture correlates with favorable social status for women. The examples I have just cited suggest that the *Devī-Māhātmya* is part of a broader Indian context whose thinking about gender is shaped by many factors other than the fact that the *Devī-Māhātmya* happens to be a text praising the Goddess. In any case, inquiries into Indian thinking about gender, and into the religious life of Indian women are well under way, and I have been unwilling to force a connection between this inquiry and those. Such a connection may come, but the part of the *Devī-Māhātmya*'s legacy that I have explored has not indicated the appropriateness of attempting such a synthesis at this time.

Secondly, it continues to be my view that careful scholarship has contributions to make—both intellectually and humanistically—to all sorts of revolutions. But it will be others, not I, who will determine whether this translation and study of the *Devī-Māhātmya* are useful in thinking about matters of gender. My role is simply to make the scholarship as reliable as I can.

In aspiring to this kind of indirect contribution, I discern both a need for caution, and then a final possibility.

The cautionary note comes from André Padoux. Having noted the aspiration of some to import Indian *mantra*s into the West for the liberation that they promise, he continues:

> Should we wish . . . to import them to the West for our own use, we should never forget the following two fundamental points: (1) Mantras are efficient forms of speech within a particular tradition, where speech is conceived of within a particular mythico-religious framework. If we pluck them from this cultural milieu, which is their nourishing soil, is "the luminous bud of mantra" . . . likely to survive? One may well doubt it. (2) We must remember that mantras, even in their higher, supposedly redemptive forms, are always part of a precise and compulsory ritual context, outside which they are useless and powerless. A mantra may be a liberating word but only in accordance to precise and binding rules.[85]

It is considerations such as Padoux's—recognizing that cultures are genuinely different, that comparative scholarship can no longer simply offer translations, as least of religious texts, without also indicating what the function of those texts has been—that has dictated that there be two parts to this book, a translation *and* a study, so as not to misrepresent the context in which the text has lived.

But things are not finally so bleak as Padoux suggests, I think, at least with regard to the *Devī-Māhātmya*.[86] For the *Devī-Māhātmya* is not *just* a *mantra*. It is also a narrative discourse, a story that can teach the reader or listener something. And even among those for whom it functions as *mantra*, it is different from other *mantra*s precisely because it can be *understood*. What this means is that while we in the West must be aware of the ritual context that has often, perhaps most of the time, sustained the text in its Indian setting, we can also note that the text has been understood in India, and understood in a variety of ways. This, in turn, leaves us open to understand the text as best we may, in ways that are not possible for most *mantra*s, precisely because they are not intelligible. Once that possibility is granted, then a host of subsequent options come into view. A. N. Jani, we recall, had an acute sense of the Goddess's presence, of how her will becomes manifest in whatever comes to pass. On learning of the enriched dream-life that was experienced by women who had read portions of my translation of the *Devī-Māhātmya*, he asked me to urge them to keep careful track of those dreams. For it is in just such a way, he said, that the Goddess makes her will known.

Appendix: Translation of the Aṅgas

Kavaca: "The Armor"

Mārkaṇḍeya said:

1. That which is the highest secret in the world, giving every kind of protection to men,
Whose account has not been told of before, tell me that, O grandfather of the universe.

Brahmā said:

2. That is the highest secret, O wise one; it benefits all creatures.
Give ear to the holy Armor (*kavaca*) of the Goddess, O great sage.

3. The first is Śailaputrī, and the second Brahmacāriṇī;
The third is Candraghaṇṭā; the fourth Kūṣmāṇḍā.

4. The fifth is the mother of Skanda, the sixth Kātyāyanī;
The seventh is Kālarātrī, and the eighth Mahāgaurī.

5. The ninth is said to be Siddhidā; these are proclaimed as the nine Durgās.
These names were uttered by the noble Brahmā.

6. One who is being burned by fire, or has gone into battle, in the midst of enemies,
Those who are afflicted by fear, in difficulty and in crisis, these folk take refuge (in the Goddess).

7. To them nothing inauspicious happens, in battle or adversity.
I do not see misfortune for such a one, neither grief nor misery nor danger.

8. Prosperity assuredly is produced for those who remember her with devotion.
Cāmuṇḍā is seated on a corpse, Vārāhī mounted on a buffalo,

9. Aindrī is astride an elephant, Vaiṣṇavī rides on Garuḍa.
On a bull is Māheśvarī mounted, while Kaumārī is borne on a peacock.

10. Brahmī, wearing all her jewels, is conveyed on a swan.
With the variegated splendor of their ornaments, shining with their diverse jewels,

11. Thus do the goddesses appear, mounted on their chariots, filled with anger.
Conch, discus, club, spear, plow, and cudgel,

12. Shield, lance, axe, and noose,
Pike, trident, and a great bow-weapon:

13. These are the weapons that they carry for the sake of destroying the demons' bodies,
For the safety of devotees, and also for the well-being of the gods.

14. O one of great might, O one of great stamina, O destroyer of great danger,
Protect me, O Goddess who is hard-to-see, who increases the fears of enemies.

15. May Aindrī protect me in the east, the goddess of Agni in the southeast.
May Vārāhī protect me in the south, the one who carries a sword in the southwest.[1]

16. May Vāruṇī protect me in the west, the one who rides a deer in the northwest.
May Kaumārī protect me in the north, the one who carries a spear in the northeast.

17. Above, O Brahmāṇī, protect me, and, O Vaiṣṇavī, below.
Just so may Cāmuṇḍā, who rides a corpse, protect the ten directions.

18. May Jayā (victory) stand in front of me, may Vijayā (triumph) stand behind,
Ajitā (the unconquered) on my left side, Aparājitā (unvanquished) on my right,

19. Let Udyotinī (lustre) guard my hair-tuft; let Umā abide on my head,

The one who wears a garland on my forehead; let the famed one protect my two eyebrows.

20. (May) the three-eyed one (stand) between my eyebrows, the one with the bell of Yama in my nose,
The one with the conch between my eyes, and the one who dwells at the threshold in my ears.

21. Let Kālikā protect my cheeks, and Śaṅkarī the base of my ears,
The sweet-smelling one my nostrils, and Carcikā my upper lip.

22. May a drop of nectar protect my lower lip, and Sarasvatī my tongue,
Kaumārī my teeth, and Caṇḍikā the middle of my neck.

23. May the one of variegated sound protect my uvula, and Mahāmāyā my palate,
Kāmākṣī my chin, and the all-auspicious one my voice.

24. (Let) Bhadrakālī (abide) in my neck, the bow-bearing one in my backbone,
The blue-throated one in my outer neck, Nalakūbarī in my esophagus.

25. May the sword-bearer protect my two shoulders, and the bearer of the thunderbolt my two arms,
The one who carries a staff my two hands, and Ambikā (abide) in my fingers.

26. May the queen with the spear protect my fingernails, the queen of nails protect my armpits.
Let the great Goddess, who destroys mental anguish, protect my two breasts.

27. Let the goddess Lalitā protect my heart, the one who carries a lance (abide) in my belly.
May Kāminī protect my navel, and the queen of secrets my private parts.

28. May the protectress of what has been born protect my penis, the one who rides a buffalo my rectum,
The blessed one my hips, Vindhyavāsinī my knees.

29. (May) she who is proclaimed to be the mighty one (protect) my shanks, Vināyakī my knee joints,
Nārasiṃhī my ankles, the one of unlimited vitality my heels.

30. (May) the bearer of fortune (protect) my toes, she who dwells down below the soles of my feet,

The one with terrible fangs my toenails, and the hair-raising one my locks.

31. (May) Kauberī (protect) my pores, and the queen of speech my skin,
Pārvatī my blood, bone-marrow, flesh-marrow, flesh, bones, and fat.

32. (May) Kālarātri (protect) my entrails, the crowned queen my bile,
The one with a lotus my fingers in lotus-calyx position, the one with a jewel in her crest my phlegm.

33. May the flame-faced one protect the lustre of my nails, the unbreakable one (abide) in all my joints.
O Brahmāṇī, protect my semen, the queen with the umbrella of royalty my shadow.

34. O you who move in *dharma*, protect my egoity, mind, and intellect,
Likewise (my five breaths), Prāṇa, Apāna, Vyāna, Samāna, and Udāna.[2]

35. Let the one with the discus always guard my fame, renown, and fortune.
May Indrāṇī protect my lineage; O Caṇḍikā, protect my cattle.

36. May Mahālakṣmī protect my sons, may Bhairavī protect my wife.
May the beneficent Vijayā, who abides everywhere, protect my lineage.

37. May the victorious, sin-destroying Goddess protect every place
That has been left unprotected, excluded from this Kavaca.

38. If one is concerned for his own wellbeing, he ought not to take a single step
Without being covered by the Kavaca; wherever (one who is protected by the Kavaca) goes,

39. There will be accomplishment of his purpose, victory, and the satisfaction of all desires.
Whatever desire he may set his heart upon, that will he certainly obtain.

40. (Such) a man will acquire unparalleled lordship over the earth.
A mortal, (but) fearless, not to be conquered in battles, he will be victorious.

41. A man who is surrounded by the Kavaca ought to be worshipped in all three worlds.

This Kavaca of the Goddess is difficult to obtain even for the gods.

42. He who would recite this Kavaca at the three intervals of the day (dawn, noon, and dusk), restrained, filled with faith,

A portion of the divine comes to be his, and he is unconquered in the three worlds.

43. He would live more than a hundred years, free from sudden or accidental death.

All (his) diseases, spider-bite, leprosy, and the like, come to an end.

44. The natural poison which is both moveable and immoveable, and also that which is unnatural,

All incantations, *mantra*s and *yantra*s in the world,

45. Those who go upon the earth, and those who go in the sky, those who are born in water, and those who are taught by another,

Those which are innate, those which are produced in one's family, Mālās, Ḍākinīs, and Śākinīs,

46. Those terrible, mighty Ḍākinīs that move through the atmosphere,

Those that possess one, spirits, demons, Yakṣas, Gandharvas, and Rākṣasas,

47. Brahmarākṣas, ghosts, Kūṣmāṇḍas, Bhairavas, and so forth,

All these perish at the sight of one in whose heart Kavaca abides.

48. (Such a man) would increasingly be honored by royalty, (for) this (Kavaca) is the greatest means of enhancing one's splendor.

He grows in fame, becoming renowned throughout the world.

49. Having first done the Kavaca, one should recite the 700-versed Caṇḍī.

For as long as the circle of the earth with its mountains, woods, and groves shall remain,

50. For so long shall (such a man's) continuity, through his sons and grandsons, remain on earth.

At his body's demise this person obtains the highest goal,

51. The eternal one, difficult of access even for the gods, because of the grace of Mahāmāyā.

Argalā: "The Stopper"

Mārkaṇḍeya said:

1. Victorious, auspicious, Kālī, Bhadrakālī, the skull-bearer,
Durgā, patience, auspicious, the supportress, Svāhā, Svadhā—hail to you!

2. O you who put Madhu and Kaiṭabha to flight, (thereby) granting a boon to Brahmā, hail to you:
Give the form/beauty (*rūpa*), give the victory, give the fame, kill the enemies.

3. O you who ordained the destruction of Mahiṣa, (thereby) granting a boon, hail to you:
Give the form, give the victory, give the fame, kill the enemies.

4. O Goddess whose feet are to be honored, Goddess who gives that which is auspicious:
Give the form, give the victory, give the fame, kill the enemies.

5. O you who killed Raktabīja, (who also) slew Caṇḍa and Muṇḍa:
Give the form, give the victory, give the fame, kill the enemies.

6. O you who are of unthinkable form and conduct, destroying all enemies:
Give the form, give the victory, give the fame, kill the enemies.

7. You grant everything to those who are bowed down with devotion; O Caṇḍikā, to me who am bowed down,
Give the form, give the victory, give the fame, kill the enemies.

8. O Caṇḍikā, who destroys the illnesses of those who are bowed down, filled with devotion to you:
Give the form, give the victory, give the fame, kill the enemies.

9. O Caṇḍikā, to those who constantly praise you here because of their devotion,
Give the form, give the victory, give the fame, kill the enemies.

10. Give good fortune, give good health, O Goddess, (give) the highest happiness:
Give the form, give the victory, give the fame, kill the enemies.

11. Ordain the destruction of enemies, ordain (in me) the utmost strength:

Give the form, give the victory, give the fame, kill the enemies.

12. Ordain what is auspicious, O Goddess, ordain vast wealth:
Give the form, give the victory, give the fame, kill the enemies.

13. Make people wise, famous, and rich:
Give the form, give the victory, give the fame, kill the enemies.

14. O Caṇḍikā, who vanquishes the pride of mighty demons, to me who am bowed down,
Give the form, give the victory, give the fame, kill the enemies.

15. O four-armed one, praised by the four-faced (Brahmā), O highest queen:
Give the form, give the victory, give the fame, kill the enemies.

16. O you who also are praised by Krishna with constant devotion, O Ambikā:
Give the form, give the victory, give the fame, kill the enemies.

17. O you who are praised by the husband of Himālaya's daughter (Śiva), O highest queen:
Give the form, give the victory, give the fame, kill the enemies.

18. O you whose feet are rubbed by the crest-jewels of gods and demons, O Ambikā:
Give the form, give the victory, give the fame, kill the enemies.

19. O you who are genuinely honored by Indrāṇī's lord, O highest queen:
Give the form, give the victory, give the fame, kill the enemies.

20. O Goddess who shatters the haughtiness of demons with your fearsome long arm:
Give the form, give the victory, give the fame, kill the enemies.

21. O Goddess Ambikā, who grants boundless bliss to those devoted to you:
Give the form, give the victory, give the fame, kill the enemies.

22. Grant me a wife, pleasing to the mind, who follows my inclinations,
Born of a good family, who helps in crossing this difficult ocean of existence.

23. Having recited this hymn, a man should then recite the great hymn,
Well-fashioned in verses, seven hundred in number; (then) he obtains (all) good things.

Kīlaka: "The Bolt"

The seer said:

1. Hail to the god whose body is pure knowledge, whose heavenly eyes are the three Vedas,
Who is the cause of acquiring what is best, who wears the half-moon.

2. One should understand everything about this foremost bolt of *mantras*.
He who is constantly intent upon repeating it attains prosperity.

3. All ritual undertakings—ruining an adversary and the like—are successful.
For those who offer praise with this hymn, the Goddess succeeds by the mere recitation (of it).

4. There is nothing, neither *mantra* nor medicine (that is not effective).
Everything—ruining an adversary and the like—should work even without recitation (of this hymn).

5. All actions will succeed; having created this uncertainty (about the relationship between recitation of this hymn and other ritual action),
Śiva ordained that all action should be successful,

6. And he made the hymn to Caṇḍikā (the *Devī-Māhātmya*) a secret.
There is no end to its merit, (so) he suitably (made) a restraint.

7. Concentrating on the eighth and fourteenth days of the dark fortnight of the moon,
He doubtless obtains every prosperity.

8. He gives (everything to the Goddess), he receives (it back from her); only in this way is she pleased.
Having such a form, (as if) with a bolt was it (the merit of reciting the hymn to Caṇḍikā) fastened back.

9. He who always recites this (Caṇḍī) expansively, having removed the restraint upon it,
He is a perfected one, he a demigod, born in delight even as a Gandharva.

10. Even when he wanders about, there is no danger for him anywhere.
He never falls victim to accidental death, and when dead, he ought to attain *mokṣa*.

11. Having known (of these restraints), having begun (to remove them), one should undertake ritual action; without action, one perishes.
Knowing thus, this fulfilment is undertaken by the wise.

12. Whatever qualities are seen to exist among women-folk, having a long-lived husband, and the like,
All that is by her grace; this auspicious hymn is to be recited.

13. Even when this hymn is recited softly, its utter success
Is resounding: therefore it is to be commenced.

14. Why should she not be praised by the populace since it is by her grace
That lordship, auspiciousness, health, success, destruction of enemies, and the highest *mokṣa* come to pass?

The Ṛg Vedic Rātrī Sūkta

We saw in chapter 5 that the material that has gathered around the *Devī-Māhātmya* often has two hymns serving as a kind of buffer at each end of the core text, standing between that text and the preceding and succeeding *aṅga*s. We also saw that there is widespread agreement that the two hymns are known as the Rātri and Devī Sūktas, but disagreement as to whether this refers to hymns within the *Devī-Māhātmya* or to two Vedic hymns with these names, *Ṛg Veda* 10.127 and 10.125. In order to represent fairly this range of interpretative possibilities, I here provide translation of the Vedic hymns, following the text of Max Müller.[3]

1. The goddess Rātrī (night) approaches, illuminating manifold places with her eyes:
She has put on all her glories.

2. The immortal goddess has filled up the broad expanse, the heights and depths;
With (her own) light, she drives out the darkness (*tamas*).

3. The goddess approaches, replacing her sister Uṣas (dawn).
May this darkness also disappear.

4. (May you stand) by us now, at whose coming we go to rest,
Like birds to their nest in a tree.

5. To rest have gone the villagers, as have all legged and winged creatures,
Even the greedy hawks.

6. Ward off the she-wolf and the wolf, ward off the thief, O Rātrī,
And be easy for us to get through.

7. Distinctly has the plastering black darkness come unto me.
O Dawn, may you collect (it) like a debt!

8. Accept, O daughter of heaven, what I have presented you as if (it were a herd of) cattle,
(Namely,) this hymn, (presented) as if to a conqueror, O Rātrī.

The Ṛg Vedic Devī Sūkta

1. I go about with the Rudras, with the Vasus, I with the Adityas, and with the All-gods.
I support both Mitra and Varuṇa, I both Indra and Agni, I the two Aśvins.

2. I support the impetuous Soma, and I Tvaṣṭṛ, Pūṣan (and) Bhaga.
I grant wealth to the skillful sacrificer who offers oblations, who presses the Soma.

3. I am the queen, who brings treasures together, wise, foremost of those worthy of worship.
The gods have put me in many places, variously abiding, of manifold presence.

4. Through me a man eats food: He who sees, who breathes, who hears what is spoken (does so through me).
Unknowing, they depend on me. Hear, O famous one—I am telling you (something) worthy of faith.

5. I myself proclaim this (state of affairs) that is approved by gods and men.
Whomsoever I wish I make mighty, a Brahman, a seer, a sage.

6. I draw the bow for Rudra, so his arrow may slay the foe of sacred speech.
I stir up quarrels among people; I pervade heaven and earth.

7. On the summit of this world, I give birth to the father; my origin is in the waters, in the ocean.
Thence I spread through all the worlds, and I touch yonder sky with my summit.

8. I blow forth like the wind, grasping all worlds.
Beyond heaven, beyond this earth, in (my) greatness such have I become.

Prādhānika Rahasya: "The Secret Pertaining to Primordial Matters"

The king said:

1. Blessed one, I have been told about the *avatāras* of Caṇḍikā by you.
Can you, O Brahman, tell me about their material nature (*prakṛti*), their primary form (*pradhāna*)?

2. O twice-born one, properly tell me, reverent before you, everything about the Goddess's very own form (*svarūpa*),
The one that is to be worshipped by me according to established pattern.

The seer said:

3. This is the highest secret. It is said that it ought not to be uttered.
But you are a man of devotion: There is nothing I cannot tell you, O best of men.

4. The foremost of all is Mahālakṣmī, constituted of the three qualities (*triguṇā*), the supreme queen.
Her very own form is both with and without characteristic marks (*lakṣyālakṣyasvarūpā*); she abides, having pervaded everything.

5. She carries a citron, club, shield, and drinking vessel.
O king, on her head she wears a snake, *liṅga*, and *yoni*.

6. She shines with the color of burned gold, with ornaments of the same golden hue.
She filled up all the emptiness with her splendor.

7. Having seen the void that was this whole world, the supreme queen
Took on another form, by means of pure *tamas*.

8. She became a woman, with wide eyes and slender waist,
Shining like cut collyrium, her fair face featuring sharp fangs.

9. Her four arms were graced with sword, blood-drinking vessel, skull, and shield,

And she wore a necklace of headless trunks, with a garland of heads around her neck.

10. Mahālakṣmī then spoke to the tamasic one, foremost of sensuous women:
"I give to you the names (and) the deeds that you will do:

11. Mahāmāyā, Mahākālī, Mahāmārī, hunger, thirst,
Sleep, hankering, the lonely warrior, Kālarātri, hard-to-surpass,

12. These are your names, to be explained by your actions.
He who, knowing your actions through them, dwells upon them, he attains happiness."

13. Having spoken to her thus, O king, Mahālakṣmī took on another of her own forms (*svarūpa*),
With the exceptionally pure quality known as *sattva*, having the lustre of the moon.

14. Carrying a garland of beads and a goad, with a *vīṇa* and book in her hand,
She became an excellent woman; to her she (then) gave names:

15. "Mahāvidyā, one of great voice, Bhāratī, Vāc, Sarasvatī,
Āryā, Brahmī, the great (nurturing) cow, womb of the Veda, queen of the gods."

16. Then Mahālakṣmī spoke to Mahākālī and Mahāsarasvatī:
"You two goddesses produce twins, with forms like your own."

17. On speaking thus, Mahālakṣmī herself then produced twins,
A man and a woman, seated on a lotus and shining, born of the golden womb.

18. The mother then called the male Brahmā, the support, Viriñca, creator,
And the woman she called Śrī, Padmā, Kamalā, Lakṣmī.

19. Mahākālī and (Mahā)sarasvatī gave birth to twins.
I tell you now of their forms and names.

20. Mahākālī produced a blue-throated, red-armed, white-limbed, moon-crested
Man, and a white woman.

21. He is Rudra, Śaṅkara, the pillar, with matted hair and three eyes.
The woman is Trayī (the three Vedas), knowledge, the wish granting cow, the letters of speech, sound (itself).

22. (Mahā)sarasvatī, O king, produced a golden woman and a blue-black man.
Their names, too, I tell you (now):

23. Viṣṇu, Krishna, Hṛṣikeśa, Vāsudeva, Janārdana (are his),
Umā, Gaurī, Satī, Caṇḍī, Sundarī, Subhagā, Śivā (are hers).

24. Thus did the two young females instantly partake of maleness (*puruṣatva*).
Those who have eyes see this, but other people do not know it.

25. Then, O king, Mahālakṣmī gave Trayī (Sarasvatī) to Brahmā as a wife,
To Rudra (she gave) Gaurī, to Vāsudeva Śrī.

26. Uniting with Sarasvatī, Brahmā produced an egg;
The mighty, blessed Rudra, together with Gaurī, broke it open.

27. In the middle of the egg, O king, appeared the constituent elements, *pradhāna* and the others,
The entire moving and unmoving universe, which consists of the gross elements.

28. Viṣṇu, together with Lakṣmī, nourished (and) protected it.
So indeed is Mahālakṣmī the mother, O king, the queen of all rulers.

29. She is both formless and possessed of form, carrying various designations:
She can be described by other names, but by no other name (can she be fully described).

Vaikṛtika Rahasya: "The Secret Pertaining to Subsequent Modifications"

The seer said:

1. The goddess who is said to be threefold, possessing the three *guṇas*, Tāmasī, Sāttvikī,
She is called Śarvā, Caṇḍikā, Durgā, Bhadrā, Bhagavatī.

2. She who is said to be the Yoganidrā of Viṣṇu, whose *guṇa* is *tamas*,
She is the one whom the lotus-seated Brahmā praised in order to slay Madhu and Kaiṭabha.

3. She has ten faces, ten arms, ten feet, with the lustre of collyrium,
Shining abroad, as if garlanded, with her thirty eyes.

4. O king, even though she is of dreadful form, with teeth and fangs aglitter,
She is the foundation of (all) form, of auspiciousness, of beauty, of the great Śrī (herself).

5. She is armed with sword, arrow, mace, spear, conch, discus, and *bhuśuṇḍi*;
She carries an iron bar, bow, and a skull dripping with blood.

6. She is the *māyā* of Viṣṇu, Mahākālī, who is hard to surpass;
When propitiated, she makes the worshipper master over all that does and does not move.

7. She who appeared with unimaginable lustre from the bodies of all the gods,
She is Mahālakṣmī, possessed of the three *guṇa*s, who slew Mahiṣa in front of their very eyes.

8. Her face is white, her arms blue, her breasts very white,
Her waist red, likewise her feet, her buttocks and thighs blue, a (true) delight.

9. Her lap is of many colors, and she wears variegated garlands and garments.
She is smeared with assorted unguents, endowed with beauty, form, and auspiciousness.

10. Although she has a thousand arms, she is to be worshipped in eighteen-armed form.
Here her weapons are set forth, beginning in the lower right (hand):

11. Garland of beads, lotus, arrow, sword, thunderbolt, and club,
Discus, trident, axe, conch, bell, and noose,

12. Spear, staff, shield, bow, drinking-vessel, and waterjar.
The one whose arms are graced with these weapons, seated on a lotus,

13. The queen who consists of all the gods, O king, this Mahālakṣmī,
Her should one worship: then one becomes lord over all gods and worlds.

14. She who was born from the body of Gaurī, depending on the single *guṇa* of *sattva*,
She is said to be Sarasvatī in bodily form, slayer of the demon Śumbha.

15. With her eight arms, O king, she carries arrow, pestle, spear and discus,
Conch, bell, ploughshare, and bow.

16. When worshipped with devotion, she grants knowledge of everything.
She is the goddess who is the crusher of Niśumbha, the destroyer of the demon Śumbha.

17. Thus have been declared to you, O king, the essential forms (*svarūpa*) of (the Goddess's) appearances (*mūrti*).
Listen (now) to how the worship of the separate forms of the mother of the universe is done.

18. When Mahālakṣmī is to be worshipped, Mahākālī and Sarasvatī
Are to be worshipped on her right and left, with the three couples in the rear.

19. Brahmā and Sarasvatī are in the middle, Rudra and Gaurī to their right,
Viṣṇu and Lakṣmī to their left, with the three goddesses in front.

20. (In the front row) the eighteen-armed form is in the middle, with the ten-faced one on the left-hand side,
The eight-armed one on the right: Lakṣmī should be worshipped as the primary deity.

21. When this eighteen-armed form is to be worshipped, O best of men,
Along with the ten-faced and the eight-armed forms, then on the right and left

22. Time (*kāla*) and death (*mṛtyu*) are to be worshipped, in order to remove all opposition.
When the eight-armed slayer of the demon Śumbha is to be worshipped,

23. Then the nine *śakti*s are to be worshipped, likewise Rudra and Vināyaka.
One should worship Mahālakṣmī with the hymnic verses that contain the phrase *namo devyai* ("hail to the Goddess . . .").[4]

24. In the worship of the three incarnations (*avatāra*s), the *mantra*s of the (respective) hymns should be employed.
This eighteen-armed slayer of Mahiṣa is to be worshipped (as foremost).

25. She is called Mahālakṣmī, Mahākālī, Sarasvatī,
The queen over virtue and wickedness, the great ruler over all worlds.

26. One who worships her as the slayer of Mahiṣa becomes master of the universe.
One should worship Caṇḍikā, who is affectionate toward her devotees, as the supportress of the universe.

27. With oblations and the like, ornaments, fragrances, and uncrushed flowers,
With perfumes and lamps, along with assorted edible offerings of food,

28. With an offering smeared with blood, with flesh, with wine, O king,
With salutations, rinsing the mouth with water, with sweet-smelling sandalwood,

29. With offerings of camphor and betelnut, and devotion filling one's very core,
One should—in front of the goddess, on the left-hand side—worship the great demon with his head cut off,

30. Mahiṣa, who has been absorbed into the goddess-queen.[5]
In front on the right, one should worship the lion, who is the entirety of *dharma*, the mighty one,

31. The vehicle of the goddess by whom all that does and does not move is supported.
A wise man should do this devoutly, with mind single-pointedly on her.

32. With folded hands he should praise her with these (three) episodes (*carita*s),
Or with the middle one alone, but not with either of the other two episodes by itself.

33. One who is reciting should not recite half an episode: this would create a weakpoint (*chidra*) in the recitation.
Offering praises while circumambulating the deity, with hands folded on the head,

34. One should unflaggingly beg forgiveness of the supportress of the universe over and over again.
At every verse one should make offering of milk, sesamum, and ghee.

35. Alternatively one should offer auspicious oblation to Caṇḍikā with hymnic verses.

Well-composed, one should worship the Goddess with the "hail, hail" verses.[6]

36. One should be restrained, with reverent gesture, humble, sunk deeply within oneself, and bowing in obeisance
To queen Caṇḍikā for a long time: One should become filled with her (*tanmayaḥ*).

37. The one who thus worships the supreme queen with devotion daily,
Having enjoyed whatever desires he may have, such a one attains to union with the Goddess.

38. One who does not always worship this Caṇḍikā, who is fond of her devotees,
His merits does the supreme queen burn up, reducing them to ashes.

39. Therefore, O king, worship the great queen of all the worlds,
Caṇḍikā, in the way that has been prescribed: you will attain (every) happiness.

Mūrti Rahasya: "The Secret Pertaining to Forms"

The seer said:

1. The goddess who will be born of Nanda, named Bhagavatī Nandā,[7]
She, when worshipped and honored with devotion, makes the three worlds subservient (to her devotee).

2. Her brilliance is that of the finest gold, with golden garments of the highest lustre.
This goddess shines with the color of gold, with magnificent golden ornaments.

3. Her four arms are adorned with lotus, goad, noose, and conch.
She is Indirā, Kamalā, Lakṣmī, Śrī, seated on a golden lotus.

4. The goddess who was declared by me to be named "Red-tooth",[8]
Her own-form will I proclaim to you: Listen, for it destroys all dangers!

5. She wears a red garment, her color is red, all her bodily ornaments are red.
Her weapons are red, her eyes red, her hair red—truly terrifying!

6. With sharp red nails, red teeth, red tusks,

This goddess will be as attached to the person who is devoted to her as is a wife to her husband.

7. She is broad like the earth, with a pair of breasts like Mount Meru,
Long, pendulent, massive, exceedingly attractive.

8. Those firm, beautiful breasts are oceans of utter bliss:
She causes her devotees to suckle at those breasts that satisfy every desire.

9. She carries a sword, drinking vessel, pestle, and plow.
This goddess is known as "red Camuṇḍā" and "queen of *yoga*."

10. By this one the entire universe is pervaded, both what moves and what is stable.
The one who worships her with devotion completely fills this universe.

11. The one who constantly reads, studies, and learns this hymn pertaining to Raktadantikā's form,
On him does the goddess attend, as a young maiden does her beloved.

12. Śākaṃbharī[9] is of blue color, with eyes like a blue lotus,
A deep navel, her slender waist adorned with three narrow ripples of skin.

13. Her breasts are firm, even, erect, round, plump, and fully developed.
Dwelling in a lotus, (she carries) a fistful of arrows, a lotus,

14. A cornucopia of edibles, flowers, sprouts, roots and the like, with abundant fruits,
Endowed with an infinity of tastes for whatever is desired, taking away hunger, thirst, death and old age.

15. The supreme queen also carries a bow of radiant beauty.
Śākaṃbharī is renowned as "the one of a hundred eyes"; she is "Durgā."[10]

16. Free from woe, subduer of the wicked, allaying all difficulty and danger,
She is Umā, Gaurī, Satī, Caṇḍī, Kalikā, Pārvatī.

17. Singing hymns to Śākaṃbharī, meditating on her, uttering prayers, doing worship, reverencing her,
One speedily obtains the unblemished fruit of food, drink, and immortality.

18. The fearsome (*bhimā*)[11] goddess is of blue color, with shining tusks and teeth,

A woman with wide eyes, and round, plump breasts.

19. She carries a glittering sword, a drum, and a bowl fashioned from a human skull.

She is called the solitary warrior, Kālarātri, hymned as the one who grants desires.

20. The queen-bee (*bhrāmarī*)[12] is at the center of an unassailable circle of light, her form of variegated brilliance,

A goddess anointed with various unguents, wearing different kinds of jewels.

21. With many-colored bees in her hand, she is sung of as "the great pestilence."[13]

In this way are these forms of the Goddess explained, O king,

22. Forms of Caṇḍikā, mother of the universe, famous for satisfying every desire.

This is the supreme secret (*rahasya*), not to be told by you to anyone.

23. You yourself ought to learn this explanation of heavenly forms by heart, with attentiveness.

In this way, making every effort you should utter prayers to the Goddess without ceasing.

24. By means of reciting the *mantras* one is released from all sins,

Even those as terrible as Brahman-killing, acquired over seven lifetimes.

25. Meditation on the Goddess is proclaimed by me to be the greatest secret of all.

By exerting yourself in this way, you will be granted the fruit of your every desire.

Notes

Preface

1. Arthur Waley, *Three Ways of Thought in Ancient China* (London: George Allen and Unwin, 1939), 32-33.

2. My account of this debate follows the recent popular version of Robert Darnton, reported in his "Toward a History of Reading," *Princeton Alumni Weekly* 87 (April 8, 1987):19-24, 32. The incident concerning the Hampshire woman appears in David Cressy, "Books as Totems in Seventeenth Century England and New England," *Journal of Library History, Philosophy, and Comparative Literature* 21 (Winter 1986):99, along with other memorable episodes. I am grateful to Professor Darnton for this reference.

Chapter 1—Introduction

1. Thomas B. Coburn, *Devī-Māhātmya: The Crystallization of the Goddess Tradition*, (Delhi and Columbia, MO: Motilal Banarsidass and South Asia Books, 1984, 1988).

2. I have discussed the editions and translations of the *Devī-Māhātmya* in my earlier volume (hereafter abbreviated *Crystallization*), 51-52; see also the Bibliography of that volume. The importance of paying attention to historical factors, and to historical process, is the third of my interests that has determined the shape of this study; to it I shall return below. The most recent complete translation by a native Anglophone is that of F. E. Pargiter, whose translation of the *Mārkaṇḍeya Purāṇa*, in which the *Devī-Māhātmya* is sometimes included, appeared in 1904. My remark on the importance of being a native speaker of English in order to effect a good, contemporary translation is not intended to disparage the translations of Agrawala (*The Glorification of the Great Goddess*,

[Varanasi: All-India Kashiraj Trust, 1963]) and Jagadīśvarānanda (*The Devī-Māhātmyam or Śrī Durgā-Saptaśatī*, [Madras: Sri Ramakrishna Math, 1969]) on stylistic grounds, though they do leave a good deal to be desired. The problem, rather, is that these, and virtually all other translations by those who stand within the tradition, rely on later commentaries or other interpretative materials in translating the text. This is a very important matter, to which I shall return shortly.

3. For a wide-ranging, but less than systematic, exploration of these roots, see Marshall McLuhan, *The Gutenberg Galaxy: The Making of Typographic Man* (Toronto: University of Toronto Press, 1962). For a more orderly discussion and bibliography, see Walter J. Ong, *Orality and Literacy: The Technologizing of the Word* (London and New York: Methuen and Co., 1982), the several works of William A. Graham and the other items cited at note 6 below.

4. James Barr, *Holy Scripture: Canon, Authority, Criticism* (Philadelphia: Westminster Press, 1983), 57.

5. J. F. Staal, "The Concept of Scripture in the Indian Tradition," in Mark Juergensmeyer and N. Gerald Barrier (eds.), *Sikh Studies: Comparative Perspectives on a Changing Tradition* (Berkeley: Berkeley Religious Studies Series, 1979), 122-123. Staal is here quoting *Aitareya Āraṇyaka* 5.5.3.

6. Worthy of note, however, are some of the areas where this movement is apparent. Within Biblical studies, there is the emerging field of "canonical criticism," associated with the work of James Barr (*Holy Scripture: Canon, Authority, Criticism*; *The Scope and Authority of the Bible* [Philadelphia: Fortress Press, 1980], Brevard S. Childs (*Introduction to the Old Testament as Scripture* [Philadelphia: Fortress Press, 1979]; *The New Testament as Canon: An Introduction* [Philadelphia: Fortress Press, 1984]; *Old Testament Theology in a Canonical Context* [Philadelphia: Fortress Press, 1985]), and James A. Sanders (*Canon and Community: A Guide to Canonical Criticism* [Philadelphia: Fortress Press, 1984]; *Torah and Canon* [Philadelphia: Fortress Press, 1972]; *From Sacred Story to Sacred Text: Canon as Paradigm* [Philadelphia: Fortress Press, 1987]). Of related interest is the January 1985 issue of *Theology Today*, in which are raised a number of important issues regarding the relationship between anthropology and theology. Anthropologists who are raising these kinds of questions include Ruth Finnegan (*Oral Poetry: Its Nature, Significance and Social Context* [Cambridge: Cambridge University Press, 1977]) and Jack Goody ([ed.], *Literacy in Traditional Societies* [Cambridge: Cambridge University Press, 1968]; *The Domestication of the Savage Mind* [Cambridge: Cambridge University Press, 1977]). A recent book by George Bond (*"The Word of the Buddha": The Tipitaka and Its Interpretation* [Columbo, Sri Lanka: M. D. Gunasena and Co., 1982]) bears mention, as does William A. Graham's extremely important *Beyond the Written Word: Oral Aspects of Scripture in the History of Religion* (New York: Cambridge University Press, 1987). See also Graham's contributions to Richard A. Martin (ed.), *Approaches to Islam in Religious Studies* (University of Arizona Press: Tucson,

1985) and to *Die Welt des Islams* (Spring 1984). We should also note Elizabeth L. Eisenstein, *The Printing Press as an Agent of Change: Communications and Cultural Transformations in Early-Modern Europe*, Two vols. (Cambridge: Cambridge University Press, 1980) and Brian Stock, *The Implications of Literacy: Written Language and Models of Interpretation in the Eleventh and Twelfth Centuries* (Princeton: Princeton University Press, 1983). A recent volume that is more descriptive than analytical is Frederick M. Denny and Rodney L. Taylor (eds.), *The Holy Book in Comparative Perspective* (Columbia: University of South Carolina Press, 1985). A stimulating, though selective, treatment of the issues is Wendy Doniger O'Flaherty (ed.), *The Critical Study of Sacred Texts* (Berkeley: Berkeley Religious Studies Series, 1979). For a wide-ranging analysis of the issues, with explicit attention to comparative concerns, see Miriam Levering (ed.), *Rethinking Scripture: Essays from a Comparative Perspective* (Albany: State University of New York Press, 1989). Though not solely responsible for launching this revolution, the single most important article is probably Wilfred Cantwell Smith, "The Study of Religion and the Study of the Bible," *Journal of the American Academy of Religion* 39 (1971):131-140. The best contemporary account of the issues is William A. Graham, "Scripture," in Mircea Eliade (ed.), *The Encyclopedia of Religion* (New York: Macmillan, 1986) 13: 133-145.

7. *The Destiny of the Veda in India*, trans. by Dev Raj Chandra (Delhi, Patna, Varanasi: Motilal Banarsidass, 1965), 218.

8. Ibid., 25, 23.

9. *Crystallization*, 63-65, 68-69, 73, 82n, 84-85.

10. To pursue the comparison and contrast one step further, we should note the provocative remark of J. F. Staal regarding the role of the reciter (*śrotriya*, master of *śruti*, sacred sounds transmitted through hearing): "The *śrotriya* who recites without understanding should not be compared with a clergyman preaching from the pulpit, but rather with a medieval monk copying and illuminating manuscripts, and to some extent with all those who are connected with book production in modern society." *Nambudiri Veda Recitation* ('s-Gravenhage: Mouton and Co., 1961), 17.

11. Failure to undertake the second half of this goal would be to produce an unwitting, and only mildly interesting, form of cultural autobiography. It would constitute a subtle continuation of the imperialistic tradition which assumes that our values (in this case, regarding the significance of written documents) are, or ought to be, universal.

12. Jean Piaget, *Structuralism*, trans. and ed. by Chaninah Maschler (New York, et al.: Harper and Row, 1970), 5-16.

13. Claude Lévi-Strauss, "The Structural Study of Myth," *Journal of American Folklore* 67 (1955):428-444, often reprinted remains the virtual charter for the structural analysis of myth. For a clear and succinct introduction to

Lévi-Strauss's work, see Edmund Leach, *Claude Lévi-Strauss*, rev. ed., (New York: Viking Press, 1976).

14. A partial listing of the contributions of these individuals would include the following. For Madeleine Biardeau: *Études de Mythologie Hindoue*, vol. 1 (Paris: École Française d'Extrême Orient, 1981); *L'Hindouisme: Anthropologie d'une Civilisation* (Paris: Flammarion, 1981); and Charles Malamoud, *Le Sacrifice dans l'Inde Ancienne*, 1st ed. (Paris: Presses Universitaires de France, 1976.) For Veena Das: *Structure and Cognition: Aspects of Hindu Caste and Ritual*, 2d ed. (New York: Oxford University Press, 1982). For Alf Hiltebeitel: *The Ritual of Battle: Krishna in the Mahābhārata* (Ithaca: Cornell University Press, 1976); "The Two Kṛṣṇas on One Chariot: Upaniṣadic Imagery and Epic Mythology," *History of Religions* 24 (1984):1-26; "Śiva, the Goddess and the Disguises of the Pāṇḍavas and Draupadī," *History of Religions* #20 (1980): 147-174. For Stella Kramrisch: *The Presence of Śiva* (Princeton: Princeton University Press, 1981). For Wendy Doniger O'Flaherty: *Dreams, Illusion and Other Realities* (Chicago: University of Chicago Press, 1984); *The Origins of Evil in Hindu Mythology* (Berkeley: University of California Press, 1977); *Śiva, the Erotic Ascetic* (New York, et al.: Oxford University Press, 1981); *Women, Androgynes, and Other Mythical Beasts* (Chicago: University of Chicago Press, 1980). For Hans Penner: "Creating a Brahman: A Structural Approach to Religion," in Robert D. Baird (ed.), *Methodological Issues in Religious Studies* (Chico: New Horizons Press, 1985), 49-66; "Structure and Religion," *History of Religions* 25 (1985):236-254. For David Shulman: *Tamil Temple Myths: Sacrifice and Divine Marriage in the South Indian Śaiva Tradition* (Princeton: Princeton University Press, 1980).

15. By "epics" I mean, of course, the *Mahābhārata* and the *Rāmāyaṇa*, both of which have been critically edited and are in the process of appearing in English translation. By "Purāṇas" I mean those encyclopedic accounts of popular Hindu traditions as they found their way into Sanskrit between roughly the fourth and fifteenth centuries C.E. Precise definition and delimitation of "Purāṇa" is a difficult matter. The best recent summation and statement of the problem that the Purāṇas have posed for Western scholarship is Ludo Rocher, *The Purāṇas* (Wiesbaden: Otto Harrassowitz, 1986). See also my "The Study of the Purāṇas and the Study of Religion," *Religious Studies* 16 (1980):341-352.

16. See Piaget, *Structuralism*, 136-143 for a fine discussion of this matter.

17. Jacob Neusner, *Method and Meaning in Ancient Judaism III* (Chico: Scholars Press, 1981), 233-234.

18. I have explored some of the issues involved in the historical study of the Purāṇas further in "The Study of the Purāṇas and the Study of Religion" (esp. 350-351). There have been a number of other efforts to provide historical leverage on Purāṇic materials, of which we may cite Paul Hacker's classic, "Prahlāda, Werden und Wandlungen einer Idealsgestalt," *Akademie der Wissenschaften und der Literatur Abhandlungen der Geistes- und Sozial-wissenschaft-*

lichen Klasse (1959 #9):517-663 and (1959 #13):889-993 and Clifford Hospital's recent *The Righteous Demon: A Study of Bali* (Vancouver: University of British Columbia Press, 1984).

19. *Crystallization*, 51-69.

20. Theodore Aufrecht, *Catalogus Catalogorum: An Alphabetical Register of Sanskrit Works and Authors* (Leipzig: F. A. Brockhaus, 1891-1903); Maurice Winternitz, *A History of Indian Literature*, trans. by Mrs. S. Ketkar, Vol. I (New York: Russell and Russell, 1971), 565n.

21. Giorgio Bonazzoli, "Composition, Transmission and Recitation of the Purāṇas," *Purāṇa* 25 #2 (July 1983):275.

22. Correspondingly, one suspects that close study of the form and content of the commentaries on the *Bhāgavata Purāṇa* would illuminate further the place of "writtenness" in Hindu devotion, as well as (more obviously) the worship of Krishna. An important first step in this direction has been taken by James Redington, *Vallabhācārya on the Love Games of Kṛṣṇa* (Delhi, Varanasi, Patna: Motilal Banarsidass, 1983).

23. This formulation is that of Harry M. Buck. For discussion, see my "'Scripture' in India: Towards a Typology of the Word in Hindu Life," *Journal of the American Academy of Religion* 52 (1984): 454.

24. This point will be further elaborated in Part II. I make this argument with full awareness that Veena Das has offered the intriguing view that the delimitation of any text is arbitrary and that, in order to understand the *Devī-Māhātmya*, one should look for parallels between its structure and those of contemporary healing rituals, where demons are constantly obtaining and losing bodily form ("Integrating Texts and Fieldwork," Paper presented at the annual meeting of the American Academy of Religion, New York, Dec. 21, 1982). She has also been instrumental in bringing to publication a wonderfully rich series of essays that explore with new sophistication the complexity of what is meant by "texts" and by "reading" them: originally appearing in *Contributions to Indian Sociology* 19 #1 (1985), they have recently been published, with a new epilogue, as Veena Das (ed.), *The Word and the World: Fantasy, Symbol and Record* (New Delhi, London, Beverley Hills: Sage Publications, 1986). Such studies make clear the great variety of methods that are germane to the study of texts and contexts, and the appropriateness of a healthy symbiosis between structural and historical approaches.

25. This is one of the concerns of the Biblical scholars cited earlier: James Barr, Brevard S. Childs, James A. Sanders. See also the previously cited article of W. C. Smith, "The Study of Religion and the Study of the Bible."

26. The fact that such a venture runs counter to certain tendencies in the intellectual movement known as deconstructionism makes it, to my mind, all the more interesting. As noted at the beginning of this chapter, it is not my

intent here to debate issues in hermeneutics, but simply to report the results of historical research. If those results ramify for others' theoretical concerns, then so be it.

Chapter 2—The Historical Setting

1. Daniel H. H. Ingalls, Foreword to my *Crystallization*, viii.

2. I draw these items from Sir John Marshall (ed.), *Mohenjo-Daro and the Indus Civilization*, 3 vols. (London: Arthur Probsthain, 1931) and E. J. H. MacKay, *Further Excavations at Mohenjo-Daro*, 2 vols. (Delhi: Government of India Press, 1938). For an instance of how diverse the interpretation of this material can be, compare the minimalist stance of David Kinsley in the appendix ("The Indus Valley Civilization") to his recent volume on *Hindu Goddesses: Visions of the Divine Feminine in the Hindu Religious Tradition* (Berkeley, et al.: University of California Press, 1986), 212-220 with the provocative (and, to my mind, more persuasive) reinterpretation offered by Alf Hiltebeitel and Thomas J. Hopkins in Mircea Eliade (ed.), *The Encyclopedia of Religion* (New York: Macmillan, 1986) 7:215-223, s.v. "Indus Valley Religion."

3. Hiltebeitel and Hopkins, "Indus Valley Religion", 222.

4. Daniel H. H. Ingalls, Foreword to Cheever Mackenzie Brown, *God as Mother: A Feminine Theology in India* (Hartford, VT: Claude Stark and Co., 1974), xiii.

5. Kinsley, *Hindu Goddesses*, 7.

6. Ibid., 17, 18.

7. Thomas J. Hopkins, *The Hindu Religious Tradition* (Encino and Belmont, CA: Dickenson Publishing Co., 1971).

8. C. Mackenzie Brown, *God as Mother*, xv.

9. Rehearsal of the evidence substantiating this assertion is one of the major concerns of my *Crystallization*. At a minimum we might say that the goddess hymns found in the *Mahābhārata* and *Harivaṃśa* (admittedly in the critical apparatus, rather than in the constituted text) are "preliminary" in a conceptual, if not strictly chronological, sense. I also strongly suspect that some of them are older than the *Devī-Māhātmya*.

10. I.e., *Crystallization*.

11. The interpretation here is based on my own reflection on a variety of sources, including the papers presented at the Conference on the Purāṇas held at the University of Wisconsin (Madison) in August 1985. It is clearly congruent with a major, recent synoptic account of the Purāṇas' status: Cornelia Dimmitt and J. A. B. van Buitenen (ed. and tr.), *Classical Hindu Mythology:*

A Reader in the Sanskrit Purāṇas (Philadelphia: Temple University Press, 1978). See also *Crystallization*, 19-50, and the many detailed views discussed by Rocher, *The Purāṇas*, 104-131.

12. J. A. B. van Buitenen, "On the Archaism of the *Bhāgavata Purāṇa*," in Milton Singer (ed.), *Krishna: Myths, Rites and Attitudes* (Honolulu: East-West Center, 1966), 35-36.

13. Ibid., 34.

14. I say "virtually" every word attests to her primordiality, because a few of the *Devī-Māhātmya*'s favored names of the Goddess—for example, Caṇḍikā, Cāmuṇḍā—occur in Sanskrit for the first time in this text. This, of course, is consistent with the view that the impetus toward worshipping her comes from outside Aryan circles. For further discussion of "Sanskritization" and bibliography, see my *Crystallization*, 9-19.

15. The material presented in this section is drawn primarily from Part I of my *Crystallization*, q.v. for detailed citation of primary texts.

16. Jan Gonda, *Aspects of Early Vishnuism* (Utrecht: N. V. A. Oosthoeck's Uitgever's Mij, 1954), 213. For further discussion of Śrī and Lakṣmī, see ibid., 176-212 and 212-225, also Kinsley, *Hindu Goddesses*, 19-34, and my *Crystallization*, 157-160, 166-169.

17. We may note here that our text explicitly *avoids* understanding the god-*śakti* relationship as merely that of consort or spouse, for each *śakti* is far more fundamental, more integral to the god's identity and aptitude. For detailed consideration of how this is apparent in the text's use of the word *aindrī*, see my *Crystallization*, 132-133.

18. The basis for this assertion is that stylistically and theologically they are much simpler than the *Devī-Māhātmya*. I have translated these and other early hymns bearing on the history of the Goddess in my *Crystallization*, Part III.

19. See Kinsley, *Hindu Goddesses*, chapters 3 and 8.

20. For fuller discussion of the Mothers, see Appendix A (313-330) of my *Crystallization*; Kinsley, *Hindu Goddesses*, 151-160; and the definitive treatment of J. N. Tiwari in his 1971 dissertation at the Australian National University, "Studies in the Goddess Cults in Northern India, with Special Reference to the First Seven Centuries A.D.," which has recently been published under the title *Goddess Cults in Ancient India* (Delhi: Sundeep Prakashan, 1985).

21. Tiwari, "Studies," 177.

22. Ibid., 184.

23. Ibid., 184, 183, 185.

24. The material presented in this section is drawn primarily from my *Crystallization*, Part II.

25. There is an exception to this enumeration, on which see my *Crystallization*, 51n; see also our discussion of Bhāskararāya's text below in chapter 6.

26. See my *Crystallization*, 27-28, 28n, 37, 123, 123n.

27. It is worth noting that the orientation of this myth is so definitively toward Viṣṇu that the later tradition continues to view it as such, the reinterpretation by the *Devī-Māhātmya* notwithstanding. As we are about to see, it is the *Devī-Māhātmya* version of the Mahiṣa myth, with its more equivocal earlier history, that is more definitive of the Goddess's identity in subsequent understanding.

28. *Mahābhārata* 3.213-221.

29. *The Mahābhārata*, trans. by J. A. B. van Buitenen (Chicago: University of Chicago Press, 1975), 2:206.

30. This interpretation of the evidence, presented in M. Seshadri, "Mahiṣāsuramardinī: Images, Iconography and Interpretation," *Journal of the Mysore University*, N. S., Section A-Arts, Vol. 22 (1963):1-28 + 42 plates, has recently been reaffirmed and pushed much further by Heinrich von Stietencron, "Die Göttin Durgā Mahiṣāsuramardinī: Mythos, Darstellung und geschichtliche Rolle bei der Hinduisierung Indiens", in *Visible Religion*, Annual for Religious Iconography, Volume II: Representations of Gods (Leiden: E. J. Brill, 1983), 118-166. Stietencron's article is the best historical study of the central mythology of the Goddess that has appeared to date. Based on a careful sifting of Purāṇic acounts of the Goddess-Mahiṣa myth, which are then correlated with evolving iconographic representations, it presents an elegant ordering of very complicated material, and also raises some important methodological issues. We shall return to Stietencron's work, and to these issues, in chapter 4.

31. *Crystallization*, 241.

32. *Bhagavad Gītā* 4.6-8.

33. "The Portrait of the Goddess in the *Devī-Māhātmya*," *Journal of the American Academy of Religion* 46 (1978):489-506.

34. *The Laws of Manu* 7.3-5, 10-11, trans. by Georg Bühler (New York: Dover Publications, 1969). Mackenzie Brown has called my attention to another similar passage at *Mahābhārata* 3.99.9-11, where Indra, grown fainthearted in his struggle with Vṛtra, is revived by an infusion of *tejas*, first from Viṣṇu, then from other gods. While this is clearly different from "creation" at the hands of the gods, the parallel use of *tejas*, particularly in the context of divine protection, is striking.

35. Though our interest here is in the specific background to the *Devī-*

Māhātmya's textual testimony regarding the worship of the Goddess, it is worth noting that this interplay of female deity and masculine secular authority may prove to be one of the important continuities in Indian religion: It is in evidence as early as the Indus Valley civilization (Hiltebeitel and Hopkins, "Indus Valley Religion," 222), appears here in the conceptual convergence of Manu and the *Devī-Māhātmya*, and seems to have been one of the decisive factors in the growth of the cult of a buffalo-killing Goddess from local to pan-Indian scope between the ninth and sixteenth centuries (Stietencron, "Die Göttin Durgā," 137). On this theme, see the essays in Madeleine Biardeau (ed.), *Autour de la Déesse Hindoue* (Paris: Éditions de l'École des Hautes Études de l'Inde et de l'Asie du Sud, 1981), *Puruṣārtha* 5; also the work of J. C. Heesterman, for example, *The Inner Conflict of Tradition: Essays in Indian Ritual, Kingship and Society* (Chicago and London: University of Chicago Press, 1985).

36. For further discussion, see Charlotte Vaudeville, "Krishna Gopāla, Rādhā, and the Great Goddess," in John Stratton Hawley and Donna Marie Wulff (eds.), *The Divine Consort: Rādhā and the Goddesses of India* (Berkeley: Berkeley Religious Studies Series, 1982), 1-12, also my *Crystallization*, 230-241.

37. See my *Crystallization*, 267-275 for a review of the textual testimony and translation of these two hymns. For the principles according to which the critical edition of the *Mahābhārata* has been constituted, see V. S. Sukthankar's "Prolegomenon" to *The Mahābhārata*, Vishnu S. Sukthankar and others (eds.), Bhandarkar Oriental Research Institute (Poona), vol. I (1933).

38. For translation of these other early hymns, see my *Crystallization*, 267-289; for comment on this recurrent motif of the Goddess as redemptress, see *Crystallization*, 304-305.

39. Śaṅkara, *Bhagavadgītābhāṣya* (Bombay: Ānandāśrama Sanskrit Series, 1936), Upodghāṭa 3-5, cited in J. A. B. van Buitenen, *The Bhagavadgītā in the Mahābhārata* (Chicago and London: University of Chicago Press, 1981), 10.

40. This interpretation is also supported by the larger argument of Madeleine Biardeau on the place of the Goddess in the Hindu tradition in her *L'Hindouisme: Anthropologie d'Une Civilisation*. See, in particular, her remarks on the linkage of the Goddess to Viṣṇu in the *Devī-Māhātmya* by virtue of the name "Nārāyaṇī" and the shared notions of *avatāra*, the warrior deity, and the divine defender of the sociocosmic order:143-144. The entire section entitled "Amours Divines" (135-171) is exceedingly rich for understanding the place of the Goddess in Indian religion. For further interpretation that builds on Biardeau, see Alf Hiltebeitel, *The Cult of Draupadī I. Mythologies: From Gingee to Kurukṣetra* (Chicago and London: University of Chicago Press, 1988), 55-56, 281, 363. The tradition of enumerating the verses of the *Devī-Māhātmya* at 700 is a matter to which we shall return later.

Chapter 3: The Text in Translation

1. For a review of the basic issues in this debate, see my "The Study of the Purāṇas and the Study of Religion." The individual who has recently had the most to say on this matter is Giorgio Bonazzoli, whose views grow out of working on the critical editions published by the All-India Kashiraj Trust and have been published in *Purāṇa* journal. See, in addition to the item cited at chapter 1, note 21, the following: "Schemes in the Purāṇas," 24 #1 (January 1982):146-189; "The Colophons in the Critically Edited Purāṇas," 24 #2 (July 1982):353-383; "Remarks on the Nature of the Purāṇas," 25 #1 (January 1983):77-113; "Some Observations on the Variant Readings in the Purāṇic Texts and Their Imports for Critical Editions," 26 #2 (July 1984):113-133; "Considerations on a New Method of Critically Editing the Purāṇas," 27 #2 (July 1985):381-434.

2. See my *Crystallization*, 226-7n for one significant editorial puzzle that should be resolved by the critical edition.

3. *Durgā-saptaśatī saptaṭīkā-samvalitā*, ed. by Harikṛṣṇaśarma (Bombay: Veṅkateśvara Press, 1916, and Delhi and Baroda: Buṭālā and Company, 1984). Actually this edition has only six commentaries on the *Devī-Māhātmya* proper, those of Bhāskararāya, Caturdharī, Śantanu, Nāgoji Bhaṭṭa (Nāgeśa), Jagaccandracandrikā, and Daṃśoddhāra. The seventh commentary, that of Durgāpradīpa, accompanies (along with that of Bhāskararāya) only the *aṅgas*, or liturgical "limbs," of the text. It is also my sense that, while popular versions of the *Devī-Māhātmya* abound, contemporary devotees with an intellectual bent are using the Buṭālā edition as standard. I am confirmed in this impression by Douglas R. Brooks, based on his recent studies of Śrī Vidyā in South India (personal communication).

4. The text might thus be compared, perhaps, to the letters of Paul in the Christian New Testament. They are intrinsically powerful and of enormous consequence theologically and otherwise, but are for the most part stylistically undistinguished.

5. More technically, a formula is "a group of words which is regularly employed under the same metrical conditions to express a given essential idea": Albert B. Lord, *The Singer of Tales* (Cambridge: Harvard University Press, 1960), 4, quoting Milman Parry.

6. The discussion is lucidly presented, with bibliography, in Ong, *Orality and Literacy.*

7. See the critique of Ong, and the rich presentation of Purāṇic evidence, provided in C. Mackenzie Brown, "Purāṇa as Scripture: From Sound to Image of the Holy Word in the Hindu Tradition," *History of Religions* 26 #1 (August 1986):68-86.

8. *Saptaśatī*, [with the Sanskrit and Gujarati commentaries of] Mahāmahopādhyaya Śrīhathībhai Śāstrījī, ed. by A. N. Jani (Baroda: Śrīsamavibhya Press, 1972 [first ed., 1934]). The alternative to this edition would have been the very well-known Gītā Press (Gorakhpur, n.d.) edition, with Hindi translation. The differences between the two are slight: they always agree on the number of verses in each chapter, though they divide them in slightly different ways. I have preferred the Śāstrījī edition because it so often reflects Bhāskararāya's judgment.

9. Mārkaṇḍeya is the chief narrator of the *Mārkaṇḍeya Purāṇa* in the chapters before and after the *Devī-Māhātmya*, as well as in the *Devī-Māhātmya* itself, providing instruction throughout to his disciple, Krauṣṭuki. Nonetheless, it is the sage, Medhas, who is the effective narrator of the text beginning with 1.34. Mārkaṇḍeya only reappears as narrator in the last chapter, although an occasional vocative (e.g., 1.27) reminds us that Krauṣṭuki remains the intended recipient of this discourse. Such "nesting" of a story within a story, like a Chinese box, is typical of Purāṇic structure, though not all instances are as satisfyingly symmetrical as is the case here.

10. In the *varṇa* theory of caste, the upper three castes are referred to as "twice-born" because, in addition to their biological birth, they are allowed access to the Veda, which is understood as a second, initiatory kind of birth.

11. The convention of describing the universe as "three-tiered," or "consisting of three worlds," can refer to the distinctions between heaven, atmosphere, and earth, or between heaven, earth, and nether region. For a convenient introduction to Purāṇic cosmology, see Dimmitt and van Buitenen, *Classical Hindu Mythology*, 24-29.

12. Yogānidrā is here personified as the Goddess. The verb *bhaj* has a rich range of meanings, from "resorted to" and "was engaged in" to "worshipped" (whence the noun *bhakti*). See glossary.

13. The notion is that there are three "instants" in the utterance of any syllable: beginning, middle, and end.

14. The notion of a primary matter that consists of three qualities or strands (*guṇa*s) is formally a conceptualization of the Sāṃkhya school of Indian philosophy, but in popular forms it is pervasive of epic and Purāṇic thinking. The basic distinction it affirms is between *sattva, rajas*, and *tamas*, which are, respectively, thought, movement, and obstruction, or intelligence-stuff, energy-stuff, and mass-stuff. Surendranatha Dasgupta, *A History of Indian Philosophy* (Cambridge: University Press, 1932) I: 242, 244. We shall see below, in chapter 5, that the *aṅga*s make a good deal of this distinction in interpreting the *Devī-Māhātmya.*

15. This half-verse is placed in parentheses in our edition as an indication that it is not attested by all commentators. It is also lacking in the Gītā Press edition. Similar annotation occurs elsewhere below.

16. This particular metamorphosis of the demon may be difficult to visualize. It consists of an attempted transformation from buffalo-form to human-form, with the latter emerging from the buffalo's mouth. However, as we are about to see, before he can fully emerge, the Goddess, placing her foot on the buffalo's throat, decapitates the human-form. For discussion and examples, see von Steintencron, "Die Göttin Durgā," 134-136 and accompanying plates.

17. The references here are to various subdivisions of the Vedic literary corpus.

18. The precise relationship between the forms of the Goddess at this juncture is admittedly puzzling. I have argued elsewhere (*Crystallization*, 99-100; and see 100n) that our text is less interested in establishing precise relationships than in glorying in the Goddess's metamorphic potential. As we shall see in chapter 6, commentators view this particular passage as problematical and deal with it in different ways. Although the *aṅga*s do not address this passage specifically, the three Rahasyas may be understood as another kind of effort at systematic understanding of the many forms of the Goddess.

19. Both the Śāstrījī and Gītā Press editions reverse the order of 10.24 and 10.25 as given in the Harikṛṣṇaśarma edition.

20. As we shall see in chapter 5, the Mūrti Rahasya expresses interest in the forms of the Goddess that our text enumerates at this juncture. I here provide the Sanskrit characterizations in parentheses since they are the basis for some of the Rahasya's elaboration.

21. Since the primary concern of our next four chapters will be—What do people *do* with the *Devī-Māhātmya*?—we should note that here in chapter 12 our text itself provides the beginnings of an answer. To facilitate our subsequent discussion, I here provide parenthetically the Sanskrit original, and sometimes a very literal translation.

22. Note that the seer here returns to the starting point of his discourse in the first chapter—see 1.47-48.

23. What is meant by the *Devī-Sūkta* is a matter on which there are different opinions, as we shall see in chapter 5.

24. The repetition of the last quarter-verse to signal the end of a composition is a common practice in Indian texts.

Chapter 4: The Legacy of a Text

1. Graham, *Beyond the Written Word*. The first half of Graham's important book explores the large issues of (and assumptions about) written and spoken words, and written and spoken scripture. The second half then looks at particular instances in the Islamic and Christian traditions.

2. Ibid., 41, 29.

3. I make such a statement for the sake of the argument that is developed in this and the following paragraph, not because I presume to resolve the complex matter of whether the Purāṇas are initially oral or written phenomena (on which, see the works of Bonazzoli cited above, chapter 3, note 1 and C. Mackenzie Brown, "Purāṇa as Scripture"). That contemporary conversational English needs refinement on these matters is apparent in the ease with which even educated speakers confuse the words "verbal" and "oral," as in the statement, "I gave so-and-so verbal instructions." Virtually *all* instructions are "verbal," insofar as they use words. The salient distinction, often unwittingly lost, is whether those instructions are spoken (oral), or written.

4. This phrase—*sāvarṇiḥ sūryatanayo yo manuḥ kathyate 'ṣṭamaḥ*—happens to be the first half-verse of the first chapter of our text, but any brief phrase, of virtually any derivation, would suffice to make my point here.

5. The classic study of bardic composition, much discussed and debated, is Lord, *The Singer of Tales*.

6. The examples here come from my own reflection on a variety of materials, with a conscious indebtedness to Georges Gusdorf, *Speaking* (*La Parole*), trans. by Paul T. Brockelman (Evanston: Northwestern University Press, 1965).

7. The typology that I propose here has been presented in somewhat different form in my "'Scripture' in India," 451-455.

8. See Ong, *Orality and Literacy*, and C. Mackenzie Brown's ("Purāṇa as Scripture") critique of Ong.

9. Stietencron, "Die Göttin Durgā."

10. Hacker, "Prahlāda"; Frank Whaling, *The Rise of the Religious Significance of Rāma* (Delhi: Motilal Banarsidass, 1980); Hospital, *The Righteous Demon*.

11. Hiltebeitel, *The Cult of Draupadī*. See chapter 2, note 40.

12. Ibid., xvii.

13. Ibid., 135.

14. Cp. Hiltebeitel, *The Cult of Draupadī*, 79 and *Devī-Māhātmya* (DM) 3.28-32.

15. Hiltebeitel, *The Cult of Draupadī*, 176.

16. Cp. Hiltebeitel, 278, 434 and DM 2.31.

17. Cp. Hiltebeitel 61, 298, 368 and DM 5.42-76.

18. Cp. Hiltebeitel 301, 351, 363 and DM 8.39-62.

19. Hiltebeitel, 307; see DM 7.4-21, 8.52-59.

20. Hiltebeitel, 317-319; cp. DM 13.9.

21. Hiltebeitel, 390-391; cp. DM 2.9ff.

22. "Die Göttin Durgā."

23. Ibid., 119-127. For important further consideration of the relation between the Goddess, Mahiṣa, and Śiva, see Shulman, *Tamil Temple Myths*, esp. 176-192.

24. Stietencron, "Die Göttin Durgā," 127-136.

25. Ibid., 137-140.

26. For a stimulating instance of this new awareness, see Joyce Irwin (ed.), *Sacred Sound: Music in Religious Thought and Practice* (Chico: Scholars Press, 1983).

Chapter 5: Encounter with the Text I

1. This nice way of describing the spatial relationship between the text and its *aṅga*s is that of J. N. Tiwari, "An Interesting Variant in the *Devī-Māhātmya*," *Purāṇa* 25 #2 (July 1983):236n.

2. The following description is based on examination of several dozen versions of our text. It does not necessarily correspond with any one version, and there are differences of opinion about some of the details. I suppose, therefore, that it is a kind of structural analysis of the *form*, rather than the content, of the text and the apparatus of its reception. It may be subsequently refined in light of Cynthia A. Humes' doctoral dissertation, currently in progress, of which I shall say more in chapter 7.

3. E.g., *Mārkaṇḍeya Purāṇa* (Bombay: Veṅkateśvara Press, 1910). For (incomplete) bibliography on the Purāṇa, see Chintaharan Chakravarti, "The Mārkaṇḍeya Purāṇa: Editions and Translations," *Purāṇa* 3 #1 (Jan. 1961), 38-45.

4. The Veṅkateśvara Press edition translated in chapter 3 includes such references, along with another common feature: the provision of names for each of the chapters, based on the events occurring there.

5. See *Kātyāyana's Sarvānukramaṇī of the Rigveda*, ed. by A. A. Macdonell (Oxford: Clarendon Press, 1886).

6. The concern that the three preliminary *aṅga*s show for protection and security is more apparent in the extended connotation of *argalā:* It is the small bolt, placed vertically at the bottom edge of a door, which keeps the door in place, either open or shut, by sliding into a hole in the floor. I am indebted to A. N. Jani for this interpretation.

7. Pratapaditya Pal, "Early Paintings of the Goddess in Nepal" in Deborah Candace Brown (ed.), *Ars Orientalis XII* (Ann Arbor: Center for Chinese and Japanese Studies, University of Michigan, 1981), 41-48 + 7 plates. This article establishes a correspondence between the illuminations in a fourteenth century manuscript and the content of the *aṅga*s.

8. *Saptaśatīsarvasvam*, ed. by Dviveda Sarayūprasādaśarma, 2d ed. (Lucknow: Yutamunśīnavalakiśora, 1899), 12.

9. See Pal, "Early Paintings," 43, 47. In a more positive vein, however, Pal's work, like Stietencron's, enables us to get some historical leverage on our material by juxtaposing textual and visual media. If the *aṅga*s are germane to the interpretation of fourteenth century paintings that deal with the subject matter of the *Devī-Māhātmya*, then they may be dated back to at least that time (passim).

10. Though some individuals offered very specific interpretations on particular points, I have here tried to adopt a general, and more phenomenological, stance. I will acknowledge variations in interpretation, here and in subsequent chapters, when it seems appropriate.

11. Lawrence Babb, *The Divine Hierarchy: Popular Hinduism in Central India* (New York and London: Columbia University Press, 1975), 31. Babb is not here speaking in general terms, but of the Chhattisgarh region of India. Nonetheless, recent work in ritual studies (e.g., Ronald L. Grimes, *Beginnings in Ritual Studies* [Lanham, New York, London: University Press of America, 1982]; Jonathan Z. Smith, *To Take Place: Toward Theory in Ritual* [Chicago and London: University of Chicago Press, 1987]) suggests a good case can be made for understanding this phrase generically.

12. This conjectural account is that of Tiwari, "An Interesting Variant in the *Devī-Māhātmya*," 243-244n.

13. 12.3, 12.6, 12.7, 12.11, 12.13, 12.14, 12.18, 12.19, 13.1.

14. *Devī Purāṇa*, ed. by P. D. Maṇḍanamiśra and D. Puṣpendrakumāra-śarmā (Śāntiniketan and New Delhi: Śrī Lālabahāduraśāstrīkendrīya Saṃskṛta-vidyāpiṭha, 1976), 91.37ff; see also 95.66. While dating Purāṇic passages is notoriously difficult, the *Devī Purāṇa* appears to have been compiled within a century or two of the *Devī-Māhātmya*. See R. C. Hazra, "The Devī-Purāṇa," *New Indian Antiquary* 5 (April 1942), 2-20 and Manabendu Banerjee, "Devī-purāṇa on Indian Art," *Purāṇa* 26 #1 (Jan. 1984):11-12. The *Nīlamata Purāṇa* is cited by Pal, "Early Paintings," 47 as: Ved Kumari, *The Nīlamata Purāṇa* (Srinagar, Jammu, 1968), 164.

15. Cf. C. Mackenzie Brown, "Purāṇa as Scripture," passim.

16. For further discussion, see my *Crystallization*, 19-50.

17. The phrase is the title of a section in Bonazzoli, "Remarks on the Nature

of the Purāṇas," 93-101. Note that two of the words he there discusses, *kavaca* and *rahasya*, appear in the titles of the *aṅga*s of the *Devī-Māhātmya*.

18. See Jagadiśvarānanda, *Devī-Māhātmya*, also *Śrī Śrī Chaṇḍī*, trans. by Swami Tattwananda (Calcutta: Nirmalendu Bikash Sen, n.d.) and *Śrī Durgā Saptaśatī*, [ed. by] Śrī Sivadatta Miśra Sāstrī (Vārāṇasī: Ṭhākur Prasād, 1975).

19. Jan Gonda, *Vedic Literature* (Wiesbaden: Otto Harrassowitz, 1977), 34.

20. See my *Crystallization*, appendix A.

21. The nine Durgās are one of the popular, numerous, and ill-defined categories of divine manifestation in Śākta and Tantric sources. See Sanjukta Gupta, Dirk Jan Hoens, Teun Goudriaan, *Hindu Tantrism* (Leiden/Köln: E. J. Brill, 1979), 65 and Pushpendra Kumar [Sarma], *Śakti Cult in Ancient India* (Varanasi: Bhartiya Publishing House, 1974), 231-233.

22. Teun Goudriaan and Sanjukta Gupta, *Hindu Tantric and Śākta Literature* (Wiesbaden: Otto Harrassowitz, 1981), 1.

23. See Agehananda Bharati, *The Tantric Tradition* (Garden City: Doubleday, 1965), 112 and Gupta, Hoens, and Goudriaan, *Hindu Tantrism*, 136-138.

24. See note 6 above.

25. Teun Goudriaan, *Māyā Divine and Human* (Delhi, Varanasi, Patna: Motilal Banarsidass, 1978), 77.

26. As we shall see in the next two chapters, there is an interesting parallel between this episode and the explanation that A. N. Jani offers of the historical process by which the *Devī-Māhātmya* came to acquire the name *Saptaśatī*.

27. In our discussion of this verse, Ambika Datta Upādhyāya observed that all *mantra*s, Ṛg Vedic and other, have placed over them a curse which renders their recitation ineffective until it is removed with a *kīlaka*, a sort of "counter-curse." An appropriate *kīlaka* exists for every *mantra*. The episode that appears here in the Kīlaka is clearly similar, but the restraint is placed on the *mantra* that is the *Saptaśatī* not as a curse, but to contain its overwhelming power.

28. This is the opinion of the well-known Sanskritist, A. N. Jani, expressed in conversation, August 1987. Jani is one of the individuals whose views we will consider in greater detail in chapter 7.

29. As with the preliminary *aṅga*s, I here provide summary and analysis of the textual material, with complete translations appearing in the appendix.

30. See 1.59 and our note on that verse.

31. A. N. Jani, "The Concept of Trinity in the Śākta Philosophy," *Journal of the Maharaja Sayajirao University of Baroda* (Humanities Number) 25-26 (1976-77):43. I have corrected one typographical error in this quotation.

32. Anticipating our discussion in the next chapter, we may note that Bhāskararāya equates Mahālakṣmī with *para brahman.*

33. *Darśan: Seeing the Divine Image in India* (Chambersburg: Anima Books, 1981).

34. Ibid., 15, 1, and passim.

35. To expect otherwise is to fall prey either to our just noticed Western bias or to the Advaitin view—often presented as normative Hinduism—that the supreme form of the ultimate is *nirguṇa brahman*, Brahman devoid of qualities. Such studies as John B. Carman, *The Theology of Rāmānuja* (New York and London: Yale University Press, 1974) present an important alternative view.

36. I here use as translation for the respective *guṇa*s the language of Dasgupta, cited in chapter 3, note 14.

37. This account is closely paralleled by *Lakṣmī Tantra* 5.8-17, where it forms part of a much more extensive, eclectic Pāñcarātra cosmology. See *Lakṣmī-Tantra: A Pāñcarātra Āgama*, ed. by Pandit V. Krishnamacharya (Madras: The Adyar Library and Research Centre, 1975) and *Lakṣmī Tantra: A Pāñcarātra Text*, trans. and notes by Sanjukta Gupta (Leiden: E. J. Brill, 1972). We shall see more of the *Lakṣmī Tantra* in chapter 6, for it is quoted by both Bhāskararāya and Nāgoji Bhaṭṭa.

38. As we shall see, the commentators distinguish between these two senses of Mahālakṣmī by calling the former *vyaṣṭi* and the latter *samaṣṭi.*

39. Figure 5.3 is adapted from the version of the *Devī-Māhātmya* edited by A. N. Jani, *Saptaśatī*, 45,to which we shall return later.

40. It is not clear whether the instructions here are given from the perspective of the devotee or that of the chief deity in the tableau. Unless we say the text blatantly contradicts itself, both perspectives are found in the Vaikṛtika: cp. verses 18 and 20. My interpretation accords with the configuration of the *yantra* (figure 5.3) to which *pūjā* is offered during recitation of the *Saptaśatī* and to which we shall return in our next two chapters.

41. See Tiwari, "An Interesting Variant in the *Devī-Māhātmya*," which explores an alternative reading of 10.4. The variant produces the translation, "Thereupon, all the goddesses . . . became absorbed into the Goddess's breasts . . . ," which Tiwari suggests reflects Bengali emphasis on the maternal aspect of the Goddess.

Chapter 6: Encounter with the Text II

1. Robert Hueckstadt has suggested (personal conversation, 1981) that this tendency may be understood as a particular instance of the general (deconstructionist) point I shall make below, namely, that each commentator brings an individual point of view to the commentarial task. But then we must go a step further: Since anyone who composed in Sanskrit had necessarily been steeped in the intricacies of Pāṇinian grammar, it is inevitable that each would evince a Pāṇinian concern with such things as syntax and etymology regardless of which text was being commented upon. For a vivid account of classical grammatical training, see Daniel H. H. Ingalls, "The Brahman Tradition" in Milton Singer (ed.), *Traditional India: Structure and Change* (Philadelphia: The American Folklore Society, 1959), 3-9.

2. See Emery Boose and Gary Tubb, "Handbook designed to aid students in the use of Sanskrit commentaries", draft manuscript, 1981, here citing the *Nyāya-kośa.*

3. I say "virtually" because we know there is some pre-Sāyaṇa precedent for commentary on the *Ṛg Veda:* see Renou, *The Destiny of the Veda*, 23. For reflection on the significance of this very late date for Sāyaṇa's *magnum opus*, see my "'Scripture' in India", 454-455.

4. For a study of one of the devotional commentaries on the *Bhāgavata*, see Redington, *Vallabhācārya.* On the distribution of Purāṇic commentaries, see chapter one, note 21.

5. I have here supplemented my own list with terms noted by Jeffrey Timm in his "Vallabha's Commentary (?) on the Bhagavad Gītā", Paper presented at the annual meeting of the American Academy of Religion, November 19, 1988.

6. See chapter 3, note 3 for specification of the commentaries included in this edition.

7. Biardeau, *L'Hindouisme*, 22, my translation. This argument is consistent with—is indeed the mirror image of—her contention that "it is necessary to abolish the epistemological dualism between 'armchair scholars' and field-workers," idem.

8. V. S. Sukthankar, *Critical Studies in the Mahābhārata* (Poona: V. S. Sukthankar Memorial Edition Committee, 1944), 264. Sukthankar's remarks occur in an essay entitled "Notes on Mahābhārata Commentators," but they apply comparably well to the commentators on the *Devī-Māhātmya.*

9. Which concern the respective merits of structural and historical approaches to the study of popular Hinduism, on which see my "The Study of the Purāṇas and the Study of Religion."

10. Bhāskararāya, *Varivasyā-Rahasya and its Commentary Prakāśa by Śrī Bhāskararāya Makhin*, ed. and trans. Pandit S. Subrahmanya Sastri (Adyar: Adyar Library and Research Centre, 1976), xvii, xxi.

11. Goudriaan and Gupta, *Hindu Tantric*, 169n.

12. Bhāskararāya, *Varivasyā-Rahasya*, xx; Goudriaan and Gupta, *Hindu Tantric*, 169n.

13. Bhāskararāya, *Varivasyā-Rahasya*, xvii-xviii.

14. Douglas Renfrew Brooks, *The Secret of the Three Cities: An Introduction to Hindu Śākta Tantrism through Bhāskararāya's Commentary on the Tripurā Upaniṣad* (Chicago and London: University of Chicago Press, forthcoming), draft manuscript, vi.

15. See Bhāskararāya, *Varivasyā-Rahasya*, xxi-xxv; Goudriaan and Gupta, *Hindu Tantric*, 169-170; also *Lalitā-Sahasranāman, with Bhāskararāya's Commentary*, trans. by R. Ananthakrishna Sastry (Adyar: The Theosophical Publishing House, 1976), viii-x, and Kanti Chandra Pandey, *Abhinavagupta: An Historical and Philosophical Study* (Varanasi: Chowkhamba Sanskrit Series Office, 2d ed., 1963), 583-590.

16. See Bhāskararāya, *Varivasyā-Rahasya*, xix-xxiv.

17. "The Śrīvidyā School of Śākta Tantrism: A Study of the Texts and Contexts of the Living Traditions in South India" (Ph.D. diss., Harvard University, 1987) and Brooks, *The Secret of the Three Cities.*

18. André Padoux, "Tantrism", in Mircea Eliade (ed.), *The Encyclopedia of Religion* (New York: Macmillan, 1986) 14:273, my italics.

19. André Padoux, "Hindu Tantrism," in Mircea Eliade (ed.), *The Encyclopedia of Religion* (New York: Macmillan, 1986) 14:274-275.

20. Gupta, Hoens, and Goudriaan, *Hindu Tantrism*, 7-9.

21. Brooks, *The Secret of the Three Cities*, draft ms., 122. Brooks takes this observation as the point of departure for a fine, lengthy discussion of "Tantric" as a "polythetic," rather than "monothetic," classification, with ten "descriptive points" that distill and develop the items enumerated by Goudriaan.

22. There is, of course, Buddhist and Jain Tantra, as well as Hindu, and the label "Tantric" applies to aspects of Chinese and Japanese religious life, as well as Indian.

23. Gupta, Hoens, and Goudriaan, *Hindu Tantrism*, 7.

24. Ibid., 6, quoting E. A. Payne, *The Śāktas* (Calcutta: Y.M.C.A. Publishing House and London: Oxford University Press, 1933), 72. For an extended discussion of the terms "Śāktism" and "Tantrism," see Brooks, *The Secret of the Three Cities*, draft ms., 112-165.

25. Goudriaan and Gupta, *Hindu Tantric*, 58.

26. Brooks, *The Secret of the Three Cities*, draft ms., 112-113.

27. Gupta, Hoens, and Goudriaan, *Hindu Tantrism*, 50.

28. Brooks, *The Secret of the Three Cities*, draft ms., 171.

29. For a picture of such an image, see the frontispiece to Brooks, *The Secret of the Three Cities*.

30. Harvey P. Alper (ed.), *Understanding Mantras* (Albany: State University of New York Press, 1989), 5, 4. This remarkable collection of essays is highly recommended for its rich exploration of the phenomenon of *mantra*. It is the natural sequel, one generation later, to Jan Gonda's classic study, "The Indian Mantra," *Oriens* 18 (1963):248-301.

31. It may appear odd to employ the neuter "Brahman" of the Upaniṣads and Vedānta here in discussing a Śākta tradition, but, as we shall see shortly, there is a striking and intentional convergence between the two.

32. This exceedingly truncated discussion may be supplemented by Brooks, *The Secret of the Three Cities*, draft ms., 244-253 and the still more extended discussion in his "The Śrīvidyā School of Śākta Tantrism," 201-268.

33. Brooks, *The Secret of the Three Cities*, draft ms., 230.

34. Ibid., draft ms., 226, 225, 233. See 225-236 passim, also Brooks, "The Śrīvidyā School of Śākta Tantrism," 269-334, and Goudriaan and Gupta, *Hindu Tantric*, 58-59.

35. For example, the Śāktas do not even merit mention in the otherwise inclusive survey (including Buddhists) that Mādhava offers in his *Sarva-darśana-saṃgraha*. On the non-confrontational nature of Śrīvidyā, see Brooks, "The Śrīvidyā School of Śākta Tantrism," 57.

36. My discussion here is indebted to the wonderfully lucid account in Eliot Deutsch, *Advaita Vedānta: A Philosophical Reconstruction* (Honolulu: University of Hawaii Press, 1969), 27-45.

37. Ibid., 37-38.

38. Ibid., 41.

39. See Brooks, *The Secret of the Three Cities*, draft ms., 204. Bhāskararāya's sense that Śaṅkara is a kindred spirit is, in part, a function of his broader sense that Śrīvidyā is a direct continuation of Vedic tradition: see Bhāskararāya, *Varivasyā-Rahasya*, x-xvi, xxv-xxvi; Goudriaan and Gupta, *Hindu Tantric*, 19. For an excellent discussion of the relation between "Veda" and "Tantra," see Brooks, *The Secret of the Three Cities*, draft ms., chapter One.

40. Recalling that Sāṃkhya starts from two primary principles—*puruṣa* and *prakṛti*—we might then attempt an aphoristic comparison of Indian views

of being and knowing. Sāṃkhya presents an ontological dualism, and so is able to affirm a single epistemology. Advaita affirms an ontological monism, but the price it pays is epistemological dualism. Śrīvidyā, too, affirms a monistic ontology, but relies on the esoteric, ritualized transformation of the material world in order to avoid epistemological dualism. See Goudriaan and Gupta, *Hindu Tantric*, 49, 51-52.

41. Brooks, *The Secret of the Three Cities*, draft ms., 195-196.

42. Ibid., 210ff.

43. Ibid., 209. More fully: "From a Śākta Tantric perspective,... the goddess is undifferentiated Brahman as well as the self-conscious result of Brahman's differentiation. The goddess then is ultimately, like Brahman itself, neuter in gender or rather genderless. At the same time, she is a divine being who assumes all three genders: neuter, masculine, and feminine."

44. P. V. Kane, *History of Dharmaśāstra* (*Ancient and Medieval Religious and Civil Law*) (Poona: Bhandarkar Oriental Research Institute, 1930-62), I:405-406, 965.

45. Ibid., I:963.

46. J. N. Farquhar, *An Outline of the Religious Literature of India* (Delhi, Patna, Varanasi: Motilal Banarsidass, 1967), 369; Haridas Bhattacharyya, "Yoga Psychology," in Haridas Bhattacharyya (ed.), *The Cultural Heritage of India* (Calcutta: The Ramakrishna Mission Institute of Culture, 1953), III:69n; Kane, *History of Dharmaśāstra*, I:963-964.

47. Ingalls, "The Brahman Tradition," 5.

48. Ibid., 8.

49. This was in conversation with Ram Shankar Bhattacharya, December 11, 1981. He identified the passage he was referring to as Nāgoji Bhaṭṭa's commentary on the *Vaiyākaraṇa-siddhānta-laghu-mañjūṣā*, in the section entitled *bauddhārtha-nirūpaṇam*, in the long section on *sphoṭa*, beginning *atha eva striyām iti sūtre* and ending *ity alaṃ prasaktānuprasaktyā*.

50. Again, as above, see Deutsch, *Advaita Vedānta*, esp. chapter 3.

51. Wilfred Cantwell Smith, *Questions of Religious Truth* (New York: Charles Scribner's Sons, 1967), 49-50.

52. As indication of how Bhāskararāya's attention is distributed across the text, the following percentage of the verses in each chapter on which he offers comment is instructive: chapter 1:45 percent; 2:35 percent; 3:29 percent; 4:58 percent; 5:62 percent; 6:30 percent; 7:16 percent; 8:29 percent; 9:31 percent; 10:25 percent; 11:45 percent; 12:48 percent; 13:41 percent.

53. Goudriaan sees the idea of *dialogue* as providing an important thread of continuity in Tantric phenomena. The texts known as Tantras consist of

conversations between deity and consort; the teaching they promulgate is considered to be "a reflection of the Supreme—still unseparated from Its Śakti—on Itself;" and this reflection is itself "the prototype of the guru-disciple relation." Gupta, Hoens, and Goudriaan, *Hindu Tantrism*, 13.

54. Brooks, "The Śrīvidyā School of Śākta Tantrism," 115.

55. Cf. Harikṛṣṇaśarma ed., 8-9 and 39-40.

56. *The Saundaryalaharī or Flood of Beauty*, trans. and ed. by W. Norman Brown (Cambridge: Harvard University Press, 1958), 6.

57. *The Rāmāyaṇa: An Epic of Ancient India*, intro. and trans. by Robert Goldman (Princeton: Princeton University Press, 1984), I.1.4.

58. *The Veda of the Black Yajus School, entitled Taittirīya Saṅhitā*, trans. by Arthur Berriedale Keith (Cambridge: Harvard University Press, 1914), IV.5.1.

59. Bhāskararāya, *Varivasyā-Rahasya*, xxvi-xxvii. This quotation from the editor's Introduction to the *Varivasyā-Rahasya* effectively summarizes Bhāskararāya's point here in his commentary. On Appayya Dīkṣita, see J. Gonda, *Medieval Religious Literature in Sanskrit* (Wiesbaden: Otto Harrassowitz, 1977), 263; Dasgupta, *A History of Indian Philosophy*, V:65ff.; also M. Krishnamachariar, *History of Classical Sanskrit Literature* (Madras: Tirumalai-Tirupati Devasthanams Press, 1937), 225-228.

60. Also *Bṛhadāraṇyaka Upaniṣad* 1.2.6, 1.2.7, 1.4.17, *Taittirīya Upaniṣad* 2.6.1.

61. Also *Taittirīya Upaniṣad* 2.6.1. The Upaniṣadic phrase here (*tapo 'tapyata, tapas taptvā*) is similar to Bhāskararāya's (*tat tapo 'kuruta*), while in the two previously cited instances the phrases are identical.

62. See Sarvepalli Radhakrishnan and Charles A. Moore (eds.), *A Source Book in Indian Philosophy* (Princeton: Princeton University Press, 1957), 487.

63. *brahmaiva cetyatām gacchatīva.*

64. This is an exceedingly complex topic, touching as it does on Tantric speculation on sound, the origin of *mantras*, and the like. For a concise introduction to the issues, see Gupta, Hoens, and Goudriaan, *Hindu Tantrism*, 90-99. For extended discussion, see André Padoux, *Recherches sur la Symbolique et L'Énergie de la Parole dans Certains Textes Tantriques* (Paris: É. de Boccard, 1963), chapters III and IV. For a helpful chart of the parallelisms in Bhāskararāya's thought, drawn from his *Guptavatī* and elsewhere, see Jani, "Concept of Trinity," 48.

65. See W. Norman Brown's introductory remarks to his edition and translation of the *Saundaryalaharī*, 25-30. Beyond what is said there, there is clearly a further logic to the convergence of Śaṅkara's *advaita* and Tantra in their shared non-dualism, which we briefly explored earlier. There is also an historical

convergence: see Brooks, "The Śrīvidyā School of Śākta Tantrism," 534. For a fascinating account of the ease with which a modern Tantric, Śrī Rāmakrishna, became posthumously understood as an Advaita Vedāntin, see Walter Neevel, "The Transformation of Sri Rāmakrishna," in Bardwell L. Smith (ed.), *Hinduism: New Essays in the History of Religions* (Leiden: E. J. Brill, 1976), 53-97.

66. *Saundaryalaharī*, Brown ed. and trans., 1. The translation which follows is Brown's, to which I have added only the parenthetical glosses on Druhiṇa, Hari and Hara.

67. For an interesting reflection on Hindu "fourths" added to Vedic triads, see Daniel H. H. Ingalls, "Dharma and Mokṣa," *Philosophy East and West* 7 (1957):45.

68. Gupta, Hoens, and Goudriaan, *Hindu Tantrism*, 103.

69. See Brooks, "The Śrīvidyā School of Śākta Tantrism," 221-222 on the notion that meaningless *mantra*s are "higher," more potent than those with semantic meaning. See also Alper, *Understanding Mantras*, passim.

70. Which appears as the *Devī Upaniṣad* in *The Śākta Upaniṣads*, trans. by A. G. Krishna Warrier (Adyar: Adyar Library and Research Centre, 1967), 77-84.

71. Bhāskararāya gives somewhat disproportionate attention to bliss (*ānanda*), including citation of the famous passage at *Bṛhadāraṇyaka Upaniṣad* 4.5.6 to the effect that every particular thing is desirable because of the desirability of *ātman*. This apparent imbalance is consistent with the Tantric integration of sensuality into spirituality: see Brooks, *The Secret of the Three Cities*, draft ms. 236-243.

72. See *Bṛhadāraṇyaka Upaniṣad* 1.2.5.

73. On this matter, see my *Crystallization*, 134-136.

74. Bhāskararāya here cites the following verses: 4.10 (twice), 1.54, 1.55, 4.3.

75. Goudriaan and Gupta, *Hindu Tantric*, 1.

76. 2.8, 9.4, 2.32, 4.18, 4.19.

77. The Gītā Press edition actually has separate meditation verses for each chapter of the *Saptaśatī*.

78. The classification of ritual as inward (*āntara*) and outward (*bāhya*) is common Tantric procedure: see Gupta, Hoens, and Goudriaan, *Hindu Tantrism*, 127-128.

79. See text, 13, line 40.

80. See my *Crystallization*, 241-249.

81. It is not clear which version of the *Mārkaṇḍeya Purāṇa* Bhāskararāya had in front of him. Several editions of that *Purāṇa* have found their way into print, and their enumeration of chapters varies. Consequently, although the text of the *Devī-Māhātmya* itself is fairly stable, the chapters of the *Mārkaṇḍeya Purāṇa* in which it appears are various. See my *Crystallization*, 51 and 51n for details, but additional notice should be taken of one other printed edition: *Mārkaṇḍeya Purāṇa*, ed. and (Hindi) commentary by Śrīrāma Śarma (Barelī: Saṃskṛti Samsthāna, 1967), two vols. This edition locates the *Devī-Māhātmya* in chapters 73-85, which comes closest of all the versions of the *Purāṇa* I have seen to Bhāskararāya's specification that the text appears in chapters 74-86. In the face of these irregularities, the Baroda Institute's forthcoming critical edition of the *Mārkaṇḍeya Purāṇa* will be most welcome.

82. These are the exact names that Bhāskararāya uses. As we have seen, chapter 11 of the text is not precise about how many forms are being enumerated, and Bhāskararāya's names differ slightly from both the text and its elaboration in the Mūrti Rahasya.

83. In his comment on 12.23 Bhāskararāya offers an interesting contrast between the "seen" quality of the hymns within the *Saptaśatī*, and the "made" quality of the *aṅga*s.

84. See *Lakṣmī Tantra* 9.12, 25, 47.

85. Bhāskararāya's first three *paṭala*s begin at the same point that the three *carita*s begin, but he then begins a fourth *paṭala* with chapter 11. There is a certain logic to breaking the text at this point, for the narrative action of the third episode has just concluded. Elsewhere (e.g., 12.1) Bhāskararāya shows an awareness of how the *Devī-Māhātmya*'s "frame story" is different from the narrative core, but is nonetheless naturally adjoined to it. It is easy to see how, with this awareness, it would be only a small step further for him to construe the *aṅga*s as an organic part of the text, as he virtually does, although he does not himself argue this point. Even with this editorial awareness, Bhāskararāya does not depart from his *ritual* commitment to three *carita*s (and three *vyaṣṭi*s, etc.).

86. This is the consensus of opinion of those (admittedly intellectual) Hindus with whom I have discussed the commentaries on the *Saptaśatī*.

87. Such as is coming to fruition in the work of C. A. Humes, of which I shall say more in our final chapter.

88. *Lakṣmī Tantra*, trans. by Sanjukta Gupta, xvi, xix, xvii. She dates the text between the ninth and twelfth centuries (xxi). Chapter 9 of the text is most often cited, for it deals explicitly with the forms and hymns of the *Devī-Māhātmya*.

89. See also Bhāskararāya's comment on 3.33.

90. See the emphasis on the physical attractiveness of the Goddess's form at 5.42ff.

91. See his comment on 3.33 and 5.38ff. We return to the latter of these citations below.

92. See Bhāskararāya's comment on 1.54.

93. As Prādhānika Rahasya 4 says (in a phrase we have seen Bhāskararāya discuss in his introduction), she is "both with and without characteristic marks."

94. See Prādhānika Rahasya 4, 7, 13 and Vaikṛtika Rahasya 1, 2, 7, 14.

95. See Bhāskararāya's comment on Vaikṛtika Rahasya 1.

96. In his commentary on Prādhānika Rahasya 29, Bhāskararāya offers a lengthy quotation from the *Lakṣmī Tantra* [9.45-51ab] in support of such correspondence.

97. See *The Māṇḍukyopaniṣad, with Gauḍapāda's Kārikā and Śaṅkara's Commentary*, trans. and notes by Swāmī Nikhilānanda (Mysore: Sri Ramakrishna Ashrama, 1968).

98. See pp. 128-129 above.

99. This multivalence is reminiscent of the way Śaṅkara uses the word *brahman* in his *Brahma-Sūtra-Bhāṣya.* The term can be understood as *saguṇa brahman* ("Brahman with qualities") in conventional discourse, or *nirguṇa brahman* ("Brahman without qualities") in the context of ultimate truth, and Śaṅkara moves easily back and forth between the two senses, as Bhāskararāya does with the two senses of Mahālakṣmī. There are, of course, critical differences between Bhāskararāya and Śaṅkara as well, given the epistemological dualism that cuts across Advaitin use of the term *brahman.* See above, note 40. I am grateful to A. N. Jani for confirming my sense of this parallel between Bhāskararāya and Śaṅkara.

100. See Nāgoji Bhaṭṭa's comment on 11.22.

101. See also 8.28 and Nāgoji Bhaṭṭa's introduction (Harikṛṣṇaśarma ed., 30, 31).

102. *brahma-jñānātiriktānivartyatva:* 1.59.

103. See Deutsch, *Advaita Vedānta*, 15-26 (s.v., "subration"); also Radhakrishnan, *Indian Philosophy* (London: George Allen and Unwin, Ltd., 1966), II:587-590; and Paul Hacker, "Eigentümlichkeiten der Lehre und Terminologie Śaṅkaras: Avidyā, Nāmarūpa, Māyā, Īśvara," *Zeitschrift der Deutschen Morgenländischen Gesellschaft* 100 (1950): 246-286, esp. 272-276.

104. Deutsch helpfully characterizes the former as "Brahman conceived by man from his limited phenomenal standpoint", and the latter as "Brahman as it is in itself": *Advaita Vedānta*, 14.

105. See Deutsch, *Advaita Vedānta*, 33-35, 43. Compare Śaṅkara's famous commentary on *Brahma Sūtra* 1.1: *The Vedānta Sūtras of Bādarāyaṇa, with*

the Commentary of Śaṅkara, trans. by George Thibaut (Oxford: Clarendon Press, 1890, 1896), two volumes.

106. E.g., 1.49, 1.53, 1.67, 5.37.

107. E.g., at 2.17, 3.33, 4.13. In a similar vein, we might note the uneasiness that Nāgoji Bhaṭṭa feels at the text's association of *tamas guṇa* with the highest deity. See his comments on 1.68, 2.8, 2.35, 5.38, 5.55, 7.24-25.

108. See Nāgoji Bhaṭṭa's comment on 1.54.

109. In the interest of brevity, I omit full consideration of the complex commentarial discussion of 5.37-42, which further substantiates the interpretation offered here. These verses raise questions about the relationship between different forms of the Goddess, and the text itself is richly ambiguous. Elsewhere, (*Crystallization*, 99-100, 109n, 154, 177, 204, 247-248n) I have argued that the text is primarily interested in celebrating the metamorphic potential of the Goddess, not in systematically sorting out her various forms. For our commentators, however, such ambiguity requires resolution, particularly since they understand the immediately preceding hymn to be addressed to the highest form of the Goddess. The way in which they impose order on these verses is, briefly, to appeal to passages found in the *Śiva Purāṇa* that deal with (1) Śiva's teasing Pārvatī about her dark (*kālī*) color, and her practice of austerities in order to slough off the dark sheath (*kośa*); and (2) Brahmā's boon to Śumbha and Niśumbha that they will be vulnerable only to a beautiful virgin who has been born, not from the womb, but from the sheath of a woman's body. Nāgoji Bhaṭṭa's basic concern is with which *guṇa* is dominant in the various forms, since *sattva guṇa* is supposed to predominate in this *carita* of the text. Bhāskararāya is more analytical and is concerned to show that both Ambikā and Pārvatī are "lower," manifest forms of the supreme, unmanifest, "fourth" form to which the hymn has just been offered. As part of this interpretation, he prefers a variant reading of the first quarter of 5.41. The passages that both commentators cite or summarize are found in *Śiva Purāṇa*, Vāyu Saṃhitā I.24-27. See *The Śiva Mahāpurāṇa*, critically ed. by Pushpendra Kumar (Delhi: Nag Publishers, 1981), and *The Śiva Purāṇa*, trans. by a Board of Scholars (Delhi, Varanasi, Patna: Motilal Banarsidass, 1970).

110. I have made note of the *Guptavatī* referring only to the author's commentaries on the *Lalitā-sahasranāma* and on Jaimini's *Pūrva-Mīmāṃsā-Sūtra*. Evidence for the converse is that Douglas Brooks has completed his two major studies of Bhāskararāya and Śrīvidyā without making any substantive use of the *Guptavatī*. I turn to Brooks's reflection on this fact just below.

111. The views presented here were conveyed in a series of conversations we had during August, 1987.

112. We may need to be reminded here of the complexity of Indian attitudes toward words: see my "'Scripture' in India," and Alper, *Understanding Mantras*. As we shall see in the next chapter, Jani also has some interesting ideas on how

this proliferation of the *Devī-Māhātmya*'s verses as instruments of power is related to their becoming called *Saptaśatī*.

113. What follows is based on a lengthy personal communication of June 19, 1987, and subsequent conversations.

114. The fact we noted earlier—that the *Guptavatī* seems to have been written toward the end of Bhāskararāya's career—increases this naturalness still further. It is the fruit of a mature, erudite scholar's reflection on one of the popular texts of his day.

Chapter 7: Encounters in the Contemporary World

1. J. N. Farquhar, *An Outline of the Religious Literature of India*, 356-357, 388 cites translations into Bengali, Gujarati, Telegu, Malayalam, and Punjabi. Goudriaan and Gupta, *Hindu Tantric*, 205 report a rendering into Hindi and Guru Gobind Singh's Hindi poem, *Durgācaritrauktivilās*, based on the *Saptaśatī*. J. Gonda, *Medieval Religious Literature in Sanskrit*, 265 takes note of Nīla-kaṇṭha's *Caṇḍīrahasya*, "an attempt to reproduce the essence" of the *Devī-Māhātmya* in thirty-six verses. See also Bāṇa's *Caṇḍīśataka*, in Mayūra, *The Sanskrit Poems of Mayūra*, ed. and trans. by George Payn Quackenbos (New York: AMS Press, 1965). There are doubtless many more instances of translating and adapting the text.

2. My summary of the text here follows that of Goudriaan and Gupta, *Hindu Tantric*, 212.

3. Idem. For study of another politically inspired encounter with a familiar myth, see Hospital, *The Righteous Demon*, esp. chapters 7 and 8.

4. See Kathleen M. Erndl, "Victory to the Mother: The Goddess Cult of Northwest India" (Ph.D. diss., University of Wisconsin-Madison, 1987), esp. chapter 2 where the *Devī-Māhātmya* and *śakti pīṭha*s ("places of power") are discussed as two "integrating devices" that connect the Punjab to the pan-Indian Goddess cult. I am indebted to Professor Erndl for calling to my attention the convergence in our scholarly interests.

5. Cynthia A. Humes, personal communication, June 25, 1989. Humes is here reporting on the research done for her Ph.D. dissertation, "The Text and Temple of the Great Goddess," that she is currently completing at the University of Iowa. Her research is focused on the Vindhyacal temple in Mirzapur.

6. Babb, *The Divine Hierarchy*, 217-226, 226-229.

7. Ibid., 218, my italics.

8. See my "'Scripture' in India" (chapter 1, note 23). See also Erndl's critique of Babb on the alleged correlation between a goddess's being benevolent or

malevolent and her being married or single. "Victory to the Mother," 337-345.

9. See C. Mackenzie Brown, "Purāṇa as Scripture."

10. Ibid., 73-76. One way of understanding the unique significance of the *Devī-Māhātmya* is that it appeals to *both* these traditions, originating as meaningful narrative (*artha*), and attracting subsequent engagement as *mantra* (*śabda*). The different ways of engaging with the *Devī-Māhātmya* may thus be seen as a microcosm of shifting Purāṇic attitudes toward verbal material. See also A. N. Jani's historical speculation cited at the end of chapter 6.

11. Not surprisingly, our proposal here that we understand encounters with the text as falling along a spectrum resembles our discussion in chapter 4 of the varied material that follows in the wake of a particular verbal utterance. What is different here is the suggested arrangement of the material along a continuum, with the two ends anchored by the two kinds of phenomena that Babb calls to our attention. As we shall see shortly, however, recent anthropological work suggests the need to see "understanding" a text as something more than mere exegesis, as a hermeneutic that "deconstructs" the text into ritual activity and social life.

12. I will describe one private recitation that I have witnessed below; see also Erndl, "Victory to the Mother," 286. Babb describes a recitation by a professional reciter, *The Divine Hierarchy*, 39-46; see also Erndl, "Victory to the Mother," 95. On Durgā Pūjā recitation, see Shib Chunder Bose, *The Hindoos As They Are* (Calcutta: Thacker, Spink and Co., London: W. Thacker and Co., 1883), 95; Erndl, "Victory to the Mother," 250; Pratapachandra Ghosha, *Durgā Pūjā: With Notes and Illustrations* (Calcutta: "Hindoo Patriot" Press, 1871), 14, 25, and note 27; Kane, *History of Dharmaśāstra*, V:171-172; Brijendra Nath Sharma, *Festivals of India* (New Delhi: Abhinav Publications, 1978), 109. I return to the broader issue of Durgā Pūja/Navarātra immediately below.

13. The information reported here is drawn from personal communications of February 26 and June 25, 1989. I am most grateful to Ms. Humes for sharing the results of her research prior to its publication. Her dissertation (see note 5 above) promises in significant measure to pick up where our present study leaves off. Since the Vindhyachal temple that stands at the center of her study is distinguished for, among other reasons, the inscription of the *Devī-Māhātmya* on its walls, it is of particular interest to those of us who have become intrigued by the media of verbal transmission.

14. Humes confirms my sense, noted in chapter 5, that Argalā 22 is the most famous of the Argalā's verses, and is one of the most popular *saṃpuṭs* used among younger men. Its goal is typical of the kind of goal (*artha*) sought by "sampuṭic" recitation of the *Saptaśatī*, a matter to which we shall return below. In light of this and our following sentence, I cannot resist citing Humes further: "In a version of the *Durgārcana-Sṛti* by Kṛṣṇa Nanda Śāstrī, it is advised that by reciting the DS [*Durgā-Saptaśatī*] 14 times one can make an unruly wife behave . . . [but] it only takes 12 recitations to defeat an enemy!"

15. Erndl, "Victory to the Mother," 281.

16. The edition referred to is the Gītā Press edition. See chapter 3, note 8. The verses of the Saptaślokī Durgā correspond, in order, to the following verses of the *Saptaśatī*: 1.42, 4.16, 11.9, 11.11, 11.23, 11.28, 11.36. They are introduced by a one-verse query from Śiva who asks about the means (*upāya*) of achieving what is desired, and a one-verse response from the Goddess who says she will proclaim the relevant discipline (*sādhana*) by revealing the "Ambā Stuti," which consists of the seven verses indicated. The verse 11.9 has an interesting history. See my *Crystallization*, 63n.

17. Beyond what we are coming to know specifically about the *Devī-Māhātmya*, the work of William A. Graham on the orality of scripture obviously has a bearing on the general issue. See chapter 1, note 6 and chapter 4, note 1 and our discussion that prompts those notes.

18. The phrases in quotation marks are Babb's. See our citation just above.

19. Veena Das, "Integrating Texts and Fieldwork." See above, chapter 1, note 24.

20. Brief accounts are found in Sharma, *Śakti Cult*, 109-112; P. Thomas, *Festivals and Holidays of India* (Bombay: D. B. Taraporevala Sons & Co., 1971), 4-7. More expansively, see Babb, *The Divine Hierarchy*, 132-141; Bose, *The Hindoos As They Are*, 92-132; C. J. Fuller and Penny Logan, "The Navarātri Festival at Madurai," *Bulletin of the School of Oriental and African Studies* 48 (1985):79-105; Ghosha, *Durgā Pūjā*, passim; Kane, *History of Dharmaśāstra*, V, 154-187; Kinsley, *Hindu Goddesses*, 106-115. Östör's account, on which I shall comment below, is found in his *The Play of the Gods* (Chicago and London: University of Chicago Press, 1980), 33-97. See also the interesting perspective in Rāmakrishna, *The Gospel of Śrī Rāmakrishna*, trans. by Swami Nikhilananda (New York: Ramakrishna-Vivekananda Center, 1952), 558-577.

21. Humes will develop this common observation further, taking note of four Navarātras.

22. We are reminded again (see chapter 2, note 35) of the repeated interplay of female deity and male secular authority, a theme that will surely repay further scrutiny. On the calendrical dimension of this convergence, see Vaudeville, "Krishna Gopāla, Rādhā, and the Great Goddess," 2-5. See also Fuller and Logan, "The Navarātri Festival," 99-101. Recent important work on Rāmlīlā includes Richard Schechner, *Between Theater and Anthropology* (Philadelphia: University of Pennsylvania Press, 1985), 151-211 and Philip Lutgendorf, "The Life of a Text: Tulsīdas' *Rāmcaritmānas* in Performance" (Ph.D. diss., University of Chicago, 1987). For an accessible introduction to performance as exegesis, see Lutgendorf, "The View from the Ghats: Traditional Exegesis of a Hindu Epic," *The Journal of Asian Studies* 48 (May 1989):272-288. On the more general matter of the performance of literature, see Schechner, *Between Theater and Anthropology*, also his *Performance Theory*, rev. and expanded ed. (New York:

Routledge, 1988); Martin Esslin, *The Field of Drama: How the Signs of Drama Create Meaning on Stage and Screen* (London and New York: Methuen Books, 1987); and Richard Hornby, *Script Into Peformance: A Structuralist View of Play Production* (Austin: University of Texas, 1977). I am indebted to Brenda Murphy for these latter references.

23. Regional variation in the celebration of Durgā Pūjā is significant. The experiences I am recounting here occurred in Varanasi in 1981.

24. Östör, *The Play of the Gods*, 10.

25. E.g., see Grimes, *Beginnings in Ritual Studies*, Jonathan Z. Smith, *To Take Place*, and the items cited at note 22 above.

26. Östör, *The Play of the Gods*, 10-15.

27. Ibid., 75-79, 83-86, 90-91, 173.

28. Ibid., 196. On the relation between the theological and the sociological, see 93-94, where Östör also offers interesting remarks on the consequences of making sacred texts readily accessible by printing them.

29. Ibid., 16-24.

30. Ibid., 53, 54. The conventions of spelling and transliteration are Östör's, following the Bengali.

31. Ibid., 88-89. One is reminded here of Geertz's famous definition of religion: "(1) a system of symbols which acts to (2) establish powerful, pervasive, and long-lasting moods and motivations in men by (3) formulating conceptions of a general order of existence and (4) clothing these conceptions with such an aura of factuality that (5) the moods and motivations seem uniquely realistic." See his "Religion as a Cultural System," in William A. Lessa and Evon Z. Vogt (eds.), *Reader in Comparative Religion* (New York, Evanston, and London: Harper and Row, 1965), 204-216.

32. V. S. Agrawala, *The Glorification of the Great Goddess*. See above, chapter 1, note 2.

33. See A. S. Gupta, "In Memoriam: Dr. Vasudeva S. Agrawala," *Purāṇa* 9 #1 (January 1967):197-201.

34. E.g., Harendra Chandra Paul, "Mystic Significances of the Madhu-Kaiṭava Myth," *Aryan Path* 37 (1966):210-215; *Glory of the Divine Mother* (*Devīmāhātmyam*), [trans. and notes] by S. Shankaranarayanan (Pondicherry: Dipti Publications, 1968). The same interpretive nature of Agrawala's translation that limits its utility for historical scholarship, as we noted in chapter 1, here makes it a fitting instance of contemporary encounter with the text.

35. "Editorial," *Purāṇa* 1 #2 (February 1960):118. The Sanskrit reads *itihāsa-purāṇābhyām vedam samupabṛṃhayet*. I am indebted to Daniel H. H. Ingalls for this reference.

36. V. S. Agrawala, "Purāṇa Vidyā," *Purāṇa* 1 #1 (July 1959):89.

37. Agrawala, "Editorial", 119. It will be interesting on some future occasion to revisit Agrawala's work in light of the stimulating recent work of Brian K. Smith, *Reflections on Resemblance, Ritual, and Religion* (New York and Oxford: Oxford University Press, 1989).

38. Agrawala, *Glorification*, xiii, 6, 15, 221.

39. E.g., ibid., ii-xi, 163, 166, 184, 192, 200, 204-205, 208.

40. Ibid., 163, 247.

41. Ibid., 3, 4.

42. Ibid., 155, citing Jung's *Commentary on the Book of the Great Liberation.*

43. Ibid., i, 3, 192. Agrawala quotes this passage without attribution. See *Atharva Veda Saṃhitā*, trans. by William Dwight Whitney and Charles Rockwell Lanman (Cambridge: Harvard University, 1905).

44. Ibid., 4, 206-7.

45. Ibid., 4, 25, 165.

46. Ibid., 23, 27; see also 190.

47. Ibid., 5-8, 160.

48. The significance of the Devī Sūkta is affirmed ibid., 2 and 156 (where the Goddess is also linked to *Ṛg Veda* 10.72). As we have seen, the Devī Sūkta is often considered an *aṅga* of the *Devī-Māhātmya.* Agrawala translates and interprets this hymn and the Rātri Sūkta (221-235, 236-238), but they seem not to have been part of his original plan for translating the text: see xiv. Reference to the Puruṣa Sūkta is found ibid., 194, 216, 240, 241.

49. Ibid., 19; see also 7.

50. Agrawala has thirty-four pages of notes on the brief first *carita*, thirteen pages on the second, and eighteen on the third.

51. See ibid., 17, 190, 194 for Mahiṣa; *Ṛg Veda* 1.164.46—*ekam sadviprā bahudhā vadanti*—is given as an unreferenced quotation ibid., 191.

52. Ibid., 19.

53. See ibid., 25, 178-179, 202-203. Typical is the analysis given of why the Goddess slew Niśumbha with the help of different forms, but acted alone in killing Śumbha: the former demon represents mind engaged with sense-objects, while the latter represents the subconscious mind that is withdrawn from matter, but still engaged with sense-objects (213).

54. Ibid., 9.

55. Ibid., 9-10, 166-167.

56. Ibid., xii.

57. Virtually all of what follows in this section comes from our correspondence and conversations, the latter occurring particularly during August 1987. Some information, such as that provided here, comes from Jani's *festschrift:* B. Datta, U. C. Sharma, Nitin J. Vyas (eds.), *Aruṇa-Bharati: Professor A. N. Jani Felicitation Volume* (*Essays in Contemporary Indological Research*) (Baroda: Professor A. N. Jani Felicitation Volume Committee, 1983), xvii.

58. *Saptaśatī*, ed. by A. N. Jani. See above chapter 3, note 8.

59. Some years ago, when I was first embarking on study of the *Devī-Māhātmya*, the late J. L. Mehta made note of a similar understanding. Recalling that during his Varanasi childhood he himself had known the text by heart, he went on to report the tradition that says mishandling of this verbal phenomenon leads the guilty party to insanity.

60. Brooks, *The Secret of the Three Cities*, draft ms., 6. Compare the different "styles" of Tantric ecstasy identified by June McDaniel, of which we shall take note in our next section. In a similar vein, one of Jani's sons, who is assuming the role of *pūjāri* in the next generation, tells of a family member who had become serious about things Tantric. After a while he began to evince peculiar behavior that was offensive to others, and his father had to tell him to give it up. He should simply do his daily *pūjā* and that would be enough because, in the son's view, it takes a strong person to handle Tantra. It can destroy one who lacks the necessary strength.

61. "This is typical of mothers. Ask a father for a rupee, and he'll give you one. Ask a mother, and she'll give you two" (A. N. Jani).

62. According to Jani, the seer for the *Gītā* is Bhagavan Veda Vyāsa, the metre is *anuṣṭubh*, the deity is Śrī Krishṇa Paramātma. The *bīja* ("seed") is Krishna's counsel at 2.11ab, the *śakti* ("power") his imperative at 18.66ab, the *tattva* his promise at 18.66cd. The *kara* ("hand") *nyāsa* that Jani described makes the following associations between digit and text: thumb, 2.23ab; index finger, 2.23cd; middle finger, 2.24ab; fourth finger, 2.24cd; little finger, 11.5ab; front and back of hand, 11.5cd. Jani offered all this analysis after noting that the *Gītā* is not a Tantra in the same way that the *Devī-Māhātmya* might be, a comment that becomes intelligible if our discussion of Tantra in chapter 6 is kept in mind.

63. Conversation with J. N. Tiwari (September 14, 1981) has suggested a parallel between the *Gītā* and the *Devī-Māhātmya* in that both are applicable to crisis situations: the former, however, addresses crises of cosmic proportion (and therefore points toward *mokṣa*), while the latter is concerned with relief from individual existential crises. See also Shankaranarayanan's quotation (*Glory of the Divine Mother*, 5) of Sri Kapali Sastriar, *Further Lights: The Veda and the Tantra.*

64. Completion of her work will correspondingly allow us to answer the question of what "typical" means with regard to recitation of the *Devī-Māhātmya.* Jani is aware of much variety in recitation, but I did not question him in detail about this matter.

65. For comparison, see the description of a recitation extending over nine days in Babb, *The Divine Hierarchy*, 39-46.

66. Jani indicated that it is possible to recite the text in as little as one hour, but that two hours is about the minimum required for the words to be *clearly heard.* (This is, as we have noted throughout, not the same as requiring that they be *understood.*) See our discussion in chapter 5 of the language that the *Devī-Māhātmya* applies in chapter 12 to its ritual usage.

67. The general scale of this kind of *pūjā* activity is nicely conveyed by the photographs in Gupta, Hoens, and Goudriaan, *Hindu Tantrism*, Plates 1-8, though the specific ritual is quite different.

68. What I report here is based on my own experience and Jani's text. For elaboration and interpretation of some of these elements, see Shankaranarayanan's notes in *Glory of the Divine Mother*, 57-70.

69. The so-called six-limbed (*ṣad-aṅga*) *nyāsa* involves identification with the head, topknot, heart, eyes, weapon, and armor of the deity. See Bharati, *The Tantric Tradition*, 273-274, and Gupta, Hoens, and Goudriaan, *Hindu Tantrism*, 140ff.

70. For alternative interpretations, see chapter 5. The meditational verses here are the same as those given in Bhāskararāya's commentary, which we translated in chapter 6.

71. The balance of this section is based primarily on conversations with Banerjea in November 1981 and August 1987. I have tried to retain some of their oral character by occasionally employing some of his distinctive phrasings. A preliminary way of understanding Banerjea in relationship to the broader Bengali scene is in terms of June McDaniel's "three strands" of Bengali Śākta Tantra—the yogic, the devotional, and the magical: "Styles of Tantric Ecstasy among the Śāktas of Bengal," Paper presented at the Society for Tantric Studies, Cleveland, N.Y., October, 1988. See also the rich body of material presented in her *The Madness of the Saints: Ecstatic Religion in Bengal* (Chicago: University of Chicago Press, 1989).

72. I shall return to these distinctions in Banerjea's thinking about the *Devī-Māhātmya* just below.

73. Since this conversation with Banerjea, I have twice had it called to my attention (by Donna Wulff and Glen Hayes) that this image in Bengali *bhakti* goes back at least as far as Rāmprasād (1718-1775). The use attributed to Rāmakrishna (*The Gospel of Śrī Rāmakrishna*, 501) is, in fact, in quotation marks, but without reference. I have found one usage by Rāmprasād, in Jadunath

Sinha, *Rāma Prasāda's Devotional Songs: The Cult of Shakti* (Calcutta: Sinha Publishing House, 1966), 12 (verse 25). The opinion expressed here by Banerjea is implicitly confirmed by Humes, who reports that out of the 125 reciters she interviewed, only three had read a Sanskrit commentary, and she considers these to be somewhat "unusual cases" on other criteria (personal communication, February 26, 1989). Clearly further research, particularly into the sociology and function of commentators, is necessary if we are to bridge the scholastic and popular engagement with our text.

74. Edward C. Dimock, Jr., "Doctrine and Practice among the Vaiṣṇavas of Bengal," in Milton Singer (ed.), *Krishna: Myths, Rites, and Attitudes*, 49.

75. Erndl arrives at a similar conclusion, contrasting Krishna and Śākta *bhakti*, in her study of the contemporary Punjab ("Victory to the Mother," 346-347).

76. For all of his antipathy to Tantra, Banerjea indicates that one of the significant episodes in his youth occurred when he was accosted by a stranger, who was also an adept, and asked why he was not yet practicing *kula-kuṇḍalinī*, a predominantly Tantric form of *yoga*. He subsequently began to do so, and it contributed significantly to his knowledge and love of the Mother. When I later asked him how I might come to know the Mother, he urged me to "rouse the *kuṇḍalinī*," a practice that he also said would deepen the spiritual life of Christians and others. On my pointing out that he seemed here to be advocating a Tantric practice, he agreed, but indicated that it was only on the surface. What was decisive was the purpose for which the *kuṇḍalinī*—a kind of spiritual energy—was aroused, and his purpose was to love the Mother, not to become one with her. This explanation is nicely consistent with our discussion in chapter 6 of how Tantric and non-Tantric contexts may be distinguished. On *kula-kuṇḍalinī*, see Gupta, Hoens, and Goudriaan, *Hindu Tantrism*, 163-180; also Lilian Silburn, *Kuṇḍalinī: The Energy of the Depths* (Albany: State University of New York Press, 1988).

77. Banerjea spoke of these five, but the enumerations and descriptions of the forms of *mokṣa* vary. See Klaus Klostermaier, *Mythologies and Philosophies of Salvation in the Theistic Traditions of India* (Waterloo: Wilfrid Laurier University Press, 1984), 84, 170; also Dasgupta, *A History of Indian Philosophy*, III:442-443n.

78. Bibliography is provided in the notes to chapter 1.

79. What I have in mind is both the past transitions that have brought us to our present situation (on which see, in particular, the work of William A. Graham, cited in chapters 1 and 4) and current ones, such as those detected by Marshall McLuhan, *The Gutenberg Galaxy*. I am also mindful of the fact

that this entire manuscript has been completed (except for the occasional correction on "hard copy") without recourse to pen or pencil.

80. Padoux, "Hindu Tantrism," 277.

81. Biardeau, *L'Hindouisme*, 168-169, my translation. The bracketed phrase follows from her earlier discussion, 164-165.

82. Humes, "The Text and Temple of the Great Goddess." See chapter 5, note 2 and chapter 7, notes 5 and 13.

83. See Hiltebeitel and Hopkins, "Indus Valley Religion" and above, chapter 2, note 2.

84. See above, chapter 2, note 35 and chapter 7, note 22. Hiltebeitel, *The Cult of Draupadī* and Shulman, *Tamil Temple Myths* also bear on the issue. See also S. Gupta and R. Gombrich, "Kings, Power and the Goddess," *South Asia Research* 6 #2 (1986):123-138.

85. André Padoux, "Mantras—What Are They?," in Alper, *Understanding Mantras*, 308.

86. For a related line of thought, see Gerald James Larson, "The *Bhagavad Gītā* as Cross-Cultural Process: Toward an Analysis of the Social Locations of a Religious Text," *Journal of the American Academy of Religion* 43 (1975): 651-669.

Appendix: Translation of the Aṅgas

1. Compare *Devī-Māhātmya* 4.24.

2. These terms are well-known categories from the philosophies of Sāṃkhya and Yoga.

3. For further discussion of these hymns, see my *Crystallization*, 255-258.

4. This is the hymn that begins at *Devī-Māhātmya* 5.7.

5. Literally, "who has attained with her the state of *sayujya*," one of several degrees of final relationship with the deity. See chapter 7, note 77.

6. The reference is to the verses of the hymn in chapter 5 of the *Devī-Māhātmya*, whose refrain ends *namo namaḥ*.

7. Cf. DM 11.38.

8. Cf. DM 11.41.

9. Cf. DM 11.45.

10. Cf. DM 11.43, 11.46.

11. Cf. DM 11.48.

12. Cf. DM 11.50.

13. Cf. DM 12.35-36.

Glossary

The primary function of this glossary is to indicate how the major names of the Goddess in the *Devī-Māhātmya* were employed in Sanskrit prior to appearing in that text. This information thus provides part of the historical background to our translation of the *Devī-Māhātmya* in chapter 3, by indicating the Vedic and epic resonance of the important designations of the Goddess. These brief entries do not necessarily provide a full "prehistory" for the names, for they do not attend to non-Sanskritic sources. When a particular name has been discussed in chapter 2, in the course of setting the *Devī-Māhātmya* in its historical context, I provide a brief definition and cross-reference to that discussion. Documentation and extended consideration of the *Devī-Māhātmya*'s names for the Goddess may be found in part I and appendix A of my *Devī-Māhātmya: The Crystallization of the Goddess Tradition.* I have included a few other technical terms here to assist the general reader.

Aindrī—The goddess or *śakti* who is related to Indra. See pages 19, 21.

Alakṣmī—Ill-fortune. See page 18.

Ambā—Mother. See page 19.

Ambikā—Mother, Mother-dear. See page 19.

Band of Mothers—See page 21.

Bhadrakālī—The auspicious dark one. See page 20.

Brahmāṇī—The goddess or *śakti* who is related to Brahmā. See pages 19, 21.

Cāmuṇḍā—Identified in the *Devī-Māhātmya* with Kālī. The name has no earlier usage in Sanskrit.

Caṇḍikā—The fierce and impetuous one. A proper noun that appears virtually for the first time in the *Devī-Māhātmya.*

Durgā—The inaccessible one, she who deals with adversity. See pages 20-21.

Gaurī—The bright and beautiful one, an occasional epithet for Śiva's consort in the *Mahābhārata.*

guṇa—Quality, characteristic, one of the three strands of primordial matter (*prakṛti*) according to the Sāṃkhya school—*sattva guṇa* (bright intelligence-stuff), *rajas guṇa* (ruddy energy-stuff), *tamas guṇa* (dark mass-stuff). This conception is widely employed and variously interpreted in different contexts, prior and subsequent to the *Devī-Māhātmya.* See pages 20, 110.

Kālī—The black one. See page 21.

Kātyāyanī—The one (fem.) from the lineage of Kātyāyana. See page 20.

Kaumārī—The goddess or *śakti* who is related to Skanda (Kumāra). See pages 19, 21.

Lakṣmī—Fortune, especially good fortune, the goddess of good fortune. See pages 18-19.

Mahākālī—The great black one. The name appears in the *Devī-Māhātmya* only at 12.35. A designation for one of the *vyaṣṭi* forms of Mahālakṣmī in the Prādhānika and Vaikṛtika Rahasyas. See figures 5.1 and 5.2.

Mahālakṣmī—The one of great fortune or auspiciousness. The name does not appear in the text of the *Devī-Māhātmya.* In the Prādhānika and Vaikṛtika Rahasyas, it is the chief designation of ultimate reality, that is, of the *samaṣṭi* form of the Goddess, and is also applied to one of her *vyaṣṭi* forms. See figures 5.1 and 5.2.

Mahāmāyā—The great illusion, she who possesses great deceptiveness. See *māyā* and page 20.

Mahāsarasvatī—The great Sarasvatī. The name does not appear in the text of the *Devī-Māhātmya,* but designates one of the *vyaṣṭi* forms of Mahālakṣmī in the Prādhānika and Vaikṛtika Rahasyas. See Sarasvatī and figures 5.1 and 5.2.

Māheśvarī—The goddess or *śakti* who is related to Śiva (Maheśvara). See pages 19, 21.

māyā—Trick, illusion, the raw material of the manifest universe. See page 20.

Mothers—See page 21.

Nārasiṃhī—The goddess or *śakti* who is related to Viṣṇu's man-lion (Narasiṃha) form. See pages 19, 21.

Nārāyaṇī—The one (fem.) who is related to Nārāyaṇa, a priestly figure in late Vedic times who, by the time of the *Devī-Māhātmya,* has been identified with Viṣṇu, Hari, Vasudeva, Krishna, and Bhagavān.

nidrā—Sleep, drowsiness. See Yoganidrā.

nityā—The inwardly eternal one. See page 20.

Pārvatī—The mountain goddess, consort of Śiva. See page 21.

Prakṛti—Primordial matter, the raw material of the manifest universe, the realm of nature in distinction (according to the Sāṃkhya school) from that of spirit (*puruṣa*), the means by which deity is both revealed and hidden. See *guṇa* and pages 20, 110.

śakti—Power, ability, capacity, power essence. See pages 19, 20, 21.

samaṣṭi—The aggregate form of ultimate reality, Mahālakṣmī prior to taking on the separate (*vyaṣṭi*) forms of Mahākālī, Mahālakṣmī, and Mahāsarasvatī. The term is applied by commentators to the process described in the Prādhānika and Vaikṛtika Rahasyas. See figures 5.1 and 5.2.

Sarasvatī—A Vedic river goddess, later associated with speech and with culture generally. The name appears only once in the *Devī-Māhātmya*, at 11.22.

Śivadūtī—She who has Śiva as messenger. In the *Devī-Māhātmya* Śivadūtī is the *śakti* of Caṇḍikā herself, a formulation that departs from the convention (also attested in the *Devī-Māhātmya*) that *śakti* is female in relationship to a deity who is male. The name is unknown prior to the *Devī-Māhātmya*.

Śrī—Wealth, good luck, fortune, the goddess of wealth. See pages 18-19.

Svadhā—The Vedic offering to deceased ancestors, the utterance accompanying that offering. See pages 19-20.

Svāhā—A Vedic ritual benediction, the personification of that benediction. See pages 19-20.

tamasī—The dark one, she who is constituted of the *guṇa* of *tamas*. See *guṇa*.

Vaiṣṇavī—The goddess or *śakti* who is related to Viṣṇu. See pages 19, 21.

Vārāhī—The goddess or *śakti* who is related to Viṣṇu's boar-form (Varāha). See pages 19, 21.

vyaṣṭī—The separate forms of ultimate reality, Mahākālī, Mahālakṣmī, Mahāsarasvatī, contrasted with the aggregate or *samaṣṭi* form. The term is applied by commentators to the evolutionary process described in the Prādhānika and Vaikṛtika Rahasyas. See figures 5.1 and 5.2.

Yoganidrā—The sleep of *yoga*, the yogic withdrawal of sensory awareness. Close approximations of this term have been employed in the *Mahābhārata* to characterize Viṣṇu's consciousness during the interval of dissolution that separates cycles of cosmic evolution. See pages 22-23.

Bibliography

I. Indian Texts and Translations

Atharva Veda Samhitā. Translated by William Dwight Whitney and Charles Rockwell Lanman. Cambridge: Harvard University, 1905.

Bāṇa. See Mayūra.

[*Bhagavadgītā.*]

1. *The Bhagavad-Gītā.* Translated and interpreted by Franklin Edgerton. 2 vols. Cambridge: Harvard University Press, 1944.
2. *The Bhagavadgītā in the Mahābhārata.* Translated by J. A. B. van Buitenen. Chicago and London: University of Chicago Press, 1981.

Bhāskararāya. *Varivasyā-Rahasya and Its Commentary Prakāśa by Śrī Bhāskararāya Makhin.* Edited and translated by Pandit S. Subrahmanya Sastri. Adyar: Adyar Library and Research Centre, 1976.

———. See *Lalitā-Sahasranāma,* also *Mārkaṇḍeya Purāṇa. Devī-Māhātmya.*

Brahma Sūtras. See *Vedānta Sūtras.*

Devī-Māhātmya. See *Mārkaṇḍeya Purāṇa. Devī-Māhātmya.*

Devī-Purāṇa. Edited by P. D. Maṇḍanamiśra and D. Puṣpendrakumāraśarmā. Śāntiniketan and New Delhi: Śrī Lālabahāduraśāstrīkendrīya Saṃskṛtavidyāpīṭha, 1976.

Durgā-Saptaśatī. See *Mārkaṇḍeya Purāṇa. Devī-Māhātmya.*

[Kātyāyana.] *Kātyāyana's Sarvānukramaṇī of the Rigveda.* Edited by A. A. Macdonell. Oxford: Clarendon Press, 1886.

Lakṣmī Tantra.

1. *Lakṣmī Tantra: A Pāñcarātra Text.* [Translated with notes by] Sanjukta Gupta. Leiden: E. J. Brill, 1972.
2. *Lakṣmī-Tantra: A Pāñcarātra Āgama.* Edited by Pandit V. Krishnamacharya. Madras: The Adyar Library and Research Centre, 1975.

Lalitā-Sahasranāman with Bhāskararāya's Commentary. Translated by R. Ananthakrishna Sastry. Adyar: The Theosophical Publishing House, 1976.

Mahābhārata.
1. *The Mahābhārata.* For the first time critically edited by Vishnu S. Sukthankar, and others. 19 vols. Poona: Bhandarkar Oriental Research Institute, 1933-1959.
2. *The Mahābhārata.* [Books 1-3] Translated by J. A. B. van Buitenen. Two vols. Chicago and London: University of Chicago Press, 1973, 1975.

[*Mānava Dharma Śāstra.*] *The Laws of Manu.* Translated by Georg Buhler. New York: Dover Publications, 1969.

Mārkaṇḍeya Purāṇa.
1. *The Mārkaṇḍeya Purāṇa.* Translated with notes by F. Eden Pargiter. Calcutta: The Asiatic Society, 1904.
2. *śrīmanmārkaṇḍeyapurāṇam.* [Bombay: Venkateśvara Press, 1910.]
3. *Mārkaṇḍeya Purāṇa.* Two vols. Edited with (Hindi) commentary by Śrīrāma Śarmā. Barelī: Saṃskṛti Saṃsthāna, 1967.

Mārkaṇḍeya Purāṇa. Devī-Māhātmya (Durgā-Saptaśatī).
1. *Śrī-durgā-saptaśatī.* Gorakhpur: Gītā Press, n.d.
2. *Śrī Śrī Chaṇḍī.* Translated by Swami Tattwananda. Calcutta: Nirmalendu Bikash Sen, n.d.
3. *Saptaśatī-sarvasvam.* [The essence of the Saptaśatī.] 2d ed. Edited by Dviveda Sarayūprasādaśarma. Lucknow: Yutamunśīnavalakiśora, 1899.
4. *Durgā-saptaśatī saptaṭīkā-samvalitā.* [The Durgā-Saptaśatī with seven commentaries, by Bhāskararāya, Caturdharī, Śantanu, Nāgojibhaṭṭa (Nāgeśa), Jagaccandracandrikā, Daṃśoddhāra, and Durgāpradīpa. Edited by] Harikṛṣṇaśarma. Bombay: Venkateśvara Press, 1916; reprint, Delhi and Baroda: Buṭālā and Company, 1984.
5. *Saptaśatī* [with the Sanskrit and Gujarati commentaries of] Mahamahopādhyaya Śrīhathībhai Śāstrījī. 3rd ed. Edited by A. N. Jani. Baroda: Śrīsamavibhya Press, 1972; first edition 1934.
6. *Devī-māhātmya: The Glorification of the Great Goddess.* [Text with English translation and annotations] by Vasudeva S. Agrawala. Varanasi: All-India Kashiraj Trust, 1963.
7. *Glory of the Divine Mother (Devīmāhātmyam).* [Text with English translation and notes by] S. Shankaranarayanan. Pondicherry: Dipti Publications, 1968.
8. *The Devī-Māhātmyam or Śrī Durgā-Saptaśatī.* 3rd ed. [Text and translation by] Swami Jagadīśvarānanda. Madras: Sri Ramakrishna Math, 1969.
9. *Śrī Durgā Saptaśatī.* [Edited by] Śrī Sivadatta Misra Śāstrī. Vārāṇasī: Ṭhākur Prasād, 1975.

Mayūra. *The Sanskrit Poems of Mayūra.* Edited and translated with introduction, text and translation of Bāṇa's *Caṇḍīśataka* by George Payn Quackenbos. New York: AMS Press, 1965.

[*Nīlamata Purāṇa*] *The Nīlamata Purāṇa.* [Edited by] Ved Kumari. Srinagar, Jammu: n. p., 1968. Quoted in Pratapaditya Pal. "Early Paintings of the Goddess in Nepal," 47. Ann Arbor: Center for Chinese and Japanese Studies, University of Michigan, 1981.

The Rāmāyaṇa: An Epic of Ancient India. Vol. I. Translated with an introduction by Robert Goldman. Princeton: Princeton University Press, 1984.

[Rāmprasād.] *Rāma Prasāda's Devotional Songs: The Cult of Shakti.* [Translated with an introduction and notes by] Jadunath Sinha. Calcutta: Sinha Publishing House, 1966.

[*Ṛg Veda.*] *Rig Veda Sanhita, with Sāyaṇa's Commentary.* Edited by F. Max Müller. 6 vols. London, 1849-74.

Śaṅkara. *Bhagavadgītā-bhāṣya.* Bombay: Ānandāśrama Sanskrit Series, 1936.

———. See *Vedānta Sūtras.*

The Saundaryalaharī or Flood of Beauty. Edited and translated by W. Norman Brown. Cambridge: Harvard University Press, 1958.

Śiva Purāṇa.

1. *The Śiva Mahāpurāṇa.* Critically edited by Pushpendra Kumar. Delhi: Nag Publishers, 1981.
2. *The Śiva Purāṇa.* 4 vols. Translated by a Board of Scholars. Delhi, Varanasi, Patna: Motilal Banarsidass, 1970.

Upaniṣads.

1. *The Māṇḍukyopaniṣad, with Gauḍapāda's Kārikā and Śaṅkara's Commentary.* Translated with notes by Swami Nikhilananda. Mysore: Sri Ramakrishna Ashrama, 1968.
2. *The Principal Upaniṣads.* Edited and translated by S. Radhakrishnan. London: George Allen and Unwin, 1968.
3. *The Śākta Upaniṣads.* Translated by A. G. Krishna Warrier. Adyar: Adyar Library and Research Centre, 1967.

The Vedānta Sūtras of Bādarāyana, with the Commentary of Śaṅkara. Two vols. Translated by George Thibaut. Oxford: Clarendon Press, 1890, 1896.

[*Yajur Veda.*] *The Veda of the Black Yajus School, entitled Taittirīya Sanhitā.* Translated by Arthur Berriedale Keith. Cambridge: Harvard University Press, 1914.

II. Secondary Sources

Agrawala, Vasudeva S. "Editorial." *Purāṇa* 1 #2 (1960):118.

———. "Purāṇa Vidyā." *Purāṇa* 1 #1 (1959):89-100.

———. See *Mārkaṇḍeya Purāṇa. Devī-Māhātmya.*

Alper, Harvey P., ed. *Understanding Mantras.* Albany: State University of New York Press, 1989.

Aufrecht, Theodore. *Catalogus Catalogorum: An Alphabetical Register of Sanskrit Works and Authors.* Leipzig: F. A. Brockhaus, 1891-1903.

Babb, Lawrence. *The Divine Hierarchy: Popular Hinduism in Central India.* New York and London: Columbia University Press, 1975.

Banerjee, Manabendu. "Devīpurāṇa on Indian Art." *Purāṇa* 26 #1 (Jan. 1984): 11-20.

Barr, James. *Holy Scripture: Canon, Authority, Criticism.* Philadelphia: Westminster Press, 1983.

———. *The Scope and Authority of the Bible.* Philadelphia: Fortress Press, 1980.

Bharati, Agehananda. *The Tantric Tradition.* Garden City: Doubleday, 1965.

Bhattacharyya, Haridas. "Yoga Psychology." In *The Cultural Heritage of India*, ed. Haridas Bhattacharyya, III:53-90. Calcutta: The Ramakrishna Mission Institute of Culture, 1953.

Biardeau, Madeleine. *Autour de la Déesse Hindoue.* Paris: Éditions de l'École des Hautes Études de l'Inde et de l'Asie du Sud, 1981.

———. *Études de Mythologie Hindoue.* vol. 1. Paris: École Française d'Extrême Orient, 1981.

———. *L'Hindouisme: Anthropologie d'une Civilisation.* Paris: Flammarion, 1981. Revised edition of *Clefs pour la Pensée Hindoue.* Paris: Seghers, 1972.

Biardeau, Madeleine and Charles Malamoud. *Le Sacrifice dans l'Inde Ancienne.* 1st ed. Paris: Presses Universitaires de France, 1976.

Bonazzoli, Giorgio. "The Colophons in the Critically Edited Purāṇas." *Purāṇa* 24 #2 (July 1982):353-383.

———. "Composition, Transmission and Recitation of the Purāṇas." *Purāṇa* 25 #2 (July 1983):225-280.

———. "Considerations on a New Method of Critically Editing the Purāṇas." *Purāṇa* 27 #2 (July 1985):381-434.

———. "Remarks on the Nature of the Purāṇas." *Purāṇa* 25 #1 (January 1983): 77-113.

———. "Schemes in the Purāṇas." *Purāṇa* 24 #1 (January 1982):146-189.

———. "Some Observations on the Variant Readings in the Purāṇic Texts and Their Imports for Critical Editions." *Purāṇa* 26 #2 (July 1984):113-133.

Bond, George D. *"The Word of the Buddha": The Tipitaka and Its Interpretation in Theravada Buddhism.* Columbo, Sri Lanka: M. D. Gunasena and Co., 1982.

Boose, Emery and Gary Tubb. "Handbook designed to aid students in the use of Sanskrit commentaries." Draft manuscript, 1981.

Bose, Shib Chunder. *The Hindoos As They Are.* Calcutta: Thacker, Spink and Co., London: W. Thacker and Co., 1883.

Brooks, Douglas Renfrew. *The Secret of the Three Cities: An Introduction to Hindu Śākta Tantrism through Bhāskararāya's Commentary on the Tripurā Upaniṣad.* Draft manuscript. Chicago and London: University of Chicago Press, forthcoming.

———. "The Śrīvidyā School of Śākta Tantrism: A Study of the Texts and Contexts of the Living Traditions in South India." Ph.D. diss., Harvard University, 1987.

———. Personal communication, June 19, 1987.

Brown, Cheever Mackenzie. *God as Mother: A Feminine Theology in India.* Hartford, VT: Claude Stark and Co., 1974.

———. "Purāṇa as Scripture: From Sound to Image of the Holy Word in the Hindu Tradition." *History of Religions* 26 #1 (August 1986):68-86.

Brown, W. Norman. See *Saundaryalaharī.*

Carman, John B. *The Theology of Rāmānuja.* New York and London: Yale

University Press, 1974.

Chakravarti, Chintaharan. "The Mārkaṇḍeya Purāṇa: Editions and Translations." *Purāṇa* 3 #1 (Jan. 1961):38-45.

Childs, Brevard S. *Introduction to the Old Testament as Scripture.* Philadelphia: Fortress Press, 1979.

———. *The New Testament as Canon: An Introduction.* Philadelphia: Fortress Press, 1984.

———. *Old Testament Theology in a Canonical Context.* Philadelphia: Fortress Press, 1985.

Coburn, Thomas B. *Devī-Māhātmya: The Crystallization of the Goddess Tradition.* Delhi and Columbia, MO: Motilal Banarsidass and South Asia Books, 1984, 1988.

———. "'Scripture' in India: Towards a Typology of the Word in Hindu Life." *Journal of the American Academy of Religion* 52 (1984):435-459.

———. "The Study of the Purāṇas and the Study of Religion." *Religious Studies* 16 (1980):341-352.

Cressy, David. "Books as Totems in Seventeenth Century England and New England." *Journal of Library History, Philosophy, and Comparative Literature* 21 (Winter 1986):92-106.

Darnton, Robert. "Toward a History of Reading." *Princeton Alumni Weekly* 87 (April 8, 1987):19-24, 32.

Das, Veena. "Integrating Texts and Fieldwork." Paper presented at the annual meeting of the American Academy of Religion, New York, 1982.

———. *Structure and Cognition: Aspects of Hindu Caste and Ritual.* 2d ed. New York: Oxford University Press, 1982.

———. ed. *The Word and the World: Fantasy, Symbol and Record.* New Delhi, London, Beverly Hills: Sage Publications, 1986.

Dasgupta, Surendranatha. *A History of Indian Philosophy.* vol. I. Cambridge: University Press, 1932.

Datta, B., U. C. Sharma, Nitin J. Vyas, ed. *Aruṇa-Bharati: Professor A. N. Jani Felicitation Volume (Essays in Contemporary Indological Research).* Baroda: Professor A. N. Jani Felicitation Volume Committee, 1983.

Denny, Frederick M. and Rodney L. Taylor, ed. *The Holy Book in Comparative Perspective.* Columbia: University of South Carolina Press, 1985.

Deutsch, Eliot. *Advaita Vedānta: A Philosophical Reconstruction.* Honolulu: University of Hawaii Press, 1969.

Dimmitt, Cornelia and J. A. B. van Buitenen, ed. and trans. *Classical Hindu Mythology: A Reader in the Sanskrit Purāṇas.* Philadelphia: Temple University Press, 1978.

Dimock, Edward C., Jr. "Doctrine and Practice among the Vaiṣṇavas of Bengal." In *Krishna: Myths, Rites, and Attitudes*, ed. Milton Singer, 41-63. Honolulu: East-West Center Press, 1966.

Divakaran, Odile. "Durgā the Great Goddess: Meanings and Forms in the Early Period." In *Discourses on Śiva: Proceedings of a Symposium on the Nature of Religious Imagery*, ed. Michael W. Meister, 271-288. Philadelphia: University of Pennsylvania Press, 1984.

Eck, Diana. *Darśan: Seeing the Divine Image in India.* Chambersburg: Anima Books, 1981.

Eisenstein, Elizabeth L. *The Printing Press as an Agent of Change: Communications and Cultural Transformations in Early-Modern Europe.* Two volumes. Cambridge: Cambridge University Press, 1980.

Eliade, Mircea, ed. *The Encyclopedia of Religion.* New York: Macmillan, 1986. S.v. "Hindu Tantrism" by André Padoux, "Indus Valley Religion" by Alf Hiltebeitel and Thomas J. Hopkins, "Scripture" by William A. Graham, "Tantrism" by André Padoux.

Erndl, Kathleen M. "Victory to the Mother: The Goddess Cult of Northwest India." Ph.D. diss., University of Wisconsin-Madison, 1987.

Esslin, Martin. *The Field of Drama: How the Signs of Drama Create Meaning on Stage and Screen.* London and New York: Methuen Books, 1987.

Farquhar, J. N. *An Outline of the Religious Literature of India.* Oxford: Oxford University Press, 1920; reprint, Delhi, Patna, Varanasi: Motilal Banarsidass, 1967.

Finnegan, Ruth. *Oral Poetry: Its Nature, Significance and Social Context.* Cambridge: Cambridge University Press, 1977.

Fuller, C. J. and Penny Logan. "The Navarātri Festival at Madurai." *Bulletin of the School of Oriental and African Studies* 48 (1985):79-105.

Geertz, Clifford. "Religion as a Cultural System." In *Reader in Comparative Religion*, ed. William A. Lessa and Evon Z. Vogt, 204-216. New York, Evanston, and London: Harper and Row, 1965.

Ghosha, Pratapachandra. *Durgā Pūjā: With Notes and Illustrations.* Calcutta: "Hindoo Patriot" Press, 1871.

Gonda, Jan. *Aspects of Early Vishnuism.* Utrecht: N. V. A. Oosthoeck's Uitgever's Mij, 1954.

———. "The Indian Mantra." *Oriens* 18 (1963):248-301.

———. *Medieval Religious Literature in Sanskrit.* Wiesbaden: Otto Harrassowitz, 1977.

———. *Vedic Literature.* Wiesbaden: Otto Harrassowitz, 1975.

Goody, Jack. *The Domestication of the Savage Mind.* Cambridge: Cambridge University Press, 1977.

———. ed. *Literacy in Traditional Societies.* Cambridge: Cambridge University Press, 1968.

Goudriaan, Teun. *Māyā Divine and Human.* Delhi, Varanasi, Patna: Motilal Banarsidass, 1978.

Goudriaan, Teun and Sanjukta Gupta. *Hindu Tantric and Śākta Literature.* Wiesbaden: Otto Harrassowitz, 1981.

Graham, William A. *Beyond the Written Word: Oral Aspects of Scripture in the History of Religion.* New York: Cambridge University Press, 1987.

———. "The Earliest Meaning of Qur'ān." *Die Welt des Islams* n.s. 23/24 (1984):361-377.

———. "*Qur'ān* as Spoken Word: An Islamic Contribution to the Understanding of Scripture." In *Approaches to Islam in Religious Studies*, ed. Richard A. Martin, 23-40. Tucson: University of Arizona Press, 1985.

———. See Mircea Eliade, ed.

Grimes, Ronald L. *Beginnings in Ritual Studies*. Lanham, New York, London: University Press of America, 1982.

Gupta, A. S. "In Memoriam: Dr. Vasudeva S. Agrawala." *Purāṇa* 9 #1 (January 1967):197-201.

Gupta, S. and R. Gombrich. "Kings, Power and the Goddess." *South Asia Research* 6 #2 (1986):123-138.

Gupta, Sanjukta, Dirk Jan Hoens, and Teun Goudriaan. *Hindu Tantrism*. Leiden, Köln: E. J. Brill, 1979.

Gusdorf, Georges. *Speaking* (*La Parole*). Translated by Paul T. Brockelman. Evanston: Northwestern University Press, 1965.

Hacker, Paul. "Eigentümlichkeiten der Lehre und Terminologie Śaṅkaras: Avidyā, Nāmarūpa, Māyā, Īśvara." *Zeitschrift der Deutschen Morgenländischen Gesellschaft* 100 (1950):246-286.

———. "Prahlāda, Werden und Wandlungen einer Idealgestalt." *Akademie der Wissenschaften und der Literatur Abhandlungen der Geistes- und Sozial-Wissenschaftlichen Klasse* (1959 #9):517-663 and (1959 #13): 889-993.

Hazra, R. C. "The Devī-Purāṇa." *New Indian Antiquary* 5 (April 1942):2-20.

Heesterman, J. G. *The Inner Conflict of Tradition: Essays in Indian Ritual, Kingship and Society*. Chicago and London: University of Chicago Press, 1985.

Hiltebeitel, Alf. *The Cult of Draupadī I. Mythologies: From Gingee to Kurukṣetra*. Chicago and London: University of Chicago Press, 1988.

———. *The Ritual of Battle: Krishna in the Mahābhārata*. Ithaca: Cornell University Press, 1976.

———. "Śiva, the Goddess and the Disguises of the Pāṇḍavas and Draupadī." *History of Religions* 20 (1980):147-174.

———. "The Two Kṛṣṇas on One Chariot: Upaniṣadic Imagery and Epic Mythology." *History of Religions* 24 (1984):1-26.

Hiltebeitel, Alf and Thomas J. Hopkins. See Eliade, Mircea, ed.

Hopkins, Thomas J. *The Hindu Religious Tradition*. Encino and Belmont, CA.: Dickenson Publishing Co., 1971.

Hornby, Richard. *Script Into Performance: A Structuralist View of Play Production*. Austin: University of Texas, 1977.

Hospital, Clifford. *The Righteous Demon: A Study of Bali*. Vancouver: University of British Columbia Press, 1984.

Humes, Cynthia A. "The Text and Temple of the Great Goddess." Ph.D. diss., University of Iowa, in progress.

———. Personal communications, February 26 and June 25, 1989.

Ingalls, Daniel H. H. "The Brahman Tradition." In *Traditional India: Structure and Change*, ed. Milton Singer, 3-9. Philadelphia: The American Folklore Society, 1959.

———. "Dharma and Mokṣa." *Philosophy East and West* 7 (1957):41-48.

———. Foreword to *God as Mother: A Feminine Theology in India*, by Cheever Mackenzie Brown. Hartford, VT: Claude Stark and Co., 1974.

———. Foreword to *Devī-Māhātmya: The Crystallization of the Goddess Tradition*, by Thomas B. Coburn. Delhi and Columbia, MO: Motilal Banarsidass and South Asia Books, 1984, 1988.

Irwin, Joyce. *Sacred Sound: Music in Religious Thought and Practice*. Chico: Scholars Press, 1983.

Jani, A. N. "The Concept of Trinity in Śākta Philosophy." *Journal of the Maharaja Sayajirao University of Baroda*. Humanities Number: 25-26 (1976-1977): 43-51.

———. See Datta, B., U. C. Sharma, Nitin J. Vyas, ed.

Kane, Pandurang Vaman. *History of Dharmaśāstra (Ancient and Medieval Religious and Civil Law)*. 5 vols. Poona: Bhandarkar Oriental Research Institute, 1930-62.

Kinsley, David. *Hindu Goddesses: Visions of the Divine Feminine in the Hindu Religious Tradition*. Berkeley, Los Angeles, London: University of California Press, 1986.

———. "The Portrait of the Goddess in the *Devī-Māhātmya*." *Journal of the American Academy of Religion* 46 (1978):489-506.

Klostermaier, Klaus. *Mythologies and Philosophies of Salvation in the Theistic Traditions of India*. Waterloo: Wilfrid Laurier University Press, 1984.

Kramrisch, Stella. *The Presence of Śiva*. Princeton: Princeton University Press, 1981.

Krishnamachariar, M. *History of Classical Sanskrit Literature*. Madras: Tirumalai-Tirupati Devasthanams Press, 1937.

Larson, Gerald James. "The *Bhagavad Gītā* as Cross-Cultural Process: Toward an Analysis of the Social Locations of a Religious Text." *Journal of the American Academy of Religion* 43 (1975):651-669.

Leach, Edmund. *Claude Lévi-Strauss*, rev. ed. New York: Viking Press, 1976.

Levering, Miriam, ed. *Rethinking Scripture: Essays from a Comparative Perspective*. Albany: State University of New York Press, 1989.

Lévi-Strauss, Claude. "The Structural Study of Myth." *Journal of American Folklore* 67 (1955):428-444. Reprinted in *Reader in Comparative Religion: An Anthropological Approach*. 2d ed. Edited by William A. Lessa and Evon Z. Vogt, 562-574. New York, Evanston, and London: Harper and Row, 1965.

Lord, Albert B. *The Singer of Tales*. Cambridge: Harvard University Press, 1960.

Losty, Jeremiah P. *The Art of the Book in India*. London: The British Library, 1982.

Lutgendorf, Philip. "The Life of a Text: Tulsidas' *Rāmcaritmānas* in Performance." Ph.D. diss., University of Chicago, 1987.

———. "The View from the Ghats: Traditional Exegesis of a Hindu Epic." *The Journal of Asian Studies* 48 (May 1989):272-288.

MacKay, E. J. H. *Further Excavations at Mohenjo-Daro*. 2 vols. Delhi: Government of India Press, 1938.

Malamoud, Charles. See Biardeau, Madeleine and Charles Malamoud.

Marshall, Sir John, ed. *Mohenjo-Daro and the Indus Civilization*. 3 vols. London: Arthur Probsthain, 1931.

McDaniel, June. *The Madness of the Saints: Ecstatic Religion in Bengal.* Chicago and London: University of Chicago Press, 1989.

———. "Styles of Tantric Ecstasy among the Śāktas of Bengal." Paper presented at the meeting of the Society for Tantric Studies, Cleveland, NY, October, 1988.

McLuhan, Marshall. *The Gutenberg Galaxy: The Making of Typographic Man.* Toronto: University of Toronto Press, 1962.

Neevel, Walter. "The Transformation of Śrī Rāmakrishna." In *Hinduism: New Essays in the History of Religions*, ed. Bardwell L. Smith, 53-97. Leiden: E. J. Brill, 1976.

Neusner, Jacob. *Method and Meaning in Ancient Judaism III.* Chico: Scholars Press, 1981.

O'Flaherty, Wendy Doniger. *Dreams, Illusion and Other Realities.* Chicago: University of Chicago Press, 1984.

———. *The Origins of Evil in Hindu Mythology.* Berkeley: University of California Press, 1977.

———. *Śiva, the Erotic Ascetic.* New York: Oxford University Press, 1981. Reprint of *Asceticism and Eroticism in the Mythology of Śiva.* London, New York, Toronto: Oxford University Press, 1973.

———. *Women, Androgynes, and Other Mythical Beasts.* Chicago: University of Chicago Press, 1980.

———. ed. *The Critical Study of Sacred Texts.* Berkeley: Berkeley Religious Studies Series, 1979.

Ong, Walter J. *Orality and Literacy: The Technologizing of the Word.* London and New York: Methuen and Co., 1982.

Östör, Akos. *The Play of the Gods.* Chicago and London: University of Chicago Press, 1980.

Padoux, André. "Mantras—What Are They?" In *Understanding Mantras*, ed. Harvey Alper, 295-318. Albany: State University of New York Press, 1989.

———. *Recherches sur la Symbolique et L'Énergie de la Parole dans Certains Textes Tantriques.* Paris: É. de Boccard, 1963.

———. See Eliade, Mircea, ed.

Pal, Pratapaditya. "Early Paintings of the Goddess in Nepal." In *Ars Orientalis XII*, ed. Deborah Candace Brown, 41-48 + 7 plates. Ann Arbor: Center for Chinese and Japanese Studies, University of Michigan, 1981.

Pandey, Kanti Chandra. *Abhinavagupta: An Historical and Philosophical Study.* 2d ed. Varanasi: Chowkhamba Sanskrit Series Office, 1963.

Paul, Harendra Chandra. "Mystic Significances of the Madhu-Kaiṭava Myth." *Aryan Path* 37 (1966):210-215.

Payne, Ernest A. *The Śāktas.* Calcutta: Y.M.C.A. Publishing House and London: Oxford University Press, 1933.

Penner, Hans H. "Creating a Brahman: A Structural Approach to Religion." In *Methodological Issues in Religious Studies*, ed. Robert D. Baird, 49-66. Chico: New Horizons Press, 1975.

———. "Structure and Religion." *History of Religions* 25 (1985):236-254.

Piaget, Jean. *Structuralism.* Edited and translated by Chaninah Maschler. New York, et al.: Harper and Row, 1970. Originally published as *Le Structuralisme.* Paris: Presses Universitaires de France, 1968.

Radhakrishnan, [Sarvepalli]. *Indian Philosophy.* Two vols. London: George Allen and Unwin, Ltd., 1966.

Radhakrishnan and Charles A. Moore, eds. *A Source Book in Indian Philosophy.* Princeton: Princeton University Press, 1957.

Ramakrishna. *The Gospel of Śrī Rāmakrishna.* Translated by Swami Nikhilananda. New York: Ramakrishna-Vivekananda Center, 1952.

Redington, James. *Vallabhācārya on the Love Games of Kṛṣṇa.* Delhi, Varanasi, Patna: Motilal Banarsidass, 1983.

Renou, Louis. *The Destiny of the Veda in India.* Translated by Dev Raj Chandra. Delhi, Patna, Varanasi: Motilal Banarsidass, 1965.

Rocher, Ludo. *The Purāṇas.* Wiesbaden: Otto Harrassowitz, 1986.

Sanders, James A. *Canon and Community: A Guide to Canonical Criticism.* Philadelphia: Fortress Press, 1984.

———. *From Sacred Story to Sacred Text: Canon as Paradigm.* Philadelphia: Fortress Press, 1987.

———. *Torah and Canon.* Philadelphia: Fortress Press, 1972.

[Sarma], Pushpendra Kumar. *Śakti Cult in Ancient India.* Varanasi: Bhartiya Publishing House, 1974.

Sastriar, Sri Kapali. *Further Lights on Tantra.* Quoted in *Glory of the Divine Mother* (*Devī-Māhātmya*), 5. [Text with English translation and notes by] S. Shankaranarayanan. Pondicherry: Dipti Publications, 1968.

Schechner, Richard. *Between Theater and Anthropology.* Philadelphia: University of Pennsylvania Press, 1985.

———. *Performance Theory.* Revised and expanded edition. New York: Routledge, 1988.

Seshadri, M. "Mahiṣāsuramardinī: Images, Iconography and Interpretation." *Journal of the Mysore University*, N. S. Section A-Arts 22 (1963): 1-28 + 42 plates.

Sharma, Brijendra Nath. *Festivals of India.* New Delhi: Abhinav Publications, 1978.

Shulman, David Dean. *The King and the Clown in South Indian Myth and Poetry.* Princeton: Princeton University Press, 1986.

———. *Tamil Temple Myths: Sacrifice and Divine Marriage in the South Indian Śaiva Tradition.* Princeton: Princeton University Press, 1980.

Silburn, Lilian. *Kuṇḍalinī: Energy of the Depths.* Albany: State University of New York Press, 1988.

Singer, Milton, ed. *Krishna: Myths, Rites and Attitudes.* Honolulu: East-West Center, 1966.

———, ed. *Traditional India: Structure and Change.* Philadelphia: The American Folklore Society, 1959.

Sinha, Jadunath. See Rāmprasād [under Indian Texts and Translations].

Smith, Brian K. *Reflections on Resemblance, Ritual, and Religion.* New York and Oxford: Oxford University Press, 1989.

Smith, Jonathan Z. *To Take Place: Toward Theory in Ritual.* Chicago and London: University of Chicago Press, 1987.

Smith, Wilfred Cantwell. *Questions of Religious Truth.* New York: Charles Scribner's Sons, 1967.

———. "The Study of Religion and the Study of the Bible." *Journal of the American Academy of Religion* 39 (1971):131-140.

Staal, J. F. "The Concept of Scripture in the Indian Tradition." In *Sikh Studies: Comparative Perspectives on a Changing Tradition*, ed. Mark Juergensmeyer and N. Gerald Barrier, 121-124. Berkeley: Berkeley Religious Studies Series, 1979.

———. *Nambudiri Veda Recitation.* 's-Gravenhage: Mouton and Co., 1961.

Stietencron, Heinrich von. "Die Gottin Durgā Mahiṣāsuramardinī: Mythos, Darstellung und geschichtliche Rolle bei der Hinduisierung Indiens." In *Visible Religion: Annual for Religious Iconography*, 118-166. Volume II: Representation of Gods. Leiden: E. J. Brill, 1983.

Stock, Brian. *The Implications of Literacy: Written Language and Models of Interpretation in the Eleventh and Twelfth Centuries.* Princeton: Princeton University Press, 1983.

Sukthankar, V. S. *Critical Studies in the Mahābhārata.* Poona: V. S. Sukthankar Memorial Edition Committee, 1944.

———. Prolegomenon to *The Mahābhārata.* For the first time critically edited by V. S. Sukthankar and others. 19 vols. Poona: Bhandarkar Oriental Research Institute, 1933-1959.

Theology Today 41 #4 (January 1985).

Thomas, P. *Festivals and Holidays of India.* Bombay: D. B. Taraporevala Sons & Co., 1971.

Timm, Jeffrey. "Vallabha's Commentary (?) on the Bhagavad Gītā." Paper presented at the annual meeting of the American Academy of Religion, November 19, 1988.

Tiwari, J. N. *Goddess Cults in Ancient India.* Delhi: Sundeep Prakashan, 1985.

———. "An Interesting Variant in the *Devī-Māhātmya.*" *Purāṇa* 25 #2 (July 1983):235-245.

———. "Studies in the Goddess Cults in Northern India, with Special Reference to the First Seven Centuries A.D." Ph.D. diss., Australian National University, 1971.

van Buitenen, J. A. B. "On the Archaism of the *Bhāgavata Purāṇa.*" In *Krishna: Myths, Rites and Attitudes*, ed. Milton Singer, 23-40. Honolulu: East-West Center, 1966.

———. See *Bhagavadgītā*, also *Mahābhārata.*

Vaudeville, Charlotte. "Krishna Gopāla, Rādhā, and the Great Goddess." In *The Divine Consort: Rādhā and the Goddesses of India*, ed. John Stratton Hawley and Donna Marie Wulff, 1-12. Berkeley: Berkeley Religious Studies Series, 1982.

Waley, Arthur. *Three Ways of Thought in Ancient China.* London: George

Allen and Unwin, 1939.
Whaling, Frank. *The Rise of the Religious Significance of Rāma.* Delhi: Motilal Banarsidass, 1980.
Winternitz, Maurice. *A History of Indian Literature.* vol. I. Translated by Mrs. S. Ketkar. New York: Russell and Russell, 1971.

Index

Advaita Vedānta. *See also* Śaṅkara
  Bhāskararāya's relation to, 128-129
  compared with Śrīvidyā, 128-131, 214-215 note 40
  historical convergence with Tantra, 216-217 note 65
  Nāgoji Bhaṭṭa's relation to, 128, 130-131
  theory of causation, 128
Agni, in *Devī-Māhātmya*, 39, 40, 41, 52. 56, 73
Agrawala, Vasudeva S., 9, 156-159, 195-196 note 2
Aindrī, 19, 201 note 17
  in *Devī-Māhātmya*, 64, 65, 66, 71, 75
Alakṣmī (ill-fortune), 18
  in *Devī-Māhātmya*, 48, 82
Ambā (mother), 19
  in *Devī-Māhātmya*, 74, 83
Ambikā (mother), 19, 144
  in *Devī-Māhātmya*, 43, 44, 45, 46, 47, 48, 50, 51, 55, 60, 63, 64, 69, 71-73, 76
Aṅgas (limbs) of the *Devī-Māhātmya*, 90, 99-117, 132. *See also* Argalā; Kavaca; Kīlaka; Mūrti Rahasya; Prādhānika Rahasya; Vaikṛtika Rahasya
  Bhāskararāya comments on, 101, 133
  chiefly concerned with ritual use of *Devī-Māhātmya*, 101, 108, 116-17
  possible relationship to the name *Durgā-Saptaśatī*, 140
  terminology pervades villagers' experience, 154-156
Appayya Dīkṣita, 134
Argalā, 100, 164. *See also Aṅgas*
  analysis of, 104-105, 106-107
  definition of, 208 note 6
  translation of, 180-181
Artha (meaning, means of living) 151, 155, 222 note 10
Artifacts, verbal and nonverbal, 1, 5, 14-15, 16, 88-90, 92-93, 154-156. *See also* Documents, written; Scripture; Texts, nature and interpretation of
Aryan(s), 13-15, 16, 17-18
Atharva Veda, 157
Aufrecht, Theodore, 121

Babb, Lawrence, 101, 150-152, 156
Baṇa, 24
Band of Mothers. *See* Mothers, the
Banerjea, C. R., 165-169, 171, 172
Benares. *See* Varanasi
Bengal, 116, 165-169
Bhadrakālī, 20
  in *Devī-Māhātmya*, 45, 52, 76

Bhagavad Gītā, 16, 20, 25, 27
historical and structural relation to *Devī-Māhātmya*, 25-27, 162-163, 226 note 63
relationship to Durgā hymns in *Mahābhārata*, 26-27
seven hundred verses of a model for *Durgā-Saptaśatī*, 27
Bhāgavata Purāṇa, commentaries on, 8, 121, 199 note 22
Bhakti, 16
and Tantra, 166-167, 228 note 76
C. R. Banerjea's views on, 166-169
contrasted with Advaita Vedānta, 166
role of, in Goddess-Mahiṣa relationship, 92
Śākta and Vaiṣṇava views of, 167
Bhāsa, 24
Bhāskararāya. *See also Guptavatī*
acknowledges other commentaries on *Devī-Māhātmya*, 133
and gender issues, 129, 133-134, 143-144, 172
as foremost intellectual authority in Śrī Vidyā, 122-123
attitude toward tradition, 147-148
breaks with Advaita Vedānta epistemology, 128
commentary on *Devī-Māhātmya* compared with Nāgoji Bhaṭṭa's, 141-148
dates and biography, 122-123
describes evolution of world in two ways, 129
discusses the name *Durgā-Saptaśatī*, 139-140
historical study of, 122, 171
hostility toward, 166
importance of his commentary on *Devī-Māhātmya*, 121
interpretation of Mahālakṣmī resembles Śaṅkara's of *saguṇa* and *nirguṇa* Brahman, 219 note 99
A. N. Jani in tradition of, 161
motives for commenting on *Devī-Māhātmya*, 133, 146-148
pays homage to Śaṅkara, 128
philosophy of, 126-129
role in developing monistic and dialectical qualities of Śāktism, 162
use of Sāṃkhya terminology, 144
use of terms *samaṣṭi* and *vyaṣṭi*, 135-139
views on *aṅgas*' relationship to *Devī-Māhātmya*, 101, 133, 218 note 85
views on causation compared with Nāgoji Bhaṭṭa's, 130-131
views on *mantra* and *yantra*, 126
Bhīmādevī (fearsome goddess), 78, 139
Bhrāmarī (queen-bee), 78, 139
Biardeau, Madeleine, 7, 171
Books, xi-xii, 3-4, 87-88, 93. *See also* Cult of the book; Scripture
Brahmā, 112-115, 135-136, 139
in *Devī-Māhātmya*, 36-39, 40, 41, 48, 56, 63, 64, 81, 82
Brahmāṇī, 64, 65, 70, 71, 75
Brahmanical synthesis, the, 16, 17
Bṛhadāraṇyaka Upaniṣad, 34
Brooks, Douglas R., 123, 147, 162
Brown, C. Mackenzie, 151
Buffalo-demon. *See* Mahiṣa

Cāmuṇḍā, 62, 67, 75, 137, 201 note 14. *See also* Kālī
Caṇḍa and Muṇḍa, 55-56, 60-63, 75
Caṇḍī. *See* Caṇḍikā. *See also Durgā-Saptaśatī.*
Caṇḍī dī Var, 149-150
Caṇḍikā, 24
Bhāskararāya's understanding of, 133, 134, 135, 137, 138, 140, 142-143, 145, 146, 147-148
in *Devī-Māhātmya*, 43, 47, 48, 51, 63, 64, 67, 68-73, 76, 81, 83, 201 note 14

Nāgoji Bhaṭṭa's understanding of, 145
Chāndogya Upaniṣad, 134, 142
Cit/Cit-śakti, Goddess as, 135, 168
Commentaries. *See also Devī-Māhātmya*, commentaries on
as indicative of *Devī-Māhātmya*'s function, 90
as understood in this study, 119, 121-122
comparative study of, 119-121
Hindu views of, 120-121
hostility to, 166
nature of, 119-122
on *Devī-Māhātmya*, 119-148
Rahasyas considered as, 109
Cult of the book, 31, 151, 222 note 9

Darśan(a) (seeing), 101, 111, 126-128, 160, 162
Das, Veena, 7, 153
Dassera, 153. *See also* Durgā Pūjā
Deutsch, Eliot, 128
Devī-Atharva-Śirṣa Upaniṣad, 136
Devī Bhāgavata Purāṇa, 90, 139, 141
Devī-Māhātmya. *See also Durgā-Saptaśatī; Māhātmya*
a *mantra* that can be understood, 173-174, 222 note 10
Agrawala translation and encounter, 9, 156-159
alternative scholarly approaches to, 90-93
and cult of the book, 222 note 10
and dreams, 2-3, 174
aṅgas on, 10, 99-117. *See also Aṅgas*
as earliest literary conceptualization of Goddess, 16
as independent text, 100
as typical and atypical Purāṇic text, 8
as written document, 1, 31
Bhagavad Gītā, relationship to, 25-27, 162-163, 226 note 63
commentaries on, 5, 8, 9, 10, 119-148.
See also Commentaries
distanced from *bhakti*, 121
Durgā Pūjā understood as one of, 153-156
relationship to *aṅgas*, 99-101, 132
unknown to most reciters, 227-228 note 73
compared with *Ṛg Veda*, 5, 100, 105
composition of, 1, 31
in Sanskrit, 17-18
editions of, 30, 31, 121, 131, 133, 195-196 note 2
frame story as integral part of, 102
function in Hindu life, how examined in this study, 89-90
gender issues in, 2-3, 172-174, 222 note 14. *See also* Gender
has two kinds of religious significance, 151, 222 note 10
historical setting of, 13-27
historical study of, 6-10, 170-172
hymns of
discussed, 113-116, 132, 140-141
translated, 36-38, 48-51, 53-55, 74-77
in relationship to Draupadī cult, 91
incontrovertible power of, 161
internal self-references, 68, 79-82
legacy of, 87-93, 170
literary merits of, 30-31
Mārkaṇḍeya Purāṇa, place in, 8, 22, 99
Navārṇa *mantra*, relationship to, 136-138
popularity of, 148-149
received text of, 99-100
recitation of, 5, 140-141, 150-152, 160-161
by Sikhs and Muslims, 150
conditions for, 107-108
description of, 163-165
discussed in the *Devī-Māhātmya* itself, 79-81, 101-102
types of, 151-152

without understanding or study of, 152-153, 170
ritual context and content of, 101-102, 170
structure of, 22, 100
terminology pervades villagers' experience, 154-156
translation of
into Indian vernaculars, 149
issues in, 3-10, 29-31, 195-196 note 2
Devī-Māhātmya/Saptaśatī Caṇḍī *yantra*, 114-115, 138-139, 163, 164, 165
Devī Sūkta, 100, 102, 105, 140, 165, 183
Ṛg Vedic, translation of, 184-185
Dharma, 16, 25, 32, 49, 76, 82
as concept in Bhāskararāya's commentary, 134, 142-143
Dhūmralocana, 59-60
Documents, written. *See also* Artifacts, verbal and nonverbal; Scripture; Understanding, media of
and religious life, 1, 3-4, 87-88, 92-93, 170
historical study of, 6-10
in Östör's study of Durgā Pūjā, 154, 155-156
structural study of, 6-9
varied crosscultural attitudes toward, xi-xii, 3-4, 8-9, 87-88
Doniger, Wendy. *See* O'Flaherty, Wendy Doniger
Draupadī cult, 90-92
Dreams, *Devī-Māhātmya* and, 2-3, 80, 174
Durgā, 20, 23-24, 139
in *Devī-Māhātmya*, 49, 50, 53, 57, 70, 71, 76, 78
Durgā Pūjā, 152-156, 170
as commentary on *Devī-Māhātmya*, 153-156
Devī-Māhātmya recited during, 152, 166
mentioned in *Devī-Māhātmya*, 80, 102
shows interplay of Goddess and kingship, 153, 172, 223-224 note 22
Durgā-Saptaśatī (Seven Hundred [Verses] to Durgā). *See also* *Devī-Māhātmya*
discussion of the name, 27, 31, 139-140, 162
preferred title of *Devī-Māhātmya* as independent text, 100

Eck, Diana, 111
Erndl, Kathleen, 152

Feminism. *See* Gender, contemporary revolution in thinking about
Fertility, 14-15
Formulaic construction, 31

Gadamer, Hans-Georg, 2
Gauḍapāda, 143
Gaurī, 112-115, 138, 139
in *Devī-Māhātmya*, 49, 52, 53, 74
Geertz, Clifford, definition of religion, 224 note 31
Gender, 14, 106, 107, 172
contemporary revolution in thinking about, 2-3, 172-174
of deity, 2, 14-15, 129, 143-144, 166-167, 172-173
of feminine nouns in *Devī-Māhātmya*, 18-19
Goddess-buffalo myth, growth and iconography of, 92-98, 102
Goddess-kingship association, 172
an important continuity in Indian culture, 171, 202-203 note 35, 203 note 40
calendrical evidence for, 153, 172, 223-224 note 22
Krishna's role in, 25-27, 77
prior to *Devī-Māhātmya*, 14, 24-27, 200 note 2

suggested in parallelism between *Devī-Māhātmya* and *Bhagavad Gītā*, 27, 162-163, 226 note 63
Goddesses, in pre-Aryan and Aryan life, 14-15
Goudriaan, Teun, 124
Graham, William A., 87
Guṇas (qualities), 110, 154-155, 205 note 14. *See also Prakṛti; Pradhāna* correlated with *vyaṣṭi* forms of Mahālakṣmī, 142-143
in Advaita Vedānta, 131
in *Devī-Māhātmya*, 48
in Prādhānika and Vaikṛtika Rahasyas, 112-114
in Sāṃkhya, 110, 205 note 14
interpreted by V. S. Agrawala, 158
Gupta, Sanjukta, 141
Guptavatī ("Containing What Is Hidden," Bhāskararāya's commentary on the *Devī-Māhātmya*), 121, 122, 131-144, 145-148. *See also* Bhāskararāya; Commentaries; *Devī-Māhātmya*, commentaries on
analysis of, 131-141
context for set by Tantras, 139-140
contrasted with Western notions of commentary, 131
date of composition, 122, 221 note 114
describes *Devī-Māhātmya/Saptaśatī* Caṇḍī *yantra*, 138-139
Devī and Rātri Sūktas discussed in, 140
dharma as concept in, 134, 142-143
discusses the name *Durgā-Saptaśatī*, 139-140
gender of deity discussed in, 143-144
guṇas discussed in, 136, 142-143, 145
includes commentary on *aṅgas*, 101
meditation verses in, 138
motives for, 133, 146-148
Navārṇa *mantra* in, 136-138, 139
nirguṇa and *saguṇa* Brahman as Mahālakṣmī in, 136
Rahasyas as understood in, 135-145
Śākta philosophy in, 133-136, 141-144
samaṣṭi and *vyaṣṭi* forms of Mahālakṣmī in, 135-139, 142-145
Śaṅkara reverenced in, 128, 133
Sāṃkhya terminology in, 144
Saundaryalaharī and, 133, 135-136
structure of, 131-133
texts cited in, 133, 134, 136, 139, 140-141, 142
turīyā in, 137, 142-144, 145, 220 note 109
understands *Devī-Māhātmya* and its verses as *mantra*, 132-133, 139-141
Guru Gobind Singh, 149-150

Hacker, Paul, 90
Harivaṃśa, 23-24, 27, 141
Heidegger, Martin, 2
Hermeneutics, 2, 199-200 note 26
Hiltebeitel, Alf, 7, 90-92
Hopkins, Thomas J., 16
Hospital, Clifford, 90
Hueckstadt, Robert, 212 note 1
Humes, Cynthia A., 152, 156, 163, 172
Hymns. *See Devī-Māhātmya*, hymns of

Iconography, 14, 24, 92-98, 202 note 30
Indo-Europeans. *See* Aryan(s)
Indra, in *Devī-Māhātmya*, 39, 40, 41, 48, 51, 56, 58, 63, 64, 66, 73
Indus Valley civilization, 14-15, 200 note 2

Jagadīśvarānanda, 9, 195-196 note 3
Jani, A. N., 109, 110, 146-147, 152-153, 159-165, 174, 210 note 28
Jung, Carl G., 157

Kālī, 21, 91. *See also* Cāmuṇḍā

in *Devī-Māhātmya*, 61-63, 65, 67, 69, 70, 71
Kālidāsa, 21, 23
Kane, P. V., 130
Kātyāyanī, 20, 65, 73, 76
Kaumārī, 64, 65, 66, 70, 75
Kauśikī, 55, 206 note 18, 220 note 109
Kavaca, 100, 164. *See also Aṅgas*
analysis of, 104-106
translation of, 175-179
Kaviraj, Gopinath, 161
Kīlaka, 100, 164. *See also Aṅgas*
analysis of, 104-105, 107-108
as countercurse, 210 note 27
as reflection of historical process, 146-147
translation of, 182-183
King. *See* Suratha, the king
Kingship. *See* Goddess-kingship association. *See also* Suratha, the king
Kinsley, David R., 15, 25
Kramrisch, Stella, 7
Krishna/Krishna Gopāla, 24, 25-27, 41, 77. *See also* Goddess-kingship association
Kubera, 40, 41, 52

Lakṣmī (good fortune), 18, 112-115, 138, 139. *See also* Śrī in *Devī-Māhātmya*, 53, 54, 75, 82
Lakṣmī Tantra, 139, 140-141
Lévi-Strauss, Claude, 6
Līlā (play), 168

Madhu and Kaiṭabha, 22-23, 36-39, 79, 138, 158
Mahābhārata, 20-24, 26, 90-92
Mahākālī. *See also* Mahākālī/Mahālakṣmī/Mahāsarasvatī
as one of Mahālakṣmī's *vyaṣṭi* forms, 135, 137, 138
in *Devī-Māhātmya*, 82
tamas guṇa predominates in, 112-114, 142-143
temple in Baroda, 159, 160, 161, 163
Mahākālī/Mahālakṣmī/Mahāsarasvatī
in *Devī-Māhātmya/Saptaśatī* Caṇḍī *yantra*, 138-139, 164
in *Guptavatī*, 135-139, 142-143
in Prādhānika and Vaikṛtika Rahasyas, 112-116
in villagers' experience, 154-155
invoked over reciter's body, 164-165
linked with myths and hymns of *Devī-Māhātmya*, 113-115
Mahālakṣmī. *See also* Mahākālī/Mahālakṣmī/Mahāsarasvatī
as ultimate reality in universe, 109-114
as unmanifest but visualizable, 111
as *vyaṣṭi* and *samaṣṭi*, 211 note 38. *See also Vyaṣṭi* and *samaṣṭi*
Bhāskararāya's interpretation of resembles Śaṅkara's of *saguṇa* and *nirguṇa* Brahman, 219 note 99
has Mahākālī and Mahāsarasvatī as her *vyaṣṭi* forms, 135, 137, 138
multivalence of name, 143
rajas guṇa predominates in, 112-114, 142-143
Mahāmāyā, 32, 35-39, 136, 166-167. *See also Māyā*
Mahāsarasvatī. *See also* Mahākālī/Mahālakṣmī/Mahāsarasvatī
as one of Mahālakṣmī's *vyaṣṭi* forms, 135, 137, 138
sattva guṇa predominates in, 112-114, 142-143
Māhātmya, understood as both "text" and "activity," 100, 102-104
Māheśvarī, 64, 65, 66, 70, 75
Mahiṣa, 91, 92, 138, 153, 158
evolving iconography and conception of, 92-98
in *Devī-Māhātmya*, 39-51, 79

in *Caṇḍī dī Var*, 150
myth's use prior to *Devī-Māhātmya*, 22-23, 102
Mahiṣāsuramardinī, iconography of, 92-98
Mantras, 89, 124, 126, 173. *See also* *Durgā-Saptaśatī*; Navārṇa *mantra*
two kinds of meaning of, 151, 173-174
verses of *Devī-Māhātmya* understood as, 31, 132-133, 139-140
Manu, Laws of, 25-26
Mārkaṇḍeya Purāṇa, 139
aṅgas ascribed to, 105
Devī-Māhātmya's relationship to, 8, 22, 99, 102, 105
editions of, 29-30, 218 note 81
version used by Bhāskararāya, 218 note 81
Mātṛgaṇa. *See* Mothers, the
Matter. *See Pradhāna; Prakṛti*
Māyā, 20, 25, 53, 82, 128, 131. *See also* *Mahāmāyā*
Medhas, the sage, 32-39, 159
Meditation verses, 138, 165
Mehta, J. L., 226 note 59
Mokṣa, 83-84, 155, 162-163, 169
Mothers, the, 21, 63-71, 106
Müller, F. Max, 3
Muṇḍa. *See* Caṇḍa and Muṇḍa
Mūrti Rahasya, 100, 165. *See also* *Aṅgas*; Rahasyas
analysis of, 109, 116
translation of, 191-193
Myths, earlier use of *Devī-Māhātmya*'s, 22-24

Nāgeśa. *See* Nāgoji Bhaṭṭa
Nāgoji Bhaṭṭa
attitude toward tradition, 147-148
chiefly a grammarian, 130
dates and biography of, 122, 129-131
his commentary on *Devī-Māhātmya* compared with Bhāskararāya's, 141-148
importance of his commentary on *Devī-Māhātmya*, 121
motives for commenting on *Devī-Māhātmya*, 146-148
philosophically an Advaita Vedāntin, 130, 144-145
views on causation compared with Bhāskararāya's, 130-131
Names of the Goddess, earlier usage of *Devī-Māhātmya*'s, 18-21
Nārasiṃhī, 64, 65, 75
Nārāyaṇī, 74-77
Navarātra. *See* Durgā Pūjā
Navārṇa *mantra*, 136-138, 163, 164, 165
Neusner, Jacob, 7-8
Nīlamata Purāṇa, 103
Nirguṇa and *saguṇa* Brahman, 110-111, 128, 130-131, 136, 144-145, 219 note 99. *See also* *Turīyā*
Niśumbha, 24, 158
in *Devī-Māhātmya*, 52, 55-59, 62, 64, 68-70, 77, 79, 81
Nityā (inwardly eternal), 19-20, 36, 37, 53, 82
Non-Aryan, 15, 18, 21, 24. *See also* Pre-Aryan
Nyāsa (placement, identification), 106, 137, 138-139, 164
Nyāyakośa, 120

O'Flaherty, Wendy Doniger, 7
Oral composition, circumstances of, 31, 88-90
Oral culture, relation to visual culture, 88-89, 93, 155, 170
Östör, Ákos, 153-156

Padoux, André, 123, 124, 125, 173
Pal, Pratapaditya, 101
Pārvatī, 21, 23, 55
Penner, Hans, 7

Philosophy, theories of causation in, 128-131
Piaget, Jean, 6
Pradhāna (matter), 110-111, 112-114, 144. *See also Prakṛti*
Prādhānika Rahasya, 100, 165. *See also Aṅgas*; Rahasyas
analysis of, 109-115
Bhāskararāya's exegesis of, 142-144
characterizes unmanifest life of Mahālakṣmī, 112-114
diagram of relationships in, 113
translation of, 185-187
Prajāpati, 39, 40, 41, 56
Prakṛti (primary matter). *See also Pradhāna*
associations prior to *Devī-Māhātmya*, 20, 25
in *Devī-Māhātmya*, 37, 48, 53, 74
in Nāgoji Bhaṭṭa's commentary on *Devī-Māhātmya*, 144-145
in Sāṃkhya, 110-111, 128
Pre-Aryan, 13-15, 18. *See also* Non-Aryan
Protection, divine
as goal of reciting *Devī-Māhātmya*, 79-81
conceptualizations prior to *Devī-Māhātmya*, 24-27
in *Devī-Māhātmya*, 36, 37, 48, 50-52, 55, 74, 76-82
in Kavaca and Argalā to protect reciter of *Devī-Māhātmya*, 106, 107, 164
Pūjā (worship), 114-116, 126, 160, 163-165, 166, 168
Purāṇas. *See also Mārkaṇḍeya Purāṇa; Upabṛṃhaṇa*
V. S. Agrawala's understanding of, 156-158
and *bhakti*, 121, 171
and Goddess mythology, 21, 90, 92
and structuralist method, 7
and Tantras, 171
characteristics and definition of, 17-18, 22, 29, 31, 198 note 15
commentaries on and critical editions of, 8, 29-30
cult of the book in, 31, 103-104, 207 note 3, 222 note 10
historical study of, 6-10, 170-172
Pūrva-Mīmāṃsā-Sūtra, 134

Rahasyas, 100, 165. *See also Aṅgas*; Mūrti Rahasya; Prādhānika Rahasya; Vaikṛtika Rahasya
analysis of, 109-117
as earliest systematic statement of Śākta philosophy, 109
Bhāskararāya's interpretation of, 135-145
considered as commentary on *Devī-Māhātmya*, 109
self-conscious monism of, 142
Rajas guṇa (energy stuff), 110, 112-114, 142-143, 154-155, 205 note 14. *See also Guṇas*
Raktabīja, 66-68, 91
Raktadantikā (Red-tooth), 78, 139
Rāmakrishna, 166, 216-217 note 65
Rāmāyaṇa, 134
Rāmlīlā, 153
Rātri Sūkta, 100, 105, 140, 165, 183
Ṛg Vedic, translation of, 183-184
Reading, private, as recent Western phenomenon, xii, 87-88, 103-104
Recitation, of religious texts, 5, 197 note 10. *See also Devī-Māhātmya*, recitation of
Religious life, varied media of, 92-93, 170. *See also* Artifacts, verbal and nonverbal; Documents, written; Scripture; Understanding, media of
Renou, Louis, 5
Ṛg Veda, 15, 105
compared with *Devī-Māhātmya*, 5,

100, 105
mentioned in *Devī-Māhātmya*, 49
Sāyaṇa's commentary on, 120-121
used by V. S. Agrawala to interpret *Devī-Māhātmya*, 157-159
Ricoeur, Paul, 2
Ritual activity, 101-102, 209 note 11
Rudra, 112-115, 135-136, 139

Śabda, 151, 168, 222 note 10
Saguṇa Brahman. *See Nirguṇa* and *saguṇa* Brahman
Śākaṃbharī, 78, 139
Śākta, 123-129, 162
Śakti, 19, 20, 21, 37, 63-67, 201 note 14
Samādhi, the *vaiśya*, 91, 159, 162-163, 167-168
in *Devī-Māhātmya*, 33-34, 82-84
Samaṣṭi (aggregate) form of Mahālakṣmī, 135-139, 142-143, 211 note 38. *See also* Mahālakṣmī
Sāṃkhya, 110, 128-129, 130, 144, 214-215 note 40
Sāṃmukhyas (presences) of the Goddess, 167-169
Śaṅkara, 128, 133, 135, 166, 219 note 99. *See also* Advaita Vedānta
Sanskrit, 1, 15, 17-18, 19, 30-31, 120, 212 note 1
Sanskritization, 17-18
Śantanu, 132
Saptaśatī. *See Durgā-Saptaśatī*
Saptaśatī Caṇḍī *yantra*. *See Devī-Māhātmya/Saptaśatī* Caṇḍī *yantra*
Sarasvatī, 75, 112-115, 138, 139
Sat-cit-ānanda, 136-137
Śatakṣī (Hundred-eyes), 78, 139
Sattva guṇa (intelligence-stuff), 110, 112-114, 142-143, 154-155, 205 note 14. *See also Guṇas*
Saundaryalaharī, 133, 135-136
Sāvarṇi, 22, 32, 84
Scholarship, contribution of to gender revolution, 2-3, 173
Scripture. *See also* Artifacts, verbal and nonverbal; Documents, written; Understanding, media of
comparative study of, xi-xii, 1, 3-6, 9, 131-132
emerging issues in, 169-170, 196-197 note 6
links texts and fieldwork, 154-156, 199 note 24
method in, 151-156
moral dimension to, 197 note 11
function of, in religious life, 89-90, 173
recitation of, 5, 197 note 10
translation of, 3, 5-6, 29, 173
Śeṣa, 36, 41
Shulman, David, 7
Śiva, 21, 23-24, 107, 140
in *Devī-Māhātmya*, 38, 39-41, 48, 49, 63, 64, 65
Śiva Purāṇa, 90, 141, 220 note 109
Śivadūtī, 65, 66, 69, 70, 71
Skanda, 21, 23-24, 63, 64. *See also* Kaumārī
Smith, Wilfred, 131, 196-197 note 6
Śrī, 18, 37, 48, 49. *See also* Lakṣmī
Śrīcakra, 126-127, 129
Śrīvidyā. *See also* Bhāskararāya
attitudes toward diverse *sādhanās*, 147-148
basic views of, 125-126
Bhāskararāya as foremost intellectual authority in, 122-123
compared with Advaita Vedānta, 128-131, 214-215 note 40
relationship between Tantra, Śākta and, 123-129
Stietencron, H. A. von, 90, 92-93, 102
Structuralism, 6-9, 122, 208 note 2
in study of Hindu myth and culture,

6-7, 8, 90-91, 122, 170
Sugrīva, 56
Śumbha, 24, 138, 158
in *Devī-Māhātmya*, 52, 55-60, 62, 63, 64, 68-73, 77, 79, 81
Suratha, the king, 91, 159, 162-163, 167-168. *See also* Goddess-kingship association
in *Devī-Māhātmya*, 32-34, 36, 82-84
Svadhā, 19-20, 36, 49, 75
Svāhā, 19-20, 36, 49
Svarūpā (own-form) of the Goddess, 36, 109, 111, 112, 136, 168. *See also* Mahālakṣmī
Śvetāśvatara Upaniṣad, 20, 134

Taittirīya Upaniṣad, 134
Tamas guṇa (mass-stuff), 110, 112-114, 142-143, 154-155, 205 note 14. *See also Guṇas*
Tāmasī, 38
Tantra, 123-125
and *bhakti*, 166-167, 171-172, 228 note 76
and Purāṇas, 171
Bhāskararāya and, 122-123, 139-140
elements in Kavaca and Argalā, 106, 107, 172
Hindu form of, 124
historical convergence with Advaita Vedānta, 216-217 note 65
multivalency of, 161-162
ontological accessibility of ultimate reality in, 128-129, 143, 145
relationship between Śākta, Srīvidyā and, 123-129
views of C. R. Banerjea on, 166-167
views of A. N. Jani on, 161-162
wariness of, 123, 166-167
Texts, nature and interpretation of, 151-156, 199 note 24. *See also* Artifacts, verbal and nonverbal; Documents, written; Scripture; Translation of religious texts; Understanding, media of
Tiwari, J. N., 21
Translation of religious texts, 3-6, 29-30, 173
Tripurā/Tripurasundarī, 125, 126, 129
Turīyā (the fourth), 137, 142-144, 145, 220 note 109. *See also Nirguṇa* and *saguṇa* Brahman

Understanding, media of, 1-2, 87-93, 156, 170, 173-174
Upabṛṃhaṇa (confirming elaboration), 22, 105, 157

Vāc, 19-20
Vaikṛtika Rahasya, 100, 165. *See also Aṅgas*; Rahasyas
analysis of, 109, 111, 114-116
diagram of relationships in, 113
links *vikṛti* forms of Mahālakṣmī with hymns of *Devī-Māhātmya*, 132
translation of, 187-191
Vaiṣṇavī, 64, 65, 66, 71, 75
Vaiśya. See Samādhi, the *vaiśya*
Vāmana Purāṇa, 24, 139, 141
Van Buitenen, J. A. B., 17, 23
Vārāha Purāṇa, 141
Vārāhī, 64, 65, 70, 75
Varanasi, xiii, 121, 153-154
Varuṇa, 39, 40, 41, 52, 56
Vaudeville, Charlotte, 24
Vāyu, 39, 41, 52
Vedāṅgas, 104-105
Vedas, 157-159. *See also Ṛg Veda*
Verbal utterance, 88-90, 92-93. *See also* Artifacts, verbal and nonverbal; Documents, written; Scripture; Understanding, media of
Viṣṇu, 18-19, 22-23, 112-115, 135-136, 139
in *Devī-Māhātmya*, 35-40, 48, 49, 53, 63, 74, 82
Viṣṇu Purāṇa, 24

Visual culture, relation to oral culture, 87-89, 92-93, 170. *See also* Books; Cult of the book; Scripture; Understanding, media of
Viśuddhānanda, 161
Vyaṣṭi (separate) forms of Mahālakṣmī, 135-139, 142-143, 211 note 38. *see also* Mahālakṣmī

Whaling, Frank, 90
Words, 88-90, 92-93, 207 note 3, 209 note 9. *See also* Artifacts, verbal and nonverbal; Documents, written; Scripture; Understanding, media of
Writing. *See* Documents, written

Yajur Veda, 134
Yama, 39, 40, 41, 52
Yantra, 124, 126, 170. *See also Devī-Māhātmya/Saptaśatī* Caṇḍī *yantra*
Yoganidrā, 35-39